D0000179

CULTURALLY COMPETENT PUBLIC CHILD WELFARE PRACTICE

KRISHNA SAMANTRAI
Smith College School for Social Work

THOMSON

BROOKS/COLE

AUSTRALIA • CANADA • MEXICO • SINGAPORE • SPAIN • UNITED KINGDOM • UNITED STATES

Executive Editor: *Lisa Gebo*
Assistant Editor: *Alma Dea Michelena*
Editorial Assistant: *Sheila Walsh*
Marketing Manager: *Caroline Concilla*
Marketing Assistant: *Mary Ho*
Advertising Project Manager: *Tami Strang*
Project Manager, Editorial Production:
Stephanie Zunich
Print/Media Buyer: *Doreen Suruki*
Permissions Editor: *Sue Ewing*

Production Service: *Andy Sieverman,*
G & S Typesetters, Inc.
Text Designer: *Jeanne Calabrese*
Copy Editor: *Kristen Cassereau*
Cover Designer: *Jennifer Mackres*
Cover Image: *Getty Images*
Cover Printer: *Webcom Ltd.*
Compositor: *G & S Typesetters, Inc.*
Printer: *Transcontinental Printing*

Printed in Canada
1 2 3 4 5 6 7 06 05 04 03 02

For more information about our
products, contact us at:
**Thomson Learning Academic
Resource Center
1-800-423-0563**
For permission to use material from this text,
contact us by: **Phone: 1-800-730-2214
Fax: 1-800-730-2215
Web:** http://www.thomsonrights.com

Library of Congress Control Number:
2002111299

ISBN: 0-534-37055-1

**Brooks/Cole–Thomson Learning
511 Forest Lodge Road
Pacific Grove, CA 93950
USA**

Asia
Thomson Learning
5 Shenton Way #01-01
UIC Building
Singapore 068808

Australia/New Zealand
Thomson Learning
102 Dodds Street
Southbank, Victoria 3006
Australia

Canada
Nelson
1120 Birchmount Road
Toronto, Ontario M1K 5G4
Canada

Europe/Middle East/Africa
Thomson Learning
High Holborn House
50/51 Bedford Row
London WC1R 4LR
United Kingdom

Latin America
Thomson Learning
Seneca, 53
Colonia Polanco
11560 Mexico D.F.
Mexico

Spain/Portugal
Paraninfo
Calle Magallanes, 25
28015 Madrid
Spain

CONTENTS

CHAPTER 4

Investigating the First Report:
Assessment in Emergency Response   83

CHAPTER 5

Maintaining Families:
When Risk Exists, but Not Enough to Remove
the Child from Home   91

CHAPTER 6

Reunifying Families:
Bringing the Child Back After an Out-of-Home
Placement   100

PART 3 | THE ORGANIZATIONAL CONTEXT OF PRACTICE

PREFACE

This book is intended for people who are working or are going to work as social workers in the public child welfare system. They may or may not already have an MSW, or they may be current MSW students, or they may be doing a specialized training in public child welfare work. Ideally, they should already have some basic knowledge of human behavior theories and basic social work practice skills. Intended for students, this book can be used by educators and trainers as the primary text for organizing specialized course(s) on public child welfare practice. It can also be used as a professional reference book by supervisors, administrators, planners, and advocates of public child welfare services.

The core of this book in part 2 is a new model of practice that is particularly suitable for the field of public child welfare. This model integrates clinical human behavior theories in the process of assessment and case planning and assesses family functioning not from the mental health/family dysfunction perspective but as the *goodness-of-fit* between the child's needs (physical, developmental, social-emotional) and the parents' ability to meet those needs adequately according to the prevailing norms of society. Public child welfare practice is conceptualized as assessment and intervention skills needed to make *different* kinds of decisions (and case plans) at *different* points in the child welfare system, with the goal of promoting a goodness-of-fit that will reduce the risk of harm to children and promote child and family well-being. For example, the decisions—and therefore case plans (and therefore practice skills)—are different when investigating an initial report of possible abuse/neglect from decisions and practice skills when the objective is to reunify a family or to facilitate a successful adoption.

The notion of cultural competence is integral to this model. Families who come to the attention of the public child welfare system come from many different cultures, with different cultural beliefs and norms about parent–child relationships and different child-rearing practices. What is goodness-of-fit for one family may or may not be goodness-of-fit for another, and what a family considers a good-enough fit for them may not be so according to the prevailing norms of society, as some traditional practices can be seen as jeopardizing the safety and well-being of the child. This model provides a conceptual framework for practice in which cultural knowledge is integrated in the assessment–intervention process, the objective being to *engage* families in the helping process, and help them achieve a goodness-of-fit that is within their cultural context as well as within the acceptable norms of society. That is, help the family adapt to the mainstream culture without necessarily losing their cultural identity or losing their children.

This model is true to what child welfare workers have to do in their jobs. It is comprehensive, integrative, and culturally-sensitive to all cultures. It provides a framework in which students can *integrate* what they have learned in previous courses on social work practice, human behavior theories, social policies, multiculturalism, any courses they might have taken on subjects related to child abuse and neglect, domestic violence, substance abuse, etc., as well as their own personal/professional experience, and *apply* this integrated knowledge to practice with clients of public child welfare agencies.

Professional practice does not take place in a vacuum. The parameters of professional, culturally competent practice are defined and constrained by the laws, rules, and regulations of federal, state, and local governments on the one hand, by the way in which the service delivery systems are organized and financed on the other, and also by the challenges of living and working in a democratic multicultural society, as well as by our 400-year history of conflicting beliefs and values about the roles of children, families, and governments. Thus the core of the book, practice, is placed firmly within the context of the federal legislative framework as it evolved over time in part 1, and in the context of the service delivery systems and their impact upon the nature and quality of professional practice in part 3.

My conceptualization of this model of practice evolved and was class-tested over a period of about seven years in my work with California Social Work Education Center on identifying and articulating Child Welfare competencies and developing and teaching a specialized course at my school for students receiving Title IV-E Child Welfare stipends. Child welfare administrators, managers, and practitioners had long been saying that the mental health model of practice—which most graduate social work programs teach—was not suitable for practice in the field of public child welfare; that it prepared students for private practice of therapy but not for the realities of public child welfare practice. The need was to teach curriculum that would specifically prepare students for public child welfare practice that involved case management and crisis intervention as the predominant, primary methods of practice. In the process of developing such curricula, I, like other educators, found an abysmal dearth of appropriate, relevant educational materials. And there was no text.

As far as I know, there is still no single text that can be used as a more-or-less comprehensive text for a course specifically on culturally competent public child welfare practice. There are numerous books on child welfare policy and child welfare practice (which focus on the *issues* in practice, not the *skills* of practice). There are books on multicultural practice and an enormous amount of literature on the various aspects, dynamics, and treatment of various forms of child abuse and neglect. All this content is usually taught as separate, discrete pieces of knowledge; students are expected to do their own integration and synthesis and translate the discrete pieces of knowledge into practice skills required to do their job.

This text does the integration and synthesis and then moves on to developing and refining skills needed in public child welfare practice. It addresses five competency areas identified by CalSWEC—Ethnic-Sensitive and Multicultural Practice, Core Child Welfare Skills, Human Behavior and the Social Environment, Workplace Management, and Child Welfare Policy, Planning, and Administration. The sixth area—Social Work Skills and Methods—is addressed in an earlier book.

Many students, their clients, and my clients have contributed much to this work. They pushed me and challenged me into new ways of thinking and different ways of seeing the world. They brought into my sphere of consciousness situations I could never have imagined, the resilience, strengths, and creativity in people I would not have thought possible. All of you shaped and influenced my thinking that is reflected in this work. To all of you, I am deeply grateful.

I also want to thank my manuscript reviewers: Lynn Adkins, Bethany College; Doug Burham, Eastern Kentucky University; Elizabeth Danto, Hunter College, City University of New York; Lisa Deason, Tulsa Community College; Pamela Higgins Saulsberry, University of Louisiana at Monroe; Amy Okamura, San Diego State University; Christie Reed, San Jose State University; and Kathy Wehrmann, Illinois State University.

Special thanks also to Lisa Gebo, Stephanie Zunich, and Alma Dea Michelena at Brooks/Cole–Thomson Learning.

And, to my family, for being there!

Krishna Samantrai

THE PHILOSOPHICAL AND LEGAL CONTEXT OF PRACTICE

FROM PARENS PATRIAE TO PERMANENCY PLANNING: THE PHILOSOPHICAL AND LEGAL CONTEXT OF PRACTICE

The term "child welfare" refers to a specialized field of social work practice adapted to the needs of children and service programs geared toward their well-being. In its narrow (residual) view, it refers to services designed to protect and care for children whose parents are unable or unwilling to care for them according to the prevailing norms of society. In its broader (institutional) view, it refers to the well-being of *all* children and their families. In the first landmark federal legislation, The Social Security Act of 1935, child welfare services were defined as services "for the protection and care of the homeless, dependent and neglected children, and children in danger of becoming delinquent" (P.L. 74-271). In the most recent landmark federal legislation, The Adoption Assistance and Child Welfare Act of 1980, child welfare services are defined as

> . . . public social services which are directed towards the accomplishment of the following purposes: (A) protecting and promoting the welfare of all children, including handicapped, homeless, dependent, or neglected children; (B) preventing or remedying, or assisting in the solution of problems which may result in, the neglect, abuse, exploitation, or delinquency of children; (C) preventing the unnecessary separation of children from their families by identifying family problems, assisting families in resolving their problems, and preventing breakup of the family where the prevention of child removal is desirable and possible; (D) restoring to their families children who have been removed, by the provision of services to the child and the families; (E) placing children in suitable adoptive homes, in cases where restoration to the biological family is not possible or appropriate; and (F) assuring adequate care of children away from their homes, in

3

cases where the child cannot be returned home or cannot be placed for adoption. (P.L. 96-272, Title V, Part 3, Sec. 425(a)(1). 42 USC 625)

PARENS PATRIAE

At the heart of all child welfare services is the doctrine of *parens patriae,* literally meaning "parent of the state," which developed in the chancery courts of medieval to late medieval England. The English social system at the time was based on the principles of feudalism, a sort of benevolent patriarchy. Nobility (the lords) owned the land. As owners of land, they had the right to revenues generated by their serfs, tenants, and others who worked and lived on their land. In return, like fathers in families, they had the duty to see to the welfare of their serfs, tenants, and those who lived on their land. Land ownership, with its accompanying rights and duties, passed from one generation to the next by inheritance.

The king also had certain prerogatives. Among these were the rights to revenue from the lands held by him, and the wardship of his tenants' infant heirs as parens patriae. Wardships were profitable because they could be sold for revenue. Parens patriae had traditionally been viewed as a prerogative, but it may also have been viewed as a duty of the king to his subjects, or it may have been devised as a restriction upon the king's prerogatives. "The King is in legal contemplation the guardian of his people; and in that amiable capacity is entitled (or rather it is His Majesty's duty, in return for the allegiance paid to him) to take care of such of his subjects as are legally unable, on account of 1st. mental incapacity: 2. idiocy: or 3. lunacy: to take care of themselves and their property" (J. Chitty, 1820, as cited in Cogan, 1970, p. 156).

This wardship by the king was invoked in litigations starting in the late 14th century involving profits from land held by children whose fathers had died and guardianship was contested. The major issues in litigations concerned custody, guardianship, and inheritance of property; concern was about loss of profits, not the ward's welfare. Parens patriae was used by the courts of chancery, as the king's representatives, to assure orderly transfer of feudal duties from one generation to the next and to ensure that there would be someone to perform those duties. By the beginning of 17th century, however, concern for the well-being of the child also began to appear. From analysis of legal writings of that time, Cogan concludes that in the 17th century the king's relation to idiots and lunatics was that of a guardian to ward, that the guardianship was a duty of care rather than a source of profit, and that the duty had at least once been described as that of a "father" (Cogan, 1970, p. 161).

While chancery was deciding the custody and property problems of the rich, a statutory scheme dealing with the child custody of the poor had also been developing. Budding industrialization and consequent economic changes in the 16th century led to the decline of feudalism. The discovery that wool instead of animal skins could be used to make warm clothing led to a demand for wool in Europe that led the English landowners to divert portions of their land from agriculture to uncultivated pastures for raising sheep, reducing the need for serfs and tenant-farmers. That in turn led to large-scale unemployment and poverty for the people who had worked and lived on the land under the benevolence of the feudal lord. Displaced from what had been their home for centuries, these people—adults, children, families—began to roam the countryside, begging and stealing, and posing a threat to other landowners. To control this threat Parliament in 1562 passed the Statute of Artificers, which provided, among other things, that the children of pauper parents were to be involuntarily separated from their parents and to be apprenticed to others. This provision was codified in The Poor Law Act of 1601; a child could be taken from pauper parents at the discretion of the overseers of the poor and bound out to a local resident as an apprentice until he or she reached the age of majority.

Coming to the New World soon thereafter in 1606, English colonists came with the English Poor Laws as their mental and legal frame of reference for dealing with the issues of poverty and dependency. They did not want to maintain the structure of feudalism, but parents and guardians held the right to treat children as they saw fit. However, the community intervened when parental treatment was considered excessively harsh or neglectful. Thomas (1972) and Bremner (1972) cite cases of parents (or masters of apprentices) being punished when they disciplined their children too harshly. When parents were considered neglectful, local officials could take children away and indenture them to another master. Neglect was defined as parental failure to provide physical sustenance, preparation for a trade, and moral, religious education.

In the 19th century, waves of immigrants coming to New York created a large population of dependent, exploited, and delinquent children. Indenturing no longer sufficed. At the same time, the idea began to take hold that children should be protected from poverty as well as from other dangerous environments so that they do not become dangerous to society. Indenturing gave way to institutions—almshouses for the poor, Houses of Refuge and Reform Schools for the delinquent—where children could be committed so that, theoretically at least, they would be raised in good moral environment and taught a trade. The Latin phrase used for legal authority for commitment was *in loco parentis*—in place of parents. "Parens patriae" was first used by the Pennsylvania Supreme Court to justify statutory commitments to a residential institution for juveniles in Ex parte Crouse. Rendleman (1971) describes it as follows:

Mary Ann Crouse, upon her mother's petition, had been committed by a justice of the peace to the House of Refuge as unmanageable. Her father sought her release and argued that commitment without a trial by jury was unconstitutional. The court held that the purpose of the House of Refuge was improvement, reformation, wholesome restraint, and protection from depraved parents and environment; and that if the statutory procedure was followed, a jury trial was not necessary. ". . . To this end (reformation, by training its inmates to industry; by imbuing their minds with principles of morality and religion; by furnishing them with means to earn a living; and above all, by separating them from the corrupting influence of improper associates) may not *the natural parents, when unequal to the task of education, or unworthy of it, be superceded by the parens patriae, or common guardian of the community*? It is to be remembered that the public has a paramount interest in the virtue and knowledge of its members, and that of strict right, the business of education belongs to it. That parents are ordinarily entrusted with it because it can seldom be put into better hands; but where they are incompetent or corrupt, what is there to prevent the public from withdrawing their faculties, held, as they obviously are, at its sufferance? *The right of parental control is a natural, but not an unalienable one.*" (Rendleman, 1971, p. 219) (Italics added)

In the New World, the doctrine of parens patriae came to mean that the state, instead of the king, as the common guardian of the community, had the right and the duty to protect. This doctrine continues as the fundamental legal basis for all public child welfare services.

FROM PARENS PATRIAE TO PERMANENCY PLANNING

Other beliefs and values have evolved over the last 150 years that have shaped and continue to shape current child welfare practice. Among these are the concepts of the rights of the child, the best interest of the child, the child's need for continuity of relationship, and permanence.

The concepts of the "rights of the child" and the "best interest of the child" had begun to develop in the mid-19th century. "Children's rights" was used in protecting children from neglect, abuse, and exploitation, in forming the Societies for the Protection of Children, and in establishing the Juvenile Court. "Best interest of the child" was used as a guiding principle in deciding custody of children in cases of separation or divorce of parents. However, when there was a custody dispute between biological parents and other adults such as grandparents or foster parents who had raised the child, the courts almost always ruled in favor of the right of the biological parent (Bremner, 1972). These practices continued unchallenged until the 1970s, though the venue of care changed from large institutions such as poorhouses and reform schools to small group homes and foster homes. (Examples are seen in popular musicals such as *Oliver* and *Annie*.)

In the 1970s, several streams of developments in the medical, social, and other fields converged and started a process of change in the thinking about child welfare and the nature of child welfare practice.

Evolution of Child Abuse Reporting Laws

While child abuse and neglect had always existed, it had always been considered a problem of the poor. However, advances in medical (X-ray) technology starting in the 1940s led to the dramatic change in thinking in the 1960s. In 1946, a radiologist by the name of Caffey first reported a number of cases in which infants had multiple long bone fractures and subdural hematomas, but did not speculate on the cause of these injuries. In 1953, Wooley and Evans, also radiologists, suggested that such injuries might be caused by children's caretakers. In 1957, Caffey re-examined his original data and concluded that the trauma might have been willfully inflicted by the parents (Nelson, 1984). Interest in this area was picked up by other members of the medical profession, as evinced by the publication of several articles in medical journals around 1959. A nationwide study of the extent of physical mistreatment, including malnutrition and other evidence of serious neglect or abuse, was undertaken by C. Henry Kempe, Chief of Pediatrics at the University of Colorado Medical School. This study culminated in his seminal article "The Battered Child Syndrome" in the *Journal of American Medical Association* (July 7, 1962).

The media took up the issue.

> The AMA press release "Parental Abuse Looms in Childhood Deaths" took the nation by storm. The message was that Kempe and his coworkers had discovered a deadly disease which menaced the nation's children. Within a week of this new release, *Time* and *Newsweek* reported it in their medicine sections. *Saturday Evening Post* and *Life* carried it to a wider audience. Television took it up in its soap operas and medical shows. Newspaper reports began to appear frequently. . . . (Nelson, 1984, p. 58)

Kempe had presented child abuse as a medical/psychiatric problem that existed in the middle and upper classes but was not being reported because of weak reporting laws and other barriers to physician reporting. Therefore, he said, knowledge regarding its magnitude and its causes was limited. He sought improved reporting laws that would make reporting mandatory and provide civil and criminal immunity to those who reported in good faith. Thereafter, model reporting laws were proposed by the U.S. Children's Bureau, the American Humane Association, the Council of State Governments, the American Medical Association, and the American Academy of Pediatrics. Between 1963 and 1967, all 50 states and the District of Columbia enacted child abuse reporting laws. However, variations in state laws, even in how child abuse was defined, created implications for individual rights and difficulties in assessing the full magnitude and scope of the problem. A need for national focus and direction led eventually to hearings before the Senate Subcommittee on Children and Youth chaired by then-Senator Walter Mondale and the enactment of the first federal legislation on child abuse, The Child Abuse Prevention and Treatment Act of 1974. This Act established a National Center on Child Abuse and Neglect (NCAAN) as the national administrative body to administer grants to states to conduct research into the causes of child abuse and neglect, its incidence and severity, and ways of identifying, preventing, and treating it, and to serve as a national information clearinghouse. Among the conditions that states had to meet to receive these grants were the existence of a state reporting law specifying who must report and granting immunity for reporting suspected abuse or neglect, and coordination of their activities with the federal government. The availability of these grants served as another incentive for the states to improve their reporting laws.

However, child abuse reporting laws created another problem. While they required reporting and therefore *identification* of children being abused or neglected, they did not provide for any *services* to children so identified or their families.

Studies on Foster Care Drift

The 1950 White House Conference on Children had sparked an interest in the needs and development of children in foster care. This led to the first, landmark exploratory study of foster children in nine selected communities between October 1957 and August 1958 (Maas and Engler, 1959). This study identified the problem now known as "foster care drift": the unnecessary placement of children in out-of-home care because there were no alternative services for even simple difficulties encountered by families. Children would linger and drift in foster homes until the age of majority, often forgotten by the system that placed them, essentially severing the family ties. Several studies thereafter confirmed these findings (Jeter, 1961; Fanshel and Shinn, 1978; Mott, 1975). These studies found that there were over a third of a million children in foster care, a large proportion coming from low-income families. They were in foster care because their parents were ill, neglectful, abusive or had abandoned them because they could not care for them. Many of these children could have been cared for in their own homes had day care or other in-home services been made available to the families. Once the child was placed, little or no contact was maintained between the parent, the child, and the caseworker. Even though the placement was intended to be temporary, the child was likely to stay there for 4–6 years and change foster homes 2–3 times. Sometimes, even though the conditions that precipitated the child's entry into foster care were long resolved, the child was not returned to the family because either the child had no caseworker at that time or the caseworker did not know of the changed circumstances. The longer the child stayed in foster care, the less likely he or she was to return to biological parents or be adopted. While about 50 to 80% of children in foster care were likely to spend the rest of their years to maturity in foster care, foster parents were discouraged, at times even prohibited, from developing emotional attachments with their foster children. Carrying very high caseloads, caseworkers often worked from crisis to crisis, unable to provide needed attention and services to children not in crisis. Caseworker burnout and turnover rate was very high.

For the children, therefore, foster care was marked by impermanence, instability, and few, if any, close emotional bonds with other people.

At the same time, there were several successful programmatic attempts, primarily on demonstration basis, both to prevent placements and to ensure permanence for children in placement. For example, in the Alameda Project—a collaborative effort between the Children's Home Society of Oakland, California, and the Alameda County Department of Human Resources—a significant number of children were moved out of foster care with early case planning, involvement of biological parents in decision-making about their children in foster care, intensive services to biological parents, and the use of contracts (Stein and Gambrill, 1977; Stein, Gambrill and Wiltse, 1977). In Oregon's "Freeing Children for Permanent Placement" project the goal was to work with the legal system, which had been reluctant to terminate parental rights to free children up for adoption. With early case planning and regular, consistent, clear, and *documented* services to parents, 36% of the 509 children were freed for adoption. In addition, 26% were able to return to their biological parents (Pike, 1976; Emlen, 1981). In the Bowen Center Project in Chicago, long-term comprehensive services were instrumental in preventing out-of-home placement in even seriously troubled families (Sullivan, Spasser, and Penner, 1977). In Detroit's "Parents and Children Together" (PACT) project, out-of home placement was prevented in families described as having problems such as money management, ineffective coping techniques, and a chaotic physical environment with intensive, comprehensive services (Callard and Morrin, 1979). And in New York's "A Second Chance for Families Project," intensive services were found to be significantly effective in preventing out-of-home care, reducing the number of days children spent in foster care, as well as in reuniting a larger number of children in foster care with their biological families (Jones, Neuman, and Shyne, 1976). A review of several studies on the effectiveness of work in these and other such programs indicated that with families receiving preventive and protective services, better outcomes were associated with a comprehensive program of services delivered over a longer period of time (two or more years), relationship with a single worker, and service programs designed to overcome a sense of isolation and provide a supportive extended family to the client family (Jones, Magura, and Shyne, 1981).

Studies on prevention of foster care drift also found that federal policies inadvertently contributed to this problem. Under the then-existing child welfare law (Title IVB of the Social Security Act of 1935), the federal government provided foster care funds to states, sharing the cost of care *after* a child was placed in out-of-home care, but gave no funds to *prevent* out-of-home care or to return the child to the parents once placed out. In addition, the Title IVA (AFDC) money could also be used to pay for foster care. States thus had no financial incentive to provide any preventive and supportive services, and no financial disincentive for separating children from their parents (Emlen, Lahti, et al., 1978; Emlen, 1981).

The Children's Rights Movement

The ideal of children's rights was formally acknowledged in the Declaration of the Rights of the Child adopted by the League of Nations in 1924. After World War II, the United Nations took up the cause again and in 1959 unanimously readopted the Declaration of the Rights of the Child.

The preamble states that ". . . the child, by reason of his physical and mental immaturity, needs special safeguards and care, including appropriate legal protection, before as well as after birth . . ." (Gross and Gross, 1977, p. 337). In 10 principles thereafter, this Declaration asserts that "all children, without any exception whatsoever"—regardless of race, gender, national origin, or the political and religious convictions of their parents—are entitled to such rights as a name and nationality at birth; adequate nutrition, housing, recreation, and medical services; protection from all forms of neglect, abuse, and exploitation; and for children with physical, mental, or social handicaps, the right to special treatment, education, and care. The declaration also states that ". . . A child of tender years shall not, save in exceptional circumstances, be separated from his mother. Society and the public authorities shall have the duty to extend partic- ular care to children without a family and to those without adequate means of support . . ." (United Nations Declaration of the Rights of the Child, reprinted in Gross and Gross, 1977, pp. 336–339).

In an accompanying resolution, The United Nations Children's Fund (UNICEF) was assigned the special responsibility of working to implement these rights, to try to make them meaningful realities for every child on earth (Geddes, 1977).

In the United States, the Supreme Court's 1967 *Gault* decision established the child's right to due process of the law. This was a case of 15-year-old Ger- ald taken into custody and placed in the Children's Detention Home because of a verbal complaint made by a neighbor that Gerald and another boy had made an obscene phone call to her. At that time, Gerald was also on six-months' pro- bation for having been in the company of a boy who had stolen a wallet from a woman's purse. Gerald's parents, who were not home at the time, were not notified of his detention. Two hearings were held; the accuser was not present at either one of them. No sworn testimony was taken, nor any transcripts or memoranda made of what was said at the hearing. At the close of the second hearing, Gerald was committed as a juvenile delinquent to the state industrial school until he reached 21, the age of majority (Costin, 1991).

Child advocates argued and the Justices agreed that Gerald was not given the due process of the law, that his liberty was taken away for six years only be- cause he was a minor. If Gerald had been over 18, he would not have been sub- ject to juvenile court proceedings and his maximum sentence for the same of- fense would have been a fine of $5 to $50 or imprisonment for not more than two months. The justices ruled that a young suspect tried in juvenile court is en- titled to have a lawyer, to cross-examine witnesses, and to enjoy all procedural safeguards guaranteed to adult defendants by the Constitution (Costin, 1991).

Civil Rights were in the forefront of American sociopolitical environment of the 1960s. To advocate for children's rights, a loose coalition formed of con- cerned parents, older students, citizens and professional advocates, and public officials. Their efforts took on the aura of a "movement." In 1974, a story in the *U.S. News and World Report* started with the line "On the rise across the United States is a 'children's liberation' movement that is forcing the nation's el- ders to sit up and take notice—often in disbelief." It goes on to state that "At least four major national organizations of attorneys and countless public wel- fare groups have joined the fray in behalf of 68 m. Americans under 18 years old—whom some libertarians call the country's most oppressed minority"

("Nationwide Drive for Children's Rights," *U.S. News and World Report,* reprinted in Gross and Gross, 1977, pp. 206–207).

Advances were made through litigation and court rulings. These included full court rights (a child could sue an adult—parent or teachers or schools); elimination of censorship in schools (ending hair and dress rules except for safety reasons, prohibiting disciplinary action over student publications, searching student lockers); banning paddlings for discipline; abolishing tracking system in education; and custody rights (courts would consider the child's best interest and personal wishes in divorce cases—even when divorces were uncontested). For children in foster care, this meant that biological parents no longer had the inalienable right to reclaim them: parental rights could be terminated for the psychological well-being of the child.

Psychological Versus Biological Parenting

In 1973, the seminal writing of Goldstein, Freud, and Solnit (a psychiatrist, an analyst, and a law professor) brought together a wealth of knowledge and experience on child development and psychological needs of the child and the risks to foster children's growth and development because of the existing child welfare laws and practices. They put forth the concepts of the primacy of "psychological" parenting over biological parenting and the child's need for continuity of relationships with psychological parents who are ideally but not necessarily biological parents in order to develop a healthy identity and self-esteem. They noted that the best-interest-of-the-child principle often does not work in the interest of the child; that in court decisions, the child's interest is balanced against and often subordinated to the interests, wishes, and legal rights of competing adults who may be equally capable of providing good care for the child, thus causing delays in placement decisions and the formation of psychological bonds. Arguing that the child has already been hurt by the situation that brings him or her before the court, they recommended the use of the "least detrimental available alternative" rather than the "best interest of the child" as a guiding principle in custody and placement decisions and the expedition of the court's decision-making process in accord with the child's rather than adults' sense of time (Goldstein, Freud, and Solnit, 1973).

Baby-Selling Scandal and Congressional Hearings

The development that precipitated the convergence of diverse streams was the baby-selling scandal of the mid-1970s. This scandal led to Congressional hearings on the problems of children in foster care, which started the process of legislative change.

The scandal was about the adoption of healthy white infants. Until about the late 1960s, the demand for healthy white infants for adoption more or less balanced their availability, as women facing unwanted births had few choices besides giving up their babies for adoption. In the late 1960s, this balance began to shift. Availability of contraceptives reduced the number of unwanted pregnancies. With the advance of the Women's Rights movement, more women could choose to and began to keep their babies instead of giving them up for adoption. Around the same time, the movement for the rights of unwed fathers also made it much more difficult to free children up for adoption. By the mid-1970s, the demand for healthy white infants far surpassed their supply, leading to a flourishing black market in independent adoptions. People wishing to adopt paid the price the market could bear, there were hints of possible unethical practices to persuade women to give up their babies, and babies were being placed with adoptive families with no background checks or efforts at matching. In effect, adoption became a profit-making business where babies were being "sold" for money (Mott, 1975).

Protests first came from families waiting to adopt who could not afford the market price. Then, the media took up the issue. There was widespread public outrage and demands for the government to do something.

In April 1975, the Senate Subcommittee on Children and Youth, chaired by then-Senator Walter Mondale, held hearings on baby-selling. These were followed in July by hearings on adoption of special-needs children—children who were four years of age or older, nonwhite, part of a sibling group, or had physical or emotional difficulties—who waited and hoped to be adopted but had little chance, facing the grim likelihood of drifting forever in the foster care system. Testimony in these hearings highlighted the barriers in the broader child welfare system that left many children lingering in foster care. Further hearings were then held on matters related to foster care and adoption. For these hearings, Senator Mondale requested a report outlining some of the key policy questions and possible solutions to them. The report, prepared by the Subcommittee consultant Paul Mott, outlined the problem of foster care drift (described above) and the federal role in creating this problem. He recommended that

> 1. Greater emphasis must be given to the rights of children: Their most fundamental rights being permanence, stability, continuity and nurture during the developmental period of their lives. 2. A basic legislative goal should be to increase the proportion of children in stable family settings by: Increasing the resources and competencies of families to cope with their problems in order to prevent the unnecessary separation of children from their families; Identifying family problems and possible breakup early and mobilizing resources to prevent breakup in those situations where the prevention of breakup is desirable and possible; Mobilizing services to restore broken families as viable units as quickly as possible where appropriate; If restoration of the family within a time period relevant to the child's needs is not possible or appropriate, freeing the child for adoption as quickly as possible and placing him or her in a suitable adoptive home; and Completing and implementing a stable foster care plan if, within a time period relevant to the child's needs, the child cannot or should not be restored to his or her original home or placed for adoption. (Mott, 1975, p. 3)

Mott also noted that many of the problems in existing laws were due to the piecemeal way in which they were created by different committees of Congress, with no one committee in either the House or the Senate having the responsibility for overseeing all legislative efforts in the child welfare area. This fragmentation was mirrored in the Executive branch; programs for children were scattered among a variety of agencies, with no efforts at any coordination or communication between them. He pointed out that there was need for a comprehensive legislation in the child welfare area and recommended that through law and administrative practices a new, "balanced" relationship be developed between the federal government and state governments. In this new relationship, the federal government should emphasize the development of national priorities while the responsibility of implementing those priorities remains with the state governments (Mott, 1975).

These recommendations introduced the concept of permanence in child welfare and set the stage for the passage of P.L. 96-272, The Adoption Assistance and Child Welfare Act of 1980.

PERMANENCY PLANNING

The concept of permanency planning is firmly rooted in the principle of the right of the child to permanence, stability, and nurturance. It takes as its major premise that the child's well-being must be paramount in any service plan and that children's well-being is best achieved in a home where they feel a sense of belonging and permanent membership. Such a home assures the continuity of relationships necessary for development of positive self-image, establishment of healthy relationships with others, and the ability to function well in society. Permanency planning thus suggests that the biological family is primary to the care and upbringing of children, for it is here that an initial sense of belonging is first developed. Disrupting this tie is therefore a major decision—one that must not be made unless there is evidence that serious harm will come to the child if left at home. If the situation is serious enough to warrant the child's removal from home, it is incumbent upon the agency that removes the child to assist the family so the child can be returned home safely. If the biological family cannot resume care of the child even with assistance, then it is incumbent upon the agency to provide an alternative permanent home for the child in which his or her needs for belonging, stability, and nurturance can be met. According to Pike (1977), permanency describes intent. A permanent home is not one that is guaranteed to last forever, but one that is intended to exist indefinitely.

Permanency planning is now the new doctrine of child welfare. It builds upon and extends the doctrine of parens patriae in that the state or community has not only the right and duty to protect, but it also has the duty to see that children have a permanent home, preferably with their biological families. Translated into practice, permanency planning is a *process* of helping a child to live in a home where lifetime caring family relationships can be established, a *program of services* delivered on behalf of children to secure such a home and family for the child, and an *intervention strategy* designed to help children live with families that offer continuity of relationships with nurturing parents or caretakers and the opportunity to establish lifetime relationships.

THE FEDERAL LEGISLATIVE FRAMEWORK

Public child welfare services exist because of the mandates and the legal authority of the federal and state laws that authorize them. Federal laws offer money to states for specific purposes and specify the conditions a state must meet in order to get that money. Each state then has to enact its own laws to comply with the federal conditions and develop its own rules and regulations to implement them before it can draw that money. These federal and state laws, rules, and regulations define the parameters of child welfare practice—what a frontline child welfare worker can or cannot do with or for the clients.

The primary legal framework that governs public child welfare practice consists of several laws. The Child Abuse Prevention and Treatment Act (P.L. 93-247), first enacted in 1974, defines child abuse and neglect and relates to reporting laws. The Adoption Assistance and Child Welfare Act of 1980 (P.L. 96-272), which embodies the doctrine of permanence, provides for services to protect children and maintain families. Matters pertaining to the welfare of Native American children come under the jurisdiction of The Indian Child Welfare Act of 1978 (P.L. 95-608). Several other laws (or sections of other larger laws) have been enacted since 1980 to reinforce the goals of P.L. 96-272 in a multicultural society. These include the Family Preservation and Family Support Services in the Omnibus Budget Reconciliation Act of 1993; The Multiethnic Placement Act of 1994 and the Interethnic Adoption Provisions of 1996 (P.L. 103-382); Sec. 505 of the Personal Responsibility and Work Opportunity Act of 1996 (P.L. 104-193); and The Adoption and Safe Families Act of 1997 (P.L. 105-89). These above laws pertain to children in foster care. In 1986, another law, the Independent Living Initiative, was enacted to provide funding to assist adolescents prepare for independent living as they phase out of the foster care system.

The following section provides an overview of the major provisions of these laws.

P.L. 93-247, The Child Abuse Prevention and Treatment Act (CAPTA)

CAPTA was first enacted in 1974 "To provide financial assistance for a demonstration program for the prevention, identification, and treatment of child abuse and neglect, to establish a National Center on Child Abuse and Neglect, and for other purposes" (P.L. 93-247, 88 STAT.4). This Act defined child abuse and neglect as ". . . the physical or mental injury, sexual abuse, negligent treatment, or maltreatment of a child under the age of eighteen by a person who is responsible for the child's welfare under circumstances which indicate that the child's health or welfare is harmed or threatened thereby, as determined in accordance with regulations prescribed by the Secretary" (P.L. 93-247; 88 STAT 5. Sec. 3).

CAPTA established the National Center on Child Abuse and Neglect (NCAAN) as the national administrative body under the Secretary of Health, Education and Welfare (HEW) to:

(1) compile, analyze, and publish a summary annually of recently conducted and currently conducted research on child abuse and neglect; (2) develop and maintain an information clearinghouse on all programs, including private programs, showing promise of success, for the prevention, identification, and treatment of child abuse and neglect; (3) compile and publish training materials for personnel who are engaged or intend to engage in the prevention, identification, and treatment of child abuse and neglect; (4) provide technical assistance (directly or through grant or contract) to public and nonprofit private organizations to assist them in planning, improving, developing, and carrying out programs and activities relating to the prevention, identification, and treatment of child abuse and neglect; (5) conduct research into causes of child abuse and neglect, and into the prevention, identification, and treatment thereof; and (6) make a complete and full study and investigation of the national incidence of child abuse and neglect, including a determination of the extent to which incidents of child abuse and neglect are increasing in number or severity. (P.L. 93-247; 88 STAT 5. Sec. 2)

In order to get these grants, states had to have in effect a state reporting law that provided immunity of the reporting person. States also had to have a system of prompt investigation of the report and protection of the child found to be abused or neglected or at risk of abuse/neglect, and multidisciplinary service programs. Money was authorized for four years.

Since 1974, CAPTA has been amended and re-authorized every four years. The greatest amount of work has been done in clarifying the definition of child abuse and neglect and expanding its scope and in making more research/demonstration monies available. For example, the 1978 Amendments added pornography to the definition of sexual abuse, amended the definition on age to give more flexibility to states on who they define as a child (". . . child under the age of eighteen, or the age specified by the child protection law of the state in question . . ." (P.L. 95-266, Sec. 3), and added Title II, Adoption Reform, to promote a national adoption and foster care information system and to maintain a national adoption exchange so that adoption of children was not restricted to in-state adoptions only. The 1984 Amendments expanded the definition of sexual abuse to cover out-of-home care (child-care or day-care facilities) and the definition of child abuse to include medical neglect—withholding medical care from handicapped children and children at risk with life-threatening conditions. This was added following a scandal involving the then-common medical practice of withholding intravenous feeding from infants born with severe brain damage and thus not expected to live. It added Title III, Family Violence Prevention and Services, to legally acknowledge the abuse of women and mothers and the elderly as a problem and to authorize money for community-based services and shelters for battered women. The 1988 Amendments added provisions for increasing adoption of minority children through outreach, public education, and media campaigns and expediting home studies and legal procedures. In 1992, homeless children and children at risk of becoming homeless were added, and money was authorized for temporary child care for disabled and chronically ill children and crisis nurseries for abused/neglected children. The last two were repealed in the 1996 Amendments. The

Child Abuse Prevention and Treatment Act Amendments of 1996 (P.L. 104-235) required states receiving grants to establish citizen review panels to evaluate the performance of state and local child protection agencies. It also required the Department of Health and Human Services (HHS, the current name for HEW) to give priority to grant applications in states that expedite termination of parental rights and adoption of abandoned infants, and it authorized appropriations for missing children's assistance and regional and local children's advocacy centers. In the most recent amendments in 2000, it authorized use of grant funds for "establishing or supporting cooperative programs between law enforcement and media organizations, to collect, record, retain, and disseminate information useful in the identification and apprehension of suspected criminal offenders" in order to make it easier for states to enforce the child abuse and neglect laws (P.L. 106-177, Sec. 103, 28). It also added Title II, Jennifer's Law, authorizing the Attorney General to provide grants to states to improve the reporting of unidentified and missing persons.

P.L. 96-272, The Adoption Assistance and Child Welfare Act of 1980

This Act, commonly also referred to as the permanency planning legislation, is a complex comprehensive law that addresses all components of public child welfare and is the mainframe of current public child welfare services. It defined child welfare services broadly (see definition, p. 3) and established public responsibility for ensuring permanence for children and assisting and supporting biological families—which was a major shift from the traditional historical approach of separating children from their families and placing them in out-of-home care. To induce states to develop needed changes, P.L. 96-272 incorporated a complex system of federal fiscal incentives and penalties.

P.L. 96-272 has three Titles. Title I—Foster Care and Adoption Assistance—is the one most relevant to child welfare practice as it defines the parameters of practice, what the frontline child welfare workers must do.

Title I amended Title IV of the Social Security Act (1935) by adding a new Part E, which set conditions for federal payment to states for foster care and adoption. To continue to receive federal foster care funds, states were required to have (1) a state plan for foster care and adoption assistance and a single state agency to administer the plan consistently in all its jurisdictions, (2) a case plan for each child, which must be a written document, show placement in the least restrictive (most family-like) setting available, close to parents' home, and consistent with the best interest and special needs of the child, and (3) a case review system for each child. It required that each case must be reviewed at least once every six months to ensure continued need for placement and its suitability to the child's needs, and the review system must provide procedural safeguards for the parents. In addition, Part E required that the state must show that (4) "reasonable effort" was made, prior to placement of the child in foster care, to prevent or eliminate the need for removal of the child from his or her home, to make it possible for the child to return home, and (5) that placement was a result of judicial determination that remaining in the home would be contrary to the welfare of the child.

Part E thus required preplacement prevention and reunification services, and it set time limits such as review every six months and, after 18 months in placement, proceeding with termination of parental rights and freeing children up for adoption so that children do not linger and drift in the foster care system indefinitely. The requirement of "reasonable effort" has been the most difficult to implement, as "reasonable effort" has not been defined in the law, so is left to the interpretation of individual judges making the determination. These two requirements—reasonable effort and judicial determination—have increased the paperwork requirements of child welfare workers. These two requirements have also made it necessary for the child welfare system to work collaboratively with the legal system.

Part E also authorized adoption assistance and subsidies for hard-to-adopt children—children who are older, part of a sibling group, of an ethnic minority, or who have medical or emotional problems—children who would not be adopted without some assistance to the adoptive parents. However, child welfare workers have to make sure that the children and the prospective adoptive parents meet the eligibility criteria, and the amount of subsidy has to be negotiated according to need.

Part B, Child Welfare Services, amended the original (1935) Title IV-B in the Social Security Act in effect at the time. The new Part B redefined child welfare services (see page 3) and utilized another complex funding system for child welfare services other than foster care payments to induce states to change. While each state was to continue getting the base sum of money depending on its child population as before, additional monies could be obtained. For additional monies, the states were to conduct an inventory of all children who had been in foster care for a period of six months or more, develop a statewide information system capable of tracking children, a case review system as defined in Part E, and a service program for reunification and adoption or legal guardianship. If states did not do this, they could lose their share of additional federal appropriations in succeeding years. Part B thus reinforced the permanency planning provisions of Part E.

Title II authorizes money for day care and treatment programs for alcohol and drug abuse. Title III provides further procedural details regarding payments to states.

P.L. 95-608, The Indian Child Welfare Act of 1978

Matters pertaining to foster care and adoption of American Indian children come under the jurisdiction of a completely different law, The Indian Child Welfare Act of 1978 (ICWA). This Act was enacted to stop the destruction of American Indian families and cultures through the historically common practice of removing American-Indian children from their birth tribes and sending them to non-Indian boarding schools, foster homes, or adoptive homes. While the movement to stop these practices had started in the 1930s, it gained further momentum and political power during the 1960s Civil Rights era. In the mid-1970s, Congress authorized the creation of the American Indian Policy Review Commission to review the history and current status of the government's policy for dealing with Indians and to make recommendations for changes. Task Force Four of this Commission dealt with the issues of federal, state, and tribal jurisdictions. In its final report to the Commission, this task force also addressed the issue of child custody. Reporting state-by-state statistics on the alarmingly high number of Indian children placed in non-Indian foster or adoptive homes, it outlined the need for what was to become The Indian Child Welfare Act (Orrantia, 1991).

ICWA gives exclusive jurisdiction to tribes over any child custody proceeding involving an Indian child who lives in or is domiciled in the reservation of that tribe or is a ward of a tribal court. With Indian children who do not live in or are not domiciled in a reservation, and are not wards of a tribal court, any state court proceeding regarding foster placement of the child or termination of parental rights are to be transferred to the jurisdiction of the tribe, unless there is objection by the parent or Indian custodian of the child or the child's tribe. If a state court hears the case, both tribes and parents or Indian custodians have the right to be notified of and to intervene in state court proceedings.

Grounds for removal of an Indian child from his or her home are much more stringent and require "clear and convincing evidence" and testimony of a qualified expert witness. For termination of parental rights, evidence "beyond a reasonable doubt" along with expert testimony are required to show "that the continued custody of the child by the parent or the Indian custodian is likely to result in serious emotional or physical damage to the child" (Sec. 1912e).

If the child must be removed from home, the law specifies a hierarchy of preferences for foster care or preadoptive placements. The first preference is to be given to a member of the Indian child's extended family; second to a foster home licensed, approved, or specified by the Indian child's tribe; third, an Indian foster home licensed or approved by an authorized non-Indian licensing authority; and fourth, an institution for children approved by an Indian tribe or operated by an Indian organization which has a program suitable to meet the Indian child's needs.

Grounds for annulment of adoption are more lenient. A birth-parent who initially agrees to the placement of an American-Indian child has a chance to withdraw consent until a decree of adoption is entered in court. If the consent to adoption was obtained by fraud or under duress, the birth-parent has at least two years to get the adoption nullified.

Subchapter II of this Act provides for grants for Indian child and family services and programs on or near reservations.

In everyday practice, this Act makes it incumbent upon the child welfare workers to ask directly whether or not the client has Indian heritage, and to not assume anything from physical appearance or accept the information in the record as absolutely accurate. If the child or family is of Indian heritage, all actions and interventions must be guided by the provisions of the ICWA.

Howard M. Metzenbaum Multiethnic Placement Act of 1994 (MEPA) and the Interethnic Adoption Provisions of 1996 (P.L.103-382)

Since about the 1970s the usual practice in adoption was to place children with parents of the same race. Racial matching was considered to be in the best interest of children. Particularly for children of color, race-matched adoptions were considered necessary for the development of identity, self-esteem, and skills to survive in an inherently racist society. However, in the 1990s, the larger social debate about affirmative action policies brought political attention to race-based adoption policies. Opponents argued that this policy discriminates against prospective adoptive parents whose application had been denied or delayed solely on the basis of race. They also argued that race-matched adoption did not serve the interest of children of color as it increases the length of time children of color have to wait in foster care, and that communities of color were being excluded from the adoption system because their suitability was judged by the values and standards of the white middle class (Barth et al., 1994). Around the same time, there were several newspaper reports of children who had been removed from long-term transracial foster placements to achieve racial matching—breaking their established bonds and ties with "psychological" parents.

The Multiethnic Placement Act of 1994 (MEPA) was enacted in the larger social context of backlash against Affirmative Action policies. It had three goals: (1) decreasing the length of time children had to wait in foster care; (2) preventing discrimination in the placement of children on the basis of race, color, or national origin; and (3) facilitating the identification and recruitment of foster and adoptive families from communities of color.

To achieve these goals, MEPA stated that federally funded agencies and entities may not (A) categorically deny to any person the opportunity to become an adoptive or foster parent solely on the basis of the race, color, or national origin of the adoptive or foster parent or the child involved; or (B) delay or deny the placement of a child for adoption or into foster care, or otherwise discriminate in making a placement decision, solely on the basis of race, color, or national origin of the adoptive or foster parent or the child involved (42 U.S.C.5115a). However, it expressly permitted the cultural, ethnic, and racial background of the child and the capacity of the prospective foster or adoptive parent to meet the needs of the child of this background *as one of a number of factors* used to determine the best interest of the child. It also required states to undertake active, creative, and diligent efforts to recruit foster and adoptive parents of every race, ethnicity, and culture in order to facilitate the placement of children in foster and adoptive homes that will best meet each child's needs.

However, this law was amended in 1996 and its provisions made more stringent. The Interethnic Adoption Provisions amending the Multiethnic Placement Act of 1994 (P.L. 104-188 110 Stat. 1903, signed Aug. 20, 1996) removed language that allowed routine consideration of these factors in assessing both the best interest of the child and the capacity of the foster or adoptive parents to meet the needs of the child. It now states that race, color, and national origin may be considered only in rare circumstances when making placement decisions (Sec. 1808, 110 Stat. 1755, 1903-04). An agency making a placement decision that uses race, color, or national origin would need to prove to the courts that the decision was justified by a compelling government interest and necessary to the accomplishment of a legitimate state purpose—in this case the best interest of the child. Thus under this law, "the best interest of the child" must be defined on a case-by-case basis (GAO/HEHS-98-204, 1998).

In addition, this amendment also added an enforcement provision. It penalizes states that violate the amended act in any quarter of a fiscal year by reducing their federal Title IV-E funds by 2–5% (Secs. 1808 b, d.). It also allows for "aggrieved individuals" to bring a lawsuit against the state [Sec. (3)(A)].

MEPA does not affect the provisions of the Indian Child Welfare Act.

The Adoption and Safe Families Act of 1997 (P.L. 105-89)

The Adoption and Safe Families Act was enacted to further promote and facilitate adoption, to move children more quickly out of foster care into permanent homes. Therefore, it makes changes in requirements for the reasonable effort and termination of parental rights. It also offers states financial incentives for increasing the number of adoptions.

This law clarifies that the child's health and safety must be of paramount concern in any aspect of the case plan for children in foster care. While states must continue to make reasonable efforts to preserve and reunify families, the reasonable effort requirement does not apply in cases where a child has been subject to "aggravated circumstances" such as (but not limited to) abandonment, torture, chronic abuse, sexual abuse; or when a parent has killed or assaulted this child or another of their children; or when a parent's rights to a sibling have been involuntarily terminated. In these cases states are required to hold a permanency planning hearing within 30 days to place the child in a permanent home.

In order to expedite the movement of children from foster care into permanent homes, ASFA changed the timeframes for making decisions regarding permanent placement. It requires that states hold the child's first permanency hearing within 12 months rather than 18 months and that states initiate termination of parental rights (TPR) proceedings for parents of children who have been in care for 15 of the last 22 months (with the certain specified exceptions). In addition, reasonable effort to place the child in a permanent home can be made concurrently with reasonable efforts to preserve or reunify a family.

In addition, this law builds in a review of states' performance. States will receive "report cards" on performance factors such as the number of adoptions and shortness of stay in foster care, and it establishes financial incentives in the form of bonus payment to states to increase adoptions; the goal is to double the annual number of children adopted by the year 2002.

Indicating that meeting procedural safeguards is no longer sufficient and that child welfare services should lead to positive results, the most striking new requirement of this Act is the requirement of accountability from the states. ASFA requires the development and implementation of performance standards. It also requires the development of an annual report to Congress on the performance of states on each outcome measure, along with an examination of the reasons for high or low performance. Outcome measures such as length of stay in foster care, number of foster care placements, and number of adoptions are to be documented through the Adoption and Foster Care Analysis and Reporting System. The Secretary of the HHS, in consultation with states, will examine the feasibility of developing a performance-based incentive system.

On January 25, 2000, DHHS published a final rule. Beginning March 2001, the federal government will conduct Child and Family Services Reviews (CFSR) that will focus on outcomes of safety, permanency, and child and family well-being. All states must complete the CFSR process within four years of the publication of the final rules (NASW '97, U.S. Department of Health and Human Services, 2000).

Other Laws and Programs

Funding for two programs came as parts of other larger Acts. The *Family Preservation and Support Services* provisions of The Omnibus Budget Reconciliation Act (OBRA) of 1993 established Part 2 of Title IV-B and added new funding "for the purpose of encouraging and enabling each state to develop and establish, or expand, and to operate a program of family preservation services and community-based family support services." Family preservation services are described essentially as preplacement prevention, reunification, adoption or other long-term placement, and follow-up services. Family support services are described as community-based services designed to increase the strength and stability of families. Funding for these programs, renamed the *Safe and Stable Families Program,* was reauthorized for three additional years under ASFA in 1997. The *Personal Responsibility and Work Opportunity Reconciliation Act of 1996 (P.L. 104-193)* includes a provision relating to foster and adoptive placement funded under Title IV-E of the Social Security Act. Section 505 amends Section 471 of Title IV-E by adding the following state plan requirement: ". . . The state shall consider giving preference to an adult relative over a nonrelative caregiver when determining a placement for a child, provided that the relative caregiver meets all relevant State child protection standards."

For adolescents aging out of the foster care system, *The Independent Living Initiative* (P.L. 99-272) was enacted in 1986 to provide funding for services to prepare them for independent living. In 1999, this program was expanded. The *John H. Chafee Foster Care Independence Program (CFCIP),* Title I of the

Foster Care Independence Act of 1999 (P.L. 106-169), provides funds to states to assist youth and young adults up to age 21 make a smoother transition to independent living. This program enables states to expand the scope and improve the quality of educational, vocational, practical, and emotional supports in their programs for adolescents in foster care and for young adults who have recently left foster care.

This framework of public laws and funding defines the boundaries of public child welfare practice. These laws reflect the dualism of the right and duty to protect, which is not always compatible with the philosophy of individualism and freedom of the parents to raise their children as they see fit without interference from the government. They also reflect the conflict between the values of the 400-year-old English Poor laws—that parents have to be fit and worthy to deserve the right to raise their own children—and the newer values of helping parents and preserving families. These conflicting values often pose intractable dilemmas in child welfare practice, where the child welfare worker's job is to protect the child and respect the rights of the parents whether or not they seem deserving by the values of society or the individual worker. Many child welfare workers experience a conflict in their role as "helper" versus that of an investigator and enforcer of law—an agent of social control.

THE SKILLS
OF PRACTICE

PART 2

INTRODUCTION TO PART 2: THE GOODNESS-OF-FIT MODEL OF PRACTICE

Public child welfare practice begins with the initial report of suspected child abuse and neglect; this is the child/family's point of entry into the child welfare "system," also commonly referred to as the "front end." It ends when the child is placed in a permanent home, when the child welfare system no longer needs to be involved in the life of the child and the family. This is the point of departure from the system, also commonly referred to as the "back end." The time between the front end and the back end can be very short or very long. During this time, the goal of practice can be different at different points; hence the nature of practice and the skills required can also be different. In this book, for the sake of ease in understanding, these points are referred to as different "phases" of work in public child welfare practice—Emergency Response, Family Maintenance, Family Reunification, and Long-Term Care, which may include adoption or legal guardianship or long-term foster care.

At the front end (referred to as Emergency Response) the immediate task is to investigate the report, quickly assess the risk of imminent physical harm to the child, and decide whether or not the child needs to be removed from the home immediately. If the risk of physical harm is not imminent or very serious (definitions of "serious" can vary), the worker must weigh the risk of possible physical harm against possible emotional harm caused by the trauma of separation from the family, and decide if immediate separation is necessary. The goal here is to protect the child while preventing unnecessary separation; the skills required most are the skills of assessment of risk of harm (physical and emotional) and crisis intervention.

If the child is to remain in the home, the next phase of work requires a thorough assessment of the factors that contributed to the existence of the risk of abuse and/or neglect in this family. These factors may be physical, emotional, or developmental; they may be caused by external environmental conditions and/or by internal psychological conditions. Assessment also needs to be made of the family's strengths and resources that can help them deal with these factors, and the factors for which they do not have sufficient resources but will need outside help. Based on this assessment, the worker must decide what services the child and the family will need and help the family access and utilize these services effectively. The goal here is to reduce the risk of harm to the child so the family can stay together safely—maintaining families—so this phase of practice is often referred to as Family Maintenance. In addition to assessment and crisis intervention, the skills most required here are the skills of case management.

If, however, the child is to be removed from the home, the task is to help the child and the family deal with the separation and to help the biological family with the factors that contribute to the risk so that the child can be reunited with the family as quickly as possible. The goal here is to reunite families, if possible, so this phase of work is often referred to as Family Reunification. In this phase, additional skills are required—skills of addressing issues of separation with the child and the family sensitively and in culturally appropriate ways; helping the foster family understand and work with possible behavior problems and emotional issues of the child; and maintaining a working alliance between the worker, the foster family, and the biological family.

If reuniting the family is not possible or desirable for the well-being of the child, then child welfare practice moves to another phase of work, that of finding an alternate permanent home for the child (referred to as Long-Term Care or Permanency Planning). In addition to all the skills required in other phases, skills that assume greater significance in this phase are working with the giving up of the hope of reunification, in the child and in the family, and preparing the child and the family to let go of each other so the child can form an attachment with another family. It involves a careful assessment of the child's needs—physical, emotional, and developmental—and finding a family that can best meet those needs. It also involves careful assessment of and decisions about the legal arrangement most appropriate for the new family—whether it should be adoption, legal guardianship, or long-term foster care, and the post-placement services needed to ease their transition into a new family arrangement and prevent disruption. This is the back end, the point at which the child is being prepared to leave the system.

Assessment, crisis intervention, and case management are the skills that form the foundation as well as the overarching framework of public child welfare practice in all its phases of work. Within this overarching framework, different skills are called for and assume greater predominance in different phases of child welfare work, depending upon the goal in that particular phase. These phases are neither linear nor occur in a set order, nor do they occur just once.

Repeated removal and return of the child to the biological family has given the name "revolving door" to the child welfare system. When placed out of home, a child can be moved from one placement to another for a variety of reasons and thus have multiple foster placements. Even long-term arrangements that are expected to be permanent can sometimes turn out not to be permanent. Thus, work relating to emergency response, family maintenance, family reunification, and long-term placement can occur more than once and occur at any point in the life of a child in the child welfare system. The more often it occurs, the more complex child welfare practice becomes.

The central core of public child welfare practice is the Case Plan—a plan of intervention and services to be provided to the child, the family, the foster parents—to prevent the removal of the child from the home, to make it possible for the child to return home when removal was necessary, or to place the child in an alternate permanent home if the child cannot return home safely. Federal law requires that each child must have a written case plan, which must show that the services to be provided are "appropriate" to the needs of the child and the family [P.L. 96-272, Secs. 475(1), 472(a)(1), 471(a)(15)].

For the case plan to be "appropriate," the child welfare worker has to know what the client—the child, the family—needs. As each client is unique and comes with his or her own strengths and limitations, the worker has to know what kind of help and services *this* client needs, what kind of help and services this client does *not* need. That is, the case plan has to be based on an accurate assessment of client needs, and it has to be individualized. If child welfare workers don't individualize their case plans, they could provide help and services that the client does not need, which would be useless—a waste of time and taxpayers' money. Or worse, they could do harm—hurt rather than help. An appropriate case plan is the best guarantee of success. An inappropriate case plan is, at best, an expensive source of frustration for all; at worst, it is a setup for failure.

In the formulation of the case plan, the enormous importance of accurate assessment cannot be underestimated. The outcomes of assessment are the decisions regarding actions to be taken by the agency—including the (sometimes legal) decisions about where the child will live, for how long, under what kind of societally imposed conditions, with what kind of taxpayer-funded services. Child welfare worker's assessment leads to decisions and (legal) actions that have profound implications not only for the safety and well-being of the child, but also for the integrity, dignity, and well-being of the family.

THE GOODNESS-OF-FIT MODEL OF ASSESSMENT AND CASE PLANNING

Families that come to the attention of public child welfare agencies usually have multiple problems and complicated lives. Rarely does one see a "simple" case. To be effective helpers, it is imperative that child welfare workers be very clear and specific about what it is that they are assessing, what it is that needs to be assessed, and what kind of information is needed in order to make that assessment. Collecting all possible information—whether or not relevant to the presenting problem—is an unnecessary intrusion into the family's privacy and dignity.

The concern in child welfare practice is children's safety and well-being, which we believe are best assured when children are raised by their families. Child welfare workers enter the life of a family when parents (or other adult caregivers) are unable to meet the needs of their child(ren), to the extent that it puts the child(ren) at risk of harm. Children's well-being depends on the individual child's needs (physical, emotional, developmental) and the parents' or caretakers' ability to meet those needs. While some needs are common to all children, such as food, shelter, love, and a sense of belonging, others can be very different in different children, and they also change in the same child at different stages of development. Similarly, parents' ability to meet the different and evolving needs of their children also varies at different points in the parents' life. Most parents can meet most of the needs most of the time, some needs some of the time, and some needs they can never meet. No parent can meet all the needs of all their children all the time.

Assessment in child welfare practice thus involves assessment of the child's needs (physical, emotional, developmental), parents' or caretakers' ability to meet those needs according to the prevailing norms of society, *and the fit between the two.* This fit can go awry for a number of reasons, for short or long durations, be it for children's needs that are out of the ordinary so that parents are unable to meet them without help, or parents having limited external and internal resources so that meeting even ordinary needs of their children becomes overwhelming. Or, it can go awry because of the larger societal conditions that are beyond parents' control.

What needs to be assessed, then, is the "goodness-of-fit" between the child's needs and the parents' ability to meet those needs according to the prevailing norms of society at that particular point in their life. In each assessment, the questions the child welfare worker needs to ask himself/herself and answer are: What does this child need—physically, emotionally, developmentally? Which of these needs can the parents meet adequately, which needs are they not able to meet adequately, and what kind of risk of harm does this pose for this child? Since no parent is ever perfect, what is adequate or good-enough parenting, keeping the cultural variations in mind? What kind of help will this parent or family need in order to be a good-enough parent for this child? From where? For how long?

What Does This Child Need? Assessing Children's Needs

Children's physical, emotional, and developmental needs are different at different ages and stages of their development. In child welfare work, four theories provide useful conceptual tools for understanding children's developmental needs, how developmental level affects a child's perception of events, coping mechanisms, and physical and psychological responses to stress and trauma. Three theories—Psychoanalytic (psychosexual theory and ego psychology), Psychosocial, and Cognitive—conceptualize child development in terms of a series of stages that occur in a fixed, pre-set, linear order. The fourth—Attachment theory—rejects the stage model and conceptualizes development from a relational perspective. These theories are normative and offer conceptual frameworks for understanding the process of "normal" development—the term "normal" being used very broadly. Research in the last several decades provides insights into the effect of maltreatment of any kind and of separation from significant attachment figures on normal development.

Parents' Ability to Meet Their Children's Needs

The McMaster model of family functioning (Epstein et al., 1993) provides a useful framework for assessing parents' or caregivers' ability to meet the needs of their child. Based on systems approach, this model groups the essential tasks of the family into three task areas. The *Basic Task Area* includes the meeting of basic physical needs such as food, shelter, clothing, physical protection, health care, and so on; the *Developmental Task Area* entails life-cycle issues—issues that arise as a result of individual and family development over time; and the *Hazardous Task Area* involves the handling of crises that arise as a result of illness, accident, loss of income, job change, and so forth. An assessment of how well the family or caregivers have functioned in each of the three task areas, currently and historically, gives an indication of the extent to which they can meet the physical, emotional, and developmental needs of their child in their normal course of life as well as in times of stress and crises.

Goodness-of-Fit

Putting together the assessment of the child's needs (based on developmental theories) and the assessment of the extent to which parents or caregivers can meet the child's needs (based on the McMaster model), the worker can identify areas where the two fit and how good that fit is, as well as areas where they don't fit and how harmful that might be to the child. Based on this assessment of the goodness-of-fit, an appropriate plan of intervention—a case plan—can be formulated.

CULTURALLY COMPETENT PRACTICE

Families who come to the attention of the child welfare system are not all the same. They come from many different cultures, have different notions of "family," have different norms about parent–child relationships, and have different child-rearing practices. Hence, what is goodness-of-fit for one family may or may not necessarily be goodness-of-fit for another.

Until very recently, child welfare practice in the United States has been driven primarily by the norms and standards of the dominant Anglo-European (i.e., white middle-class) culture. Historically this has resulted in the destruction rather than preservation of African-American and Native-American families. Over the last two decades, the dangers of the exclusive use of the Anglo-European perspective in defining the "normal family" and "maltreatment" have come into increasingly sharp focus. Numerous studies have been published documenting that children of color are becoming the majority of children brought into the child welfare system and that the number of African-American and Latino children in out-of-home placements is disproportionately high. These studies have raised very serious concerns about insidious racism. Furthermore, the resettlement in the last couple of decades of large numbers of refugees and new immigrants from such diverse parts of the world as Southeast Asia, the Middle East, Africa, the former Soviet Union, Central and Southeastern Europe, Central and South America—people whose cultures are very different from that of the dominant culture of United States as well as from each other—has exposed further problems in the exclusive use of the dominant culture perspective with all families regardless of their unique culture. Since the early 1990s numerous stories have been appearing in newspapers around the country of people's normal child-rearing practices being misinterpreted as "child abuse," resulting in unnecessary removal of children from their families, causing further trauma to families already traumatized by the experiences of war, refugee camps, and migration to a land where the ways of life are so alien to them, as well as befuddling, and further overwhelming a system that is already struggling desperately to fulfill its legal mandate.

These developments have made it profoundly obvious that effective child welfare practice has to take the family's culture into account and build it into every aspect of work with families. That is, child welfare practice has to be culturally competent, and child welfare services, programs, and policies have to be culturally relevant to the people they serve. Cultural incompetence on the part of the worker can weaken the engagement of the client in a working alliance (or worse, result in no engagement or even alienation of the client), an inaccurate understanding of the client's needs and strengths, and an inappropriate and ineffective case plan. Cultural incompetence on the part of the policy makers, planners, administrators, and organizers can lead to designing programs and services that are incongruent with the realities and needs of culturally diverse clients. Programs and services that ignore the cultural components of the lives of their clients are often un-utilized or under-utilized; they may even exacerbate the problems they aim to resolve. "Programs and practice interventions born outside of the appropriate cultural context pursue erroneous targets, squander scarce resource, and help few" (McPhatter, 1997, p. 274).

The family's culture, therefore, is a very important factor in the assessment of the goodness-of-fit between the child's needs and the family's ability to meet those needs adequately, and in the interventions provided to the family. Some cultural factors may contribute to the difficulties that bring a family to the attention of the child welfare system; others may contribute to the resolution of such difficulties. Cultural factors impact the interaction between the worker and the client and influence the selection of appropriate interventions with the family.

Culture

Culture is the way of life of a group, an integrated way of thinking, believing, doing, and being in the world that is passed on from one generation to the next. It encompasses shared knowledge, values, beliefs, customs, rituals, traditions, language, communication styles, prescribed (and proscribed) ways of behaving, norms of social and interpersonal relationships, food, music, art, etc. Culture is the ethos and philosophy of a people, their view of the world, their orientation to the problems of human existence. Shared culture creates a form of group identity, a sense of "peoplehood."

Everybody has culture. People's cultural beliefs and views at any given time are an amalgam of the beliefs, values, norms, and so forth of their race, ethnicity, religion, geographic location, socioeconomic status, and any of the other characteristics they share with others that gives them a sense of peoplehood, and the beliefs, values, norms, and so forth of the dominant mainstream culture of the society in which they live. People's cultural values and beliefs become the filter (the cultural lens) through which they perceive, understand, and relate with people who are like themselves and those who are different.

Culture influences all aspects of individual and family life. ". . . This means personality, how people express themselves (including shows of emotion), the way they think, how they move, how problems are solved . . ." (Hall, 1976, as cited in Lynch and Hanson, 1992, p. 37). Culture defines who is "family" and how families are supposed to function. Culture defines the concept of what is a "good" person. These definitions influence the roles and relationships within a family, the goals parents have for their children, and their child-rearing practices.

Diversity and Difference

Culture is often equated with ethnicity and sometimes with race, but these are different though linked concepts that can be subsumed under the generic notion of groups with a sense of peoplehood. Culture creates a sense of group identity (peoplehood) through shared values, beliefs, and worldview. Ethnicity is a quality of group identity that comes from shared history, ancestry, and language usually tied to a place and time. Race, on the other hand, is a sense of group identity that comes from similar physical characteristics.

Race is a broad general category that can permit visible distinction between different groups. However, within any given racial group there are many ethnic groups, and within any given ethnic group there can be many different cultural groups. Thus even though they may look similar physically and may share some aspects of their cultural heritage, all Latino or African-Americans or Asian-Americans or Native-Americans or Caucasian-Americans are not the same and do not have the same culture. In some cultures, factors other than race and ethnicity are the defining characteristic of their group identity. These include factors such as geographic region (for example, the Southern culture), social class (for example, the "country club" culture), religion and faith (for example, the Jewish culture, the Islamic culture), or any of the numerous other interests and characteristics that people share that gives them a sense of peoplehood, for example, the deaf culture, the biker culture, the gay culture, the adolescent culture, the gypsy culture . . . and so on.

Thus there are many different cultures. Different cultures have different norms about family life and parent–child relationships. Differences exist even in how they define "family." Cultural differences also exist in the way a "problem" is defined, perceived, and expressed, in solutions considered acceptable, and in the choice of treatment providers. Differences also exist in help-seeking behaviors and healing practices, in language, communication styles, and patterns of relating with helping systems.

It is precisely the different ways in which culture becomes manifest that is pivotal in child welfare practice. To achieve the goals of protecting children and preserving families, preventing unnecessary out-of-home placement, and ensuring permanence for the child, child welfare workers have to be able to engage families in a collaborative relationship in order to assess their needs and strengths and formulate an appropriate case plan. To do so, workers have to be able to "start where the client is" and understand where the family is coming from—the cultural norms and beliefs that may underlie their current situation—and work with them in culturally appropriate ways. This is important even when the worker and the client come from the same cultural background; it becomes even more important when the worker and the client are from different cultures. Failure to do so can have very tragic consequences for children and families and be very expensive for the child welfare system and the larger society.

Cultural Competence

The term "cultural competence" refers to ways of thinking and behaving that enable members of one cultural, ethnic, or linguistic group to work effectively with members of another. It is "the ability to transform knowledge and cultural awareness into health and/or psychosocial interventions that support and sustain healthy client system functioning within the appropriate cultural context" (McPhatter 1997, p. 261). It is used to describe a set of values, knowledge, and skills that workers in helping professions must develop in order to be effective with culturally diverse clients.

In child welfare practice, cultural competence can be conceptualized in terms of three dimensions—value base, knowledge base, and skill base (Manoleas, 1994). *Values* necessary for cultural competence include acknowledgement and acceptance of cultural differences, and respect for all cultures as equal. Different cultural beliefs are not right or wrong but just different, and they impact upon service delivery and service utilization. *Knowledge* required includes an understanding of one's own cultural identity and how culture has shaped one's own values, practices, and beliefs; a basic understanding of the client's culture; and an understanding of the dynamics of "difference" and "power" in professional helping relationships. *Skills* required are the skills of cross-cultural communication, engagement of the culturally different client in a collaborative relationship, culturally appropriate interviewing skills, the skills of creating a culturally appropriate assessment process and using culturally appropriate interventions.

Cultural competence in child welfare practice can also be viewed in terms of three levels—worker level, agency level, and community level (Miley, O'Melia, and Dubois, 1998). At the worker level, cultural competence implies that the worker has the values, knowledge, and skills described above. At the agency level, cultural competence implies that the agency's policies, practices, staff composition, and organizational structure are based on the same value system and are designed for multicultural interchanges within the agency, between the agency and its clients, and between the agency and the community in which it exists. At the community level, cultural competence implies the same value system manifested in the celebration of diversity, promotion of cross-cultural interactions, and social justice.

BECOMING CULTURALLY COMPETENT

Cultural competence does not mean knowing everything about every culture. Rather, it means acceptance of and respect for difference, and willingness to adapt one's practice approaches to make them culturally appropriate and relevant to one's clients. Within the context of this value base, becoming culturally competent involves developing self-awareness—an awareness of one's own cultural lenses and filters; acquiring basic knowledge of the culture of the client; acquiring an understanding of the dynamics of "difference," "power," and "authority" in worker–client relationship; and developing the ability to adapt practice skills to the client's cultural context.

Self-Awareness

Everyone has culture, and all cultures have built-in biases. Often people are not aware of the ways in which their culture influences their behavior and interactions with others. This may be even truer of Anglo-Europeans who are part of the mainstream dominant U.S. culture because Anglo-Europeans have predominated in the United States, and their cultural norms have shaped the norms of American society more than any other single group.

Workers' own cultural beliefs may affect the manner in which they interact with clients. Workers therefore need to examine their own firmly held beliefs about families and children and how they play out in relation to the beliefs and practices of their culturally diverse clients. This means examining one's own cultural lens and cultural filters through which one views others, especially those who are different in any way.

Self-awareness can begin with learning about the history of one's own cultural group, the beliefs, values, customs, practices, legends, myths, music, art, folklore, etc., as they evolved over time. Exploring one's own culture and examining how culture has shaped one's values, beliefs, behaviors, conceptions of "family," and notions of others who are different help reduce personal biases and stereotyping of others. Identifying and accepting both the positive and the negatively perceived aspects of one's own culture increase one's ability to accept these aspects in the culture of others.

Basic Knowledge About the Client's Culture

This includes (1) knowledge of the other group's religious/spiritual orientations and views of metaphysical harmony, (2) cultural views of children, (3) cultural style of communication—whether information is transmitted primarily through spoken words or through the context of the situation, the relationship, and physical cues, (4) culturally prescribed and proscribed behaviors in formal and informal relationships, (5) family structure and roles; child-rearing practices including nurturing, meeting physical and psychosocial needs, methods of discipline (including use of corporal punishment), (6) norms of interdependency, mutuality, and obligation within families and kinship networks, (7) health and healing practices, and (8) views of change and intervention.

Culture-specific knowledge can be acquired by studying and reading about the culture, talking and working with individuals from the culture who can act as cultural guides or mediators, participating in the daily life of another culture, and learning the language of another culture.

Understanding the Dynamics of "Power," "Authority," and "Difference" in the Helping Process

Child welfare workers hold an enormous amount of power over their clients—the power to bestow or withhold resources and services, the power to decide what the families must do when, the power to take their children away from them. This power is vested by law in the role of a child welfare worker as representative of the state.

Power differential between the worker and client is a potent issue in the engagement of the client even when the worker and client are from the same cultural background. When they come from different cultural backgrounds, the relationship becomes more complicated by the nature of their respective cultural groups' historical experiences of power (or powerlessness) in relation to each other and in relation to the rest of society. In order to understand the client's behavior in the worker–client relationship and respond appropriately, the worker needs to know the group's history of and experiences with power, dominance, subjugation, and oppression—be they due to race and ethnicity or other factors such as class, religion, gender, sexual orientation, disability, lor any other reason. Along with the history, the worker also needs to know the culture's coping strategies and survival behaviors, and how the group has weathered adversities and survived over time.

Workers also possess the authority that comes with professional knowledge and competence. While power may be respected in some cultures and feared in others, the authority of professional knowledge and competence is usually respected in all cultures; it usually inspires trust in the client even if the worker is of a different cultural group. In many cultures, authority is also vested in people by virtue of their age, gender, or role in the family and community. To use authority appropriately in the interest of the client, the worker needs to know the meaning attached to the concepts of difference, power, and authority, and where power and authority are vested, in the client's culture as well as in one's own culture.

Developing the Ability to Adapt Practice Skills to the Client's Cultural Context

One of the most crucial skills for culturally competent practice is the ability to engage a culturally different client in an accepting, genuine, nonoffensive manner. This requires the skill of cross-cultural communication, that is, being able to communicate with the client even when the styles of communication are different. Some cultures communicate primarily via the spoken word; other cultures place less emphasis on words and communicate more via body language and other subtle cues. Different languages and different meanings attached to particular words and gestures pose their own unique difficulties. When the worker and the client come from cultures with different communication styles or languages, the risk of misunderstanding is very high. The onus is upon the worker to understand the client's messages, however they are communicated, and to respond in a way that will foster client's trust.

Interviewing, assessment, and intervention skills grow out of the knowledge base above. Culturally appropriate interviewing techniques consider the manner in which questions are asked, level of intrusiveness, directness, social distance, formality, and forms of address. In assessment and intervention, the questions to pursue and the interventions to offer must be informed by substantial understanding of the client's cultural reality.

Becoming culturally competent is an evolutionary process that begins with self-awareness and increases with each interaction with culturally diverse clients. It is a journey that must be undertaken consciously. As in all professional development, there is no ideal completion.

GUIDING PRINCIPLES FOR CULTURALLY COMPETENT PRACTICE

Knowing everything about all cultures is an impossible goal. Therefore, some general principles are proposed below to guide culturally competent practice.

1. Start with some level of self-awareness and basic knowledge about the client's culture. Be particularly careful about knowing what words, ges-

tures, and body language may be perceived as pejorative or complimentary, and the significance to the client of nonverbal behaviors such as eye contact, proximity, touching, silence. Learn cultural strengths as well as weaknesses.

2. Recognizing the great variety of mixture of races, ethnicities, and cultures, make no assumptions from the clients' physical appearance about their racial/ethnic/cultural identity, or their concerns, priorities, and resources. Ask the clients how they identify themselves, how closely or not they follow their traditional cultural beliefs, customs, and practices, and what their culture means to them. Understand the differences between individual family practices and broader cultural traditions.

3. Assess the level of cultural assimilation, acculturation, and culture conflict—of the family with their environment, and between members of the family. Assess the role cultural factors may be playing in the creation of the client's current difficulties and the role they may play in the resolution of those difficulties.

4. Use the authority of professional knowledge and competence to gain the client's trust and cooperation, rather than the power of law to induce fear and coerce compliance. The use of legal authority does become necessary sometimes; use it judiciously when needed.

5. Despite best intentions, mistakes will be made, cultural faux pas will be committed. It's best to acknowledge them, and perhaps ask the client what might have been a more appropriate word or action under the circumstances. Respect for the client and worker intent can be conveyed not only in words but also in the worker's intonations and nonverbal behaviors.

In working with culturally diverse families, Lynch and Hanson (1998) point out, "It is our obligation to work with families to develop interventions that are culturally competent. It is also our obligation to interpret the new (i.e., mainstream) culture to families and help them find ways to negotiate it effectively" (p. xv).

This is the challenge of culturally competent child welfare practice in a multicultural society.

STRUCTURE OF PART 2

Chapter 3, "Assessment," presents selected concepts from theories and research that are particularly relevant to child welfare practice and discusses how they can be integrated in culturally competent practice to formulate appropriate assessments. Chapters 4–7 illustrate the use of the goodness-of-fit model of assessment and case planning in the four phases of public child welfare practice—Emergency Response, Family Maintenance, Family Reunification, and Long-Term Care. Chapter 8, Intervention, discusses the two predominant practice methods in child welfare—Case Management and Crisis Intervention, and then presents the principal features of four culturally responsive program models that have evolved in recent years—Family Preservation and Support,

Kinship Care, Family Group Decision-Making, and Shared-Family Foster Care/ Whole-Family Foster Care.

Case materials used for illustrations reflect family situations commonly encountered in child welfare practice anywhere in the country; they do not describe any specific family in any specific location. All names are fictional. Discussion of the case material is intended to stimulate reader's thinking and class discussions and hence is, by design, neither complete nor comprehensive. For the sake of ease in reading, the pronoun "he" is used consistently for the child or client.

3 CHAPTER   ASSESSMENT

Assessment is the process of finding out what each client needs in order to alleviate the conditions that bring the client to the attention of the child welfare system.

Assessment is not static but dynamic. It is a continuous, multimodal, culturally skilled process necessary to ensure appropriate services over time as client needs change, modified as more or different information becomes available. (The word "culture" includes all cultures, not just ethnic minorities.) It must be done nonjudgmentally, neither blaming nor absolving any of the people involved, but objectively recognizing and understanding the strengths and limitations, successes and failures, constructive and destructive patterns of behavior of the client as well as of all those affecting the client's life, and the conditions that led to the involvement of the child welfare system in this family's life.

The process of assessment involves *gathering* information that is relevant to the reason for referral of the client to the agency and to the worker, *organizing* this information in a clear chronological order, and *analyzing* the (organized) information to glean a clear understanding of the factors that contributed to the situation that brings this client into the child welfare system. An accurate assessment leads to a clear understanding of the kind of help (intervention) the client will need in order to alleviate that situation, and the agency's service plan.

Sorting out the often massive information about the complex lives of families can be a daunting task. Theories provide a way of thinking about and organizing large amounts of information in a systematic, logical way in order to make sense of what otherwise might be a confusing mass of interrelated data and events. Like lenses of a camera, theories can be used to get a clear picture of the client and the situation at hand; and, like any one lens, no one theory can give a clear picture of all the complexities of clients and their situations.

This chapter presents selected concepts from different theories that are useful in assessing the needs of the child and the ability of the family to meet the needs of the child. It also demonstrates how these theoretical concepts can be integrated in practice to formulate assessments and case plans.

ASSESSING THE NEEDS OF THE CHILD— THEORETICAL CONCEPTS

In child welfare practice, four theories offer useful conceptual frameworks for understanding children's developmental needs. Three theories—Psychoanalytic theory, Psychosocial theory, and Cognitive theory—view development as occurring in a series of fixed, predetermined stages. Though they all subscribe to the stage model of development, each of these theories views development from a different perspective. Psychoanalytic theory focuses on the child's internal emotional (psychosexual) development; Psychosocial theory stems from and extends psychoanalytic theory by underscoring the social and environmental conditions necessary for healthy internal emotional development; Cognitive theory focuses on the intellectual, cognitive development of the child. The fourth—Attachment theory—rejects the stage model and views development as occurring in the context of significant human relationships.

Each theoretical perspective provides insight into the development of one facet of a child's personality. To understand the whole child, development must be viewed from all of these perspectives.

Stages of Development

According to the stage model, development occurs in specific stages that coincide with chronological age. Each stage builds upon the one before; each stage has its own characteristic, typical behaviors seen in most children, which are therefore considered "normal" or "age-appropriate"; and each stage has its own particular developmental tasks to be accomplished, issues to be faced, and challenges to be met. When a child cannot master developmental tasks of the stage at the appropriate age, the accomplishment of later tasks becomes more difficult.

PSYCHOANALYTIC THEORY

Psychoanalytic theory, developed by Sigmund Freud over the course of almost half a century, was the first systematic theory of human development.

A physician specializing in disorders of the nerves, Freud (1856–1939) was often called upon to treat patients whose symptoms did not seem to have any physiological explanations. Trying to understand the cause of their symptoms, Freud would talk to his patients and explore their life histories and their childhood memories using various different techniques. He began to find that many of the symptoms and problems of adulthood originated from the emotional conflicts children experience in the process of growing up. From this work Freud pieced together, over the course of about 50 years, his theory of how the mind (psyche) works and how children develop.

The theory of psychosexual development of the child begins with the premise that all human beings are born with two instinctual drives—the sexual drive and the aggressive drive. The aim of the sexual drive, also known as the erotic instinct, is the preservation of the life of the individual and of the species. The aim of the aggressive drive, also known as the death or destructive instinct, is to destroy, to return from the animate into the inanimate state of being. These drives are unconscious. Seldom present in pure form, they usually appear in varying degrees of mixture of one with the other. They are also biologically based. That is, they are usually experienced as physical tension (for example, hunger), and the discharge of this tension usually occurs in some form of behavior (for example, eating). At birth they are untamed—demanding instant gratification, seeking pleasure, and avoiding pain. However, infants are not able to meet their own demands and needs; they have to depend on their external environment in the form of the parents or caregivers to do so. In the reality of the external environment, parents or caregivers cannot and do not always meet these demands. This creates a conflict between internal demands and external reality. This conflict produces frustration, pain, and anxiety. To defend itself against this frustration and anxiety, the infant's budding ego begins to develop internal, psychological mechanisms of defense.

With this underlying premise, human development is seen as the taming of these two conflicting drives as they come in contact with the external environment. Sigmund Freud introduced the notion of defense mechanisms at each stage; it was developed further and refined by Anna Freud and other subsequent ego psychologists.

Freud perceived childhood development as occurring in five distinct stages and phases. He called them oral, anal, phallic-oedipal, latency, and genital stages.

The Oral Stage (Birth to about 18 Months)   The first stage of development is called oral because at this time the mouth is the most sensitive part of the human body, the primary organ for the expression of drives. Infants experience and explore their world through their mouths. They experience pleasure in the acts such as sucking and swallowing, and they express anger and aggression in behaviors such as biting and spitting. The most common behavior seen at this age, across cultures, is infants putting everything in their mouth, edible or not.

The experience of feeding in early infancy is deeply profound and has lasting effects. Feeding relieves the physiological tension of hunger (which can become emotionally distressing very quickly and even overwhelming when food takes long to arrive), and it brings the pleasure and delight of the mouthing behaviors such as sucking, tasting, and swallowing. The experience of the mouth as the organ of tension-relief and pleasure, repeated several times a day, day after day, for several months, becomes etched in the unconscious and becomes a powerful presence throughout life. As adults, many people seek food for tension-relief when they are stressed, for solace when they are sad, or simply for pleasure. Resorting to the mouth in other ways (for example, sucking or chewing the thumb or cigar or pencil or candy) to cope with stress or simply for pleasure is a common form of behavior in children and in adults.

A landmark development of this stage is the appearance of separation anxiety and stranger anxiety. Somewhere between the ages of 6 and 11 months, children begin to show a definite preference for their mother (primary caregiver). They want to be held by her, fed and changed by her, to play with her. Mother is the center of their universe. Physical proximity to mother, being in her arms or in her lap, feels safe. Being away from her feels unsafe; it makes them anxious. In the presence of strangers infants of this age become wary, show signs of fear, and begin to cry.

The developmental task of this stage is to give up the breast or the bottle, not to put everything in the mouth, not to be too distraught when food or comfort does not arrive instantly. In families and cultures that believe in weaning by a specific age and specific methods, it can become a major source of conflict and frustration, a developmental challenge for the infant.

Anxiety at this stage is related to fear of survival. Anxiety arises automatically in response to excessive levels of frustration (such as prolonged hunger) or other threatening kinds of situations. Ego psychologists believe that infants experience this anxiety as excruciating physical distress accompanied by vague, amorphous fears that terrify and overwhelm them. To capture the depth of the overwhelming terror involved, they refer to it as "annihilation anxiety."

At this stage, the infant has little to protect himself from such anxiety. He can neither escape from nor change the situation, so he protects himself by developing the (defense) mechanism of *repression*—banishing any memory of this fear, anxiety, and pain into the deep, dark chasms of his mind, the unconscious—never to be brought into the conscious mind again. First beginning at this stage, repression—a forcible ejection from consciousness of those ideas and feelings that are not acceptable to the conscious ego—remains the most frequent way of dealing with a great number of the problems of childhood. It continues into adulthood, also in the form of suppression and selective memory.

The Anal Stage (18 Months to about 3 Years)   Toward the end of the first year, the center of pleasure begins to shift to the other end of the body, the anal region. Mouthing behavior still occurs, but it is generally sought when the baby needs comfort or tension-relief—when he is tired, hurt, or on the way to sleep. Now children begin to become increasingly aware of their bowel action. They attempt to investigate their own anal area, looking, touching, feeling it, and often attempt to investigate the anal area of animals (pets), siblings, and other children. For young children between the ages of about 18 months to 3 years, the anus becomes the most sensitive area of the body, the primary organ through which the child experiences pleasure and expresses aggression, anger, hostility.

Several kinds of behavior are typical of this stage. The first is the fascina-
tion with feces and toilets. Children play with their feces, smear it—on walls,
toys, themselves—on anything and anybody, and even eat it. Toilets are fascinating; they will play with the water, splash in it, drink it if allowed. Flushing
toilets can be frightening.

The second most common behavior is "getting into everything." The ability to crawl, pull themselves up, and walk expands their horizons. The world
looks a lot different now than it did from the earlier prone position, and there
is much to discover. At the start of this period the toddler is endlessly busy exploring his world—looking, touching, feeling, handling everything he can
reach; he is fascinated by the novelty of the world he is discovering and brings
much of it back to show it to mother. During later toddlerhood, learning and
practicing new motor skills take up much more of his time. So behaviors such
as pulling everything out of cupboards and drawers, dropping and throwing
objects, opening and closing drawers and doors, standing things up and knock-
ing them down, pouring spillable materials into and out of containers, climb-
ing up and down the stairs, and so on are very common and typical of this age.
These activities are repeated endlessly, over and over and over again, sometimes
to the utter fatigue of the adults around them.

Physical proximity to the mother figure is still very important, but there is
also the attraction of the world beyond. So the child will wander away in his
explorations, but he will often look back to make sure the mother is still there,
within sight or at least within sound. Often, he will stop doing whatever he is
doing, come back and physically touch her, stay close for a few moments, then
return to his activity.

Somewhere around 13–16 months, a pattern of negativism begins to appear. The child begins to say "no" to everything, repeatedly, regardless of the
context. At times he will do precisely what has been forbidden, even as he re-
peats the parent's words to himself, complete with intonation, "no no,
don't . . ." (Fraiberg, 1959).

Children are impulsive during the anal stage. When an impulse strikes, they
tend to act upon it instantly, without thought. Thus they are quick to get into
everything, prone to break things, to wander off, to have accidents. The tendency to act impulsively, to get into everything, to say no and do what is forbidden can get a toddler into a great deal of conflict with the parents and caregivers. Depending on the beliefs and practices of the family and the culture
about parental authority and control, this age can become a period of intense
battle for power and control between the toddler and the caregiver. In some cultures, toilet training becomes the focal point of this battle.

Two other developments are typical of this stage. One is the beginnings of
narcissism—self-love and self-centeredness. The child engages in his own individual play and is indeed totally self-absorbed even when playing next to other
toddlers (who are similarly self-absorbed and self-engaged). If another child
has something he wants, he has no compunction about taking it or snatching
it, and little awareness of or concern for the distress caused to the other child.
The word "mine" begins to appear in the child's vocabulary. He marks out his

own territory—*his* toys, *his* mother, *his* bed—there can be no sharing. Feelings of omnipotence (he is all-powerful, his mother is all-powerful) and omniscience (mother is not only all-powerful, she is also all-knowing!) also begin to become evident in his behavior, as does a sense of grandiosity and entitlement, a need to "show off" ("look at me, see what I can do . . .").

The other is the development of magical thinking. The child seems to believe that all things—rocks, furniture, toys—are alive. Such beliefs, part of many mythological stories in many cultures, are conveyed in everyday interactions and games between adults and toddlers. (For example, if a toddler bumps into a chair and falls, the adult will often say "bad chair . . . chair made baby fall. . . .") Another common belief is that body parts are alive and capable of moving about, that body parts attached in one way can be rearranged, if only one knows how. This belief is also often reflected in many games between children and adults ("I'll take your nose from here and put it over there," pulling a coin out of the ear). These beliefs can lead to a fear of toilets and become a possible cause of constipation. To the child, feces are a part of himself, alive and capable of feeling. When let go, they are flushed by a noisy, whirling, fast-moving water, and they disappear, gone forever. At times it seems better not to let them go.

The exploratory behavior of the anal stage serves many developmental needs. The child tests out his capacities—what he can do physically and interpersonally, how far he can stretch himself, and where his limits are. This ultimately gets woven into his sense of himself, of who he is. This stage also poses major challenges for the child. He wants to be close to the powerful and reassuring mother, but he also wants to explore. He wants to cling, but he also wants to be free and unfettered in acting on his curiosity. He is caught in what seems to be an intractable conflict. At times it is too much for him, he does not know what to do. At times he is compliant, agreeable; at other times he is defiant and erupts into temper tantrums. The developmental task now is to develop controls—physical control over his bowel and bladder muscles, and psychological control over his impulses.

The fears and anxieties typical of this age are about abandonment—of losing mother's love and being abandoned by her, especially if he wanders too far away, asserts himself too much, or displeases her in any other way. This can be quite terrifying, since he depends on mother for his physical and emotional well-being. The defense mechanisms typical of this stage are *denial* ("I didn't do it . . . this isn't happening . . .") and *projection* ("somebody else did it . . ."). If, however, anxiety gets to be too high to be allayed by these defenses, *regression* to an earlier stage of development, at least temporarily, becomes the defense of last resort.

In the resolution of conflicts of this stage, growth occurs in the area of body mastery and regulation of impulses, and in the child's ability to tolerate frustration and delay gratification.

The Phallic-Oedipal Stage (Approximately 3–6 Years)   The period between the ages of about 3 and 6 years is marked by much emotional turmoil and much emotional growth. Beginning with sexual curiosity and taking the child through the development of capacity to fantasize and the oedipal conflict, this stage culminates in the formation of the superego.

Sexual Curiosity   Around the age of three, children begin to discover their own genitals. They begin to masturbate—touching, manipulating, or rubbing the penis or the clitoris repeatedly. Generally, it is both normal and universal for children to handle their genitals; they will engage in it at frequent intervals, at any time or place, in or out of the presence of adults (unless they are told not to). Many children masturbate at bedtime before going to sleep, or when bored and otherwise not occupied.

In addition to touching, interest also develops in looking and showing. Children this age want to exhibit themselves; they are curious and they want to see others. They want to go into the bathroom with parents, to shower with parents and touch parents' genitals, to watch babies being bathed and changed. A favorite game is the game of "doctor." It allows children to look at and "examine" each other's body, to handle it, touch it. In this way, they begin to become aware of gender differences.

Curiosity about everything is a typical characteristic of this age. It continues the exploratory interests of the toddler, but with a difference. At 18 months to 2 years the child is fascinated by the novelty of the world he is discovering; at 3, he wants to understand it. Thus a new word—"why?"—enters his vocabulary, replacing the ubiquitous "no" of the anal stage. Children will engage adults in conversations that are studded with "whys," even when adults have no more answers.

Play, Fantasy, and Make-Believe   The nature of play with other children changes from the self-centered, self-absorbed individual play to cooperative and interactive play. The 3-year-old begins to show a capacity to share, will join another child or children in building a house or playing a game, will even show active gestures of comfort and consolation if another child is crying or distressed. With this increased capacity to participate in shared undertakings there also comes a desire to vie with others, to outdo others, to be the best, the biggest, the prettiest. In this way, children learn both to cooperate and to compete.

The ability to fantasize and play make-believe also begins to appear. Children begin to use toys to tell a story, and the story is usually about something of importance to their inner life. Play thus becomes a vehicle for expression of inner concerns and interests, for re-experiencing and mastering the many baffling and sometimes painful experiences of life. A very common game among children this age across cultures is "playing house." Many children have imaginary friends.

There are two other aspects of fantasy. One is the belief that wishing something hard enough can make that thing happen—an extension of the earlier feeling of omnipotence (hence the importance of fairy tales at this age). The other is castration fears.

In the course of getting acquainted with their bodies, children quickly notice the obvious anatomical difference—some people have a penis, others don't. In their efforts to understand why, they draw upon explanations given by adults, if any; the warnings, threats, and injunctions against masturbation; and the earlier magical thinking about body parts being movable and removable. Many children come to the conclusion that the absence of penis must be a punishment for something—that some people never got it while from others it got taken away as a punishment for some known or unknown transgression. To the little boy, this means he, too, could lose his penis, or somebody could take it away from him. In some families and cultures, this fear is reinforced in verbal comments from adults, in the threats against masturbation or even in playful teasing comments.

Castration fears are not confined to penises or little boys only. For both boys and girls, the fantasy and the fear is that *any* body part could be cut off, taken away, or damaged. Thus children this age tend to be fearful of doctors and hospitals, and particularly fearful of any surgeries on any part of the body. Sometimes even a haircut will produce a hysterical reaction. Often, castration fears manifest as nightmares and fear of monsters under the bed or in the closet.

The Oedipal Conflict   During this stage, children seem to go through a period of deep love and attraction for the parent of the opposite sex. This parent becomes the target of their passion and fantasies—the object of their first erotic love. This attraction reaches such proportion that the child wants this parent all to himself, to the exclusion of everybody else in the family, especially the same-sex parent. Many children (depending on the culture and the family) will talk of wanting to marry this parent, act jealous of the same-sex parent, want to get in bed with the opposite-sex parent. Girls begin to act coy and coquettish with their fathers; boys begin to act like lovers with their mothers. To the girl, the mother becomes a rival for the affections of the father, someone to be eliminated and vanquished. At the same time, she also loves her mother, wants her mother to love her, and fears her mother's disapproval and punishment. To the boy, the father becomes a rival for the affections of the mother, someone to be displaced and vanquished. At the same time, he also loves his father and wants his father to love him; fathers can be good, they look big and powerful and can be protective and comforting. At the same time, he also fears his father's disapproval, anger, and possibly punishment. Among the punishments that are feared is the threat of harm to the genitals.

Thus both girls and boys are caught in a mixture of intense love for the opposite-sex parents who cannot be available as the lover they desire, and the simultaneous love–hate (ambivalent) feelings toward the same-sex parent whom they cannot and don't always want to displace and depose. This situation produces enormous guilt, fear, and anxiety—guilt about hating and having other aggressive thoughts and fantasies about the same-sex parent whom they also love, about masturbation and possibly sex-play with other children, about doing and wanting all the things that are forbidden by the external environment. This guilt is accompanied by fear of punishment—from parents, from God, or from some other unknown forces with power and authority. Anxiety now is re-lated to the fear of losing the love and esteem of the love-object (opposite sex parent) and the fear of bodily harm as punishment from the same-sex parent (castration fears). The defense mechanisms of repression, denial, and projec-tion no longer suffice, so new and more sophisticated defense mechanisms have to be developed.

If parents can provide an environment in which the child can experience and work out his love feelings without too much encouragement or disparage-ment of the oedipal fantasies, the child soon comes to the realization that this wish and fantasy have to be renounced. The boy does not want to give up the feeling he has for his mother, but since he cannot depose his father he decides to become like his father (*identification*) in the hope that by becoming like his father he will be able to marry a woman like his mother. Similarly, the girl de-cides that the way to marry a man like her father is to become like her mother, to identify with her.

Other common defenses appear typical during this period. *Displacement*, the transfer of feelings toward one object (person) are displaced onto another object, is the basis of child's play. Feelings of anger with the parent, if expressed directly, can be dangerous and can bring retribution or guilt. However, that same feeling can be transferred to a toy (or to another person) and played out very safely (for example, child punishing a doll or kicking the dog). *Reaction-formation*, changing an instinctual drive into its opposite, is particularly useful when a new sibling arrives. The anger, jealousy, the wish to kill, are trans-formed into excessive love and solicitousness. Similarly, when a feeling of erotic attraction toward someone is prohibited, it can be transformed into and ex-pressed safely as its opposite. The most constructive defense is *sublimation*, the transformation of an unacceptable, destructive impulse into creative activity, achievement, and behavior that is more socially acceptable, desirable, and val-ued. For example, the desire to make a mess may be transformed into an inter-est in art or pottery-making; or its opposite, an interest in keeping things neat, clean, and orderly. *Fantasy* remains a major defense of this period. Through fantasy play, the child works out many feelings of hurt, anger, pain, and fear. *Regression* to an earlier stage of development when anxiety gets too high and cannot be managed by age-appropriate defenses remains a defense of last resort throughout life.

Superego Development   Somewhere around the age of 5–6 years, a new en-tity of the mind begins to emerge. Now, all the separate no-nos heard from the first days of life, the prohibitions, injunctions, warnings, and teachings about goodness and badness heard from parents, grandparents, the babysitter, the teacher, the religious leader, the policeman—indeed from any adult in position of authority—begin to come together. Some of them are real memories, others are fantasy-related. These memories and fantasies mesh with the precepts, val-ues, and symbols of the culture, forming an entity that becomes a dynamic pres-ence within the child. The external voices become his own inner voice. This new entity—the superego—serves as an inner regulatory agency.

The superego consists of two elements, the conscience and the ego ideal. The conscience is the seat of morality, a censor of morals. It tells the child what is right and wrong. It warns against temptations, forbids unacceptable thoughts and actions (for example, "you must not do this"), and can block action when warnings and forbidding fail (for example, "at the last minute I just couldn't pull the trigger"). It can stop indulgence in forbidden pleasures or giving in to enticing temptations. When it is harsh, it can stop the individual from engaging in even permitted pleasures. When all else fails, it can criticize and demean, torment and punish. Sometimes the conscience can become too punitive. Because there is no evading the conscience, the child seeks to escape his inner tension through some conscious or unconscious act of self-punishment. Some children tend to develop unexplainable symptoms like headaches and stomachaches; some children become accident-prone.

The ego ideal is a sort of model of the ideal self held up to the child of what he should be—the qualities, characteristics, traits, or possessions he should have in order to be loved, valued, considered successful, to feel good about himself. It is, thus, a regulator of self-esteem. This model of the ideal self—something that he should strive to live up to—is formed by the numerous verbal and nonverbal, conscious and unconscious messages from parents and family about their expectations and hopes for the child, their values, and their worldview. It is also shaped to a very large extent by the ethos and values of the larger society in which the child lives, the numerous direct and indirect messages conveyed in everyday interactions with other people as well as through TV and other forms of media. The child internalizes them; they become part of his system of ideals. In addition to these external elements exists the internal sense of grandiosity first evidenced in the anal stage, now reinforced by the very popular common belief (or myth?) of "you can be anything you want to be. . . , you can do anything you want to do. . . ." In the process of development, this feeling of grandiosity is tempered and tamed by the growing capacity for reality testing and social judgment, but it never really goes away completely. So for many people, the ego ideal remains far too inflated, unrealistic, and elusive. They are never thin enough or rich enough or good enough; they can never live up to their own ego ideal and hence never feel good enough about themselves.

The formation of the superego makes it possible for the child to have a new level of self-regulation and hence a new level of autonomy. It prepares the child for the tasks of the next stage of development, latency.

Latency Stage (Approximately 6–11 Years)   As the child begins to move beyond the world of the immediate family into the world of school, his attentions and interests begin to shift to new people—teachers, peers, other adults. Sexual and aggressive drives previously directed toward parents are now directed toward gaining mastery of physical skills, cognitive learning, and competition with peers.

The shift begins with the transformation of the feelings of love for the opposite-sex parent into idealization of the same-sex parent. Same-sex parents are rivals no more; they become heroes and role models. In early latency, boys and girls will often insist that their fathers or mothers are the strongest, the bravest, the best in the world. Boys seek physical and emotional closeness with their fathers, do things together, share interests. They want to please their fathers and seek their love, acceptance, and approval. They want to become like their fathers. Similarly, girls want to be like their mothers. They want to do things with their mothers, seek physical and emotional closeness, acceptance, and approval. During middle latency adults outside the family—real or fictional; for example, teacher, coach, scout leader, sports stars, TV/movie stars, or characters in books or electronic games—begin to become heroes and objects of idealization. Valued characteristics and traits of these heroes become incorporated into the child's image of the ego ideal. The fantasy of the earlier years turns into daydreams in which the child *is* the hero in the image of his hero. Daydreams are studded with themes of glory, rescue, adventure; characters like Harry Potter and Nancy Drew become fascinating, absorbing.

In early latency, oedipal conflicts are still close to the surface, superego is still in the process of crystallizing, and it is still easy to give in to temptation and knowingly do what is not right. When a transgression occurs, it is followed by severe self-reproaches. So children still need and look to the adults around them to reinforce the dos and don'ts, the rights and the wrongs, not only in themselves but also in other children—their siblings and their peers. That is, adults need to provide external controls when internal controls, the superego, falter. Therefore, rules and the enforcement of rules rigidly and equally to all become very important. Children expect and demand that the adult be strict and be "fair." The failure of the idealized adult to live up to this expectation is judged very harshly; it takes the child into the process of disappointment, disillusionment, hurt, and anger. Ideally, this process should culminate in a tempering of the idealization, an acceptance of the idealized adult (and therefore of the self) as a person with both positive and negative qualities.

Children at this age become much more group-oriented; they tend to define their identity by virtue of their place among their peers. In early latency, they often cleave to same-sex groups, each with its own secret rules, rituals, routines. Organized team sports such as baseball—once available exclusively to boys— become very important. These groups compete (and fight) with each other in supervised and unsupervised games. In this way, they acquire mastery over physical skills and work off much of their aggression. The ability to cooperate as well as compete, first manifest in the phallic stage, is now further advanced.

Aggression also shows up in other, less acceptable forms. Children this age can be very cruel to each other. They form cliques, punishing those they dislike by excluding them, castigating them verbally, beating them up physically, or bullying them. It is important to them that they affect other persons, and affect them rather painfully. There is pleasure in hurting others. Cruelty is not limited to other children; it can also be expressed against animals and against adults, especially if the adult is too weak or helpless to retaliate. Sometimes it manifests in the form of harmless or not-so-harmless pranks; other times it is expressed in more serious forms.

On the other hand, some latency-age children develop an intense, all-consuming love for a pet. They will shower this pet with infinite tenderness and care. (This is the theme of many Disney movies.) Sometimes a latency-age child develops an all-consuming love for a younger sibling and becomes fiercely protective of that sibling.

Anxiety at this stage is related to loss of self-esteem and the sense of competence, the I-can-do-it feeling about himself in relation to his peers. To deal with this anxiety, the child tends to use all the defense mechanisms of the earlier years to greater or lesser extent, depending on the situation and the extent of stress in the environment. A new defense that is seen very often is *acting-out*—acting behaviorally on an impulse to avoid the pain of the feeling that accompanies that impulse, without thought about possible negative consequences. Such behavior is usually aggressive—getting into fights. Other behaviors also seen frequently are *passivity*—doing nothing—and *counterphobic behavior*—deliberately doing what he is afraid of. Two other defenses also begin to emerge: *rationalization,* the use of convincing reasons to justify unacceptable ideas, feelings, or actions, and *intellectualization,* dealing with anxiety cognitively, analyzing and understanding it instead of experiencing it affectively.

The Genital Stage (Approximately 11–18 Years)   Adolescence is a stage of rapid biological and psychological changes again. Biologically, sex glands begin to mature and produce sex hormones. The release of sex hormones spurs an upsurge in aggressive and sexual impulses. All the issues and conflicts of all the earlier developmental stages, resolved and unresolved, re-emerge and necessitate re-working, now at a different level. In early and mid-adolescence particularly, this can flood the ego and stretch the defenses to the extreme.

First of all, dramatic changes begin to occur in the body. Bones begin to grow, height changes suddenly and unpredictably. Sex-related body changes— appearance of pubic hair, unpredictable uncontrollable erections, nocturnal emissions and voice change in boys, menstruation and breast development in girls—make young adolescents acutely aware of their own bodies and the bodies of their peers of both sexes. Suddenly, they begin to be flooded with new, often unacceptable and forbidden sexual/aggressive feelings and fantasies over which they seem to have little control, which they do not dare reveal to anybody else. This sudden flooding of the senses with sexual/aggressive stimuli requires time for processing, but there is no such time, the flooding continues. Unprepared to deal with this onslaught, the adolescent becomes moody, fidgety, restless, easily upset. School performance becomes erratic. When he can deal with it no more, his (beleaguered) ego closes itself off from further sensory stimuli until it has assimilated the previous flood of intake. This state may last for several days or weeks, to be followed again by a period of alertness and interest. Behaviorally, some days the adolescent is bright, alert, interested in the world; other days he may be apathetic, disinterested, unable to learn, often unable to hear the simplest statement or see the most obvious detail.

Bodies don't grow at the same rate in all children, so peers who were more or less the same size during latency are not that similar anymore. With different rates of physical growth, the level of motor skills also becomes different. This shakes up the adolescent's recently acquired sense of mastery, his sense of himself in relation to his peers. In addition, different parts of the body growing at different times, not in synchrony, produces clumsiness and awkwardness. All these changes are confusing and frustrating; they affect his self-image and his self-esteem. The adolescent may begin to feel inferior and inadequate because he does not match his own image of himself and is not what he thinks other people would admire. He defends against this anxiety in many ways; he may *overcompensate* by ridiculing other people or by trying through exercise or diet to force the body to do the impossible, or devoting an inordinate amount of time and energy to the body with beauty products, hair styles, tattoos, body piercings. Some adolescents develop *annoying behaviors* in order to attract attention even if that attention is negative; some turn to devouring knowledge so that the intellect will offset the physical condition. Some *withdraw* from all social activity when there is any possibility of comparison between themselves and others; some alternate between overcompensation and withdrawal.

In any case, belonging to, being accepted and affirmed by a group of peers becomes even more important, but now the groups don't have to be same-sex groups. Members of the group dress alike, act alike, hold the same values and beliefs. The security is in the sameness; differences bring excommunication from the group.

Perception of parents and other adults also begins to change again, creating demands for changes in relationships. Physically, the parents/adults are no longer the big and strong people they seemed to be when the child was young and little. Often the adolescent is as tall as his parent, if not taller, and is physically stronger than the parent; parents are no longer the heroes—the idealized people of early latency. Then he wanted to be like his same-sex parent; now he wants to be as different as possible. So he no longer wants to share any activities or thoughts or feelings with either parent. Physically and emotionally the adolescent can now do more, can take more responsibility for his own well-being, can be more independent. So he wants to be recognized as an adult. At the same time, he is uncertain about his ability to fend for himself; the very idea produces anxiety. He still wants to be a child, to be protected and cared for by his parents. Thus a conflict is created between the wish to be independent like an adult and the simultaneous wish to be dependent like a child. Behaviorally, one day he will behave as if he needs no advice, suggestions, or help from anyone; there is nothing he is not capable of doing all by himself. The next day he behaves and speaks as if he is hardly able to decide the simplest question for himself.

There are two major developmental tasks at this stage. One is the resolution of the conflict between dependence and independence. Ready or not, the outside world expects him to become independent and self-sufficient soon, at least economically if not emotionally. The other is the development of identity. As the child enters late adolescence, the resolutions and derivatives of all the previous developmental stages, the various and preferred defenses developed over the years, begin to gel together into a more or less predictable pattern of behavior—a personality—that becomes the core of his identity. While issues of identity are addressed at each developmental stage, and at each developmental stage a distinct facet of identity is developed and formed, now all these different facets begin to come together to fit like pieces of a puzzle and form a whole that gives the adolescent a coherent, integrated sense of himself. Identity defines who he is, how he relates himself to both the inner and the outer worlds, how he fits into his large social world. Once established, identity confirms for the child a sense of being a distinctive person. It carries him through his adult life.

Fixations, Regressions, and Developmental Arrests   The course of development is not a smooth, even process of progress from the oral stage to the genital stage. Growth in different areas of functioning—from suckling to independent eating, from wetting and soiling to bladder and bowel control, from egocentricity to relationships, from play to work, from emotional dependence to emotional self-reliance—does not always occur in synchrony with the chronological age considered appropriate in the child's culture; nor do the different areas grow in harmony with each other. At any given age, a child can be far advanced in one area while lagging far behind in another. This unevenness creates innumerable individual differences in children's personalities and makes each child unique.

Tackling the conflicts of each developmental stage takes emotional energy. An optimal resolution of the conflict occurs when parents (caregivers) provide an environment in which there is neither too much frustration nor too much gratification of the child's instinctual needs. However, as parents generally cannot do that, most children do not resolve all their developmental conflicts optimally. Unresolved issues remain and are carried within the individual throughout life, manifesting themselves in behaviors and attitudes that may or may not be adaptive. When there is too much frustration (or too much gratification) at any stage, an excessive amount of emotional energy gets bound in the issues of that stage, creating what is called a "fixation point." When more energy gets bound at any one developmental stage, less is left to tackle the conflicts and tasks of the next stage. The child's emotional growth is therefore weakened.

Fixations can be caused by any type of traumatic experience. The presence of a fixation at any stage is indicated when behavior typical of that stage continues to persist much beyond the age at which it is considered age-appropriate (for example, thumbsucking or bedwetting continuing well into the latency stage). The child manifests an unusual degree of preoccupation with issues of that stage in the themes of his games and play, in his interests and fantasies, and in his clinical symptoms.

In binding and retaining energy at a particular point of development, fixations engender a certain degree of arrest in development at that point. They also exert a constant regressive pull in the process of development, as these are the

points to which an individual regresses in times of stress. The stronger the fixation, the stronger is the pull exerted from such point. Sometimes even slight
difficulties at the higher levels lead to regressions quickly.

Human development, therefore, is seen as an uneven process of maturation
from a state of immaturity and dependence to a state of gradual mastery of
one's internal and external world. This process is marked by a varying pace of
development of different dimensions of psychosocial functioning, as well as
with the push-and-pull between the innate progressive and regressive forces
with some forces pushing the child forward in growth, others pulling him back.

> On this basis it becomes easier to understand why there is so much deviation from
> straightforward growth and from the average picture of a hypothetically "normal"
> child. With the interactions between progression and regression being as complex
> as they are, the disharmonies, imbalances, and intricacies of development, in short
> the variations of normality, become innumerable. (Freud, 1963, p. 139)

PSYCHOSOCIAL THEORY

Erik Erikson (1902–1994), a child psychoanalyst with an interest in cultural
anthropology, extended psychoanalytic theory by asserting that culture and social environment play a significant role in the development of a healthy personality. He reframed the conflict at each stage as "crisis" of development and
identified the social/environmental conditions necessary for a healthy resolution of that crisis.

Erikson based his theory on the epigenetic principle, which is derived from
the growth of an organism *in utero*. This principle states that "anything that
grows has a *ground plan,* and that out of this ground plan the *parts* arise, each
part having its *time* of special ascendancy, until all parts have arisen to form a
functioning whole . . ." (Erikson, 1980, p. 53). How the maturing organism unfolds depends on the opportunities and constraints in its social environment.

Based on this principle, human development is seen as a gradual differen-
tiation of parts over time according to a "ground plan," which Erikson also referred to as "the inner laws of development." Each part exists in a rudimentary
form at birth. At its proper time, each part rises to ascendancy, has a "decisive
encounter" with its environment during which it must work on a specific developmental issue and, toward the end of that stage, find a lasting solution. In
the working through of this issue, the potential exists for the development of
both syntonic (positive) qualities and dystonic (negative) qualities. Syntonic
qualities support growth and expansion, offer goals, sustain individuals
through the challenges of life; dystonic qualities make the individual more vulnerable to life's challenges. The potential of growth in any developmental area
therefore also leaves the child vulnerable in that area.

Erikson conceptualized personality development in terms of eight psychosocial stages over the life cycle—five in childhood corresponding to the five
psychosexual stages of Freud, and three in adulthood. He located each psychosocial stage "between a psychosexual one and an expanded social radius"
(Erikson, 1997, p. 80). For each stage, he listed a core crisis during which both

the syntonic quality (for example, trust) and its opposite dystonic quality (for example, mistrust) can develop to varying degrees. The resolution of the crisis results in the emergence of a basic strength or ego quality, which also has its own opposite counterpart (for example, Hope versus Despair). He pointed out that for a healthy personality, the syntonic quality must outweigh its dystonic opposite, and the resulting strength must outweigh its opposite counterpart, but all four are necessary for humans' adaptation to their social and physical environment.

The syntonic and dystonic qualities manifest as a series of alternative basic attitudes. Erikson used the term "basic" to signify that these attitudes are not conscious, and for attitudes he used the term "a sense of," which he described as follows:

> Like "a sense of health" or a "sense of well being" such "senses" pervade surface and depth, consciousness and the unconscious. They are ways of conscious *experience,* accessible to introspection (where it develops); ways of *behaving,* observable by others, and unconscious *inner states* determinable by test and analysis. It is important to keep these three dimensions in mind as we proceed. (Erikson, 1980, p. 58)

The stages of Psychosocial Development are as follows: A Sense of Basic Trust Versus Basic Mistrust, A Sense of Autonomy Versus Shame and Doubt, A Sense of Initiative Versus Guilt, A Sense of Industry Versus Inferiority, A Sense of Identity Versus Identity Diffusion, A Sense of Intimacy and Distantiation Versus Self-Absorption, A Sense of Generativity Versus Stagnation, and A Sense of Integrity Versus Despair.

A Sense of Basic Trust Versus Basic Mistrust (0 to about 12 Months)   The first component of a healthy personality is a sense of basic trust, a reasonable trustfulness of others and a sense of one's own trustworthiness. In adults, the impairment of trust is expressed in the form of basic mistrust.

This attitude toward oneself and the world derives from experiences in the first year of life—the oral stage. At birth, as the newborn infant is separated from the mother's body, his more or less coordinated ability to take in by mouth meets the mother's more or less coordinated ability to feed him. The child's ability is highly dependent on the anatomy and physiology he is born with; the mother's ability is highly dependent on her own development as a woman, her conscious and unconscious feelings about her child, cultural and societal norms and child-rearing practices, and the responses of the newborn baby. In the early days, both learn to adjust to each other. The groping and unstable newborn learns to coordinate his ways of receiving food and nurturance with the methods of the mother, who is simultaneously developing and coordinating her ways of giving. Trust begins to develop when there is a mutual coordination and regulation of rhythms between mother and child. As the child grows, he experiences his world through not only what he receives through the mouth, but also through his eyes, ears, and skin—in what he sees and hears, in the kind of touching, holding, caressing he receives. In the first six months or so, he primarily takes in (receives) what is given to him, but in the second six months as his capacity to reach, hold, grab, and bite develops, he actively attempts to get what he wants. Mother's response to these behaviors is influenced by her own individual circumstances and child-rearing practices, as well as by the beliefs, norms, child-rearing practices, and expectations of the larger culture and environment in which they live. These early interactions set up the prototypes of attitudes about "giving," "receiving," and "getting" what one needs. For trust to continue to develop, there must be mutual regulation and coordination between mother and child.

The amount of trust derived from these early infantile experiences thus depends on the quality of the mother–child relationship. Mother creates a sense of trust in her child with interactions that reflect not only her sensitivity to the baby's individual needs, but also a firm sense of her own trust in herself and her trustworthiness as a mother. When her child-rearing practices are in conflict with those around her, when they are depreciated by her family, by experts, or by other people in authority, her sense of her own trustworthiness is undermined. This, in turn, impairs her ability to foster a sense of basic trust in her child. This can be particularly pertinent in a place like America—a land of immigrants—where traditional child-rearing practices often conflict with the norms and practices of the new world.

The crisis of the oral stage comes with the convergence of three developments in the second half of the year: (1) teething and the accompanying biting behavior cause the mother to be angry and perhaps take the breast away; (2) the infant begins to become increasingly aware of himself as a separate person; and (3) the mother begins to return to pursuits she might have given up during pregnancy and after birth. These developments create a sense of separation, a sense of loss of closeness with mother. These early impressions of loss leave a residue of basic mistrust.

The ego quality that emerges from the resolution of this conflict is a sense of hope for the future; the counterpart of hope is a sense of hopelessness and despair.

A Sense of Autonomy Versus Shame and Doubt (about 1–3 Years)   During the anal stage when instinctual energy is centered in the anal region, the maturation of the sphincter muscles permits the child a new ability—to flex and relax his muscles voluntarily, to control his bowels and bladder, to be able to hold and let go, to withhold and to expel *at will*. As he progresses in this stage, the wish to exercise his will manifests not only in his control of his bowels but also in other aspects of life—in eating (or spitting) what the parents give, choice of clothes and play materials (including feces), getting into everything, generally doing what is forbidden. It is seen in the ubiquitous "no" in parent–child interactions at this stage—parents saying "no-no" to the child, child saying "no" to whatever the parents want.

For the child, the developmental push according to the inner laws of development is to exercise his will and develop autonomy; the developmental task is to learn to *control*—his muscles and his impulses—to begin to learn the socially appropriate behaviors. The issue for the parents is how much *autonomy*, if any, they will grant to the child. How they deal with this issue depends on what, in their personal and cultural beliefs, is considered appropriate— whether or not a child should have a will of his own, how much authority and control the parents should exercise over the child, what child-rearing prac- tices and disciplinary methods should be used to teach the child what he needs to learn to become a social being. Often toilet training becomes a focal point at this stage. Frequently shame and punishment are used as methods of toilet training.

To develop autonomy, early trust is necessary. The child must have faith that his wish to have a will and a choice will not result in loss of parental love. How- ever, parental firmness is necessary to protect him from the potential anarchy of his untrained impulses and unformed sense of social proprieties. While being firm, parents must also back him up in his wish to be autonomous, to be able to make his own decisions and choices. The task for the parents then is to set the limits and boundaries within which the child can be permitted to make a choice.

Given reasonable limits and boundaries, the inner developmental push moves the child into acquiring inner controls gradually at his own pace and learning socially acceptable behaviors without crisis. Crisis comes when outer controls are too rigid. Early and rigid toilet training prevents the child from learning to control his bowels and other functions gradually and willingly. Sim- ilarly, rigid outer controls in other aspects of life deprive him from developing a capacity to think for himself. When the child must submit to the will of those on whom he is dependent in every way, when compliance brings praise and non-compliance brings shame and punishment, the child faces the alternatives of complying and submitting to the will of others, or going with the develop- mental push for autonomy according to the inner laws of development and be- coming stubborn, defiant, rebellious. Mutual regulation is once again of utmost importance, for this is a decisive period for the development of a balance be- tween cooperation and willfulness, between the capacity to think for oneself or depend on others to make decisions, and between freedom of self-expression and its suppression.

"From a sense of self control without loss of self-esteem comes a lasting sense of autonomy and pride; from a sense of muscular and anal impotence, of loss of self-control, and of parental overcontrol comes a sense of doubt and shame" (Erikson, 1980, pp. 70–71).

Erikson pointed out that the kind and degree of a sense of autonomy par- ents can grant to their children depend on how much dignity and sense of per- sonal independence they experience in their own lives. Granting autonomy

> . . . necessitates a relationship of parent to parent, of parent to employer, and of par- ent to government which reaffirms the parents' essential dignity within the hierar- chy of social positions. It is important to dwell on this point because much of the shame and doubt, much of the indignity and uncertainty which is aroused in chil- dren is a consequence of parents' frustrations in marriage, in work, and in citizen- ship . . . . (Erikson, 1980, p. 76)

A Sense of Initiative Versus Guilt (about 4–7 Years)   The core conflict at this stage is the oedipal conflict. Boys attach their first love to mothers and develop their first rivalry with their fathers. Girls become attached to their fathers and become jealous of their mothers. This first love begets many (sometimes terrifying) fantasies about ways of eliminating the rival, and many fears about retribution and bodily harm from the rival. But the rival parent is also loved, so the child is caught in this dilemma of intense hate–love–fear for the same-sex parent who has become a rival and an enemy. The consequence is a deep sense of guilt and anxiety. The newly developing conscience is cruel, moralistic, and unforgiving, and it knows all. The child therefore automatically feels guilty about his inner thoughts and feelings whether or not anybody else is aware of them. Some children develop a conviction that they themselves (not just their sexual impulses) are bad.

Guilt and anxiety inhibit thought and action and restrict initiative. Some children become too obedient, too afraid. In many cases the consequences of guilt aroused at this stage do not show until much later, when conflicts over initiative impose a sort of self-restriction that keeps an individual from living up to his inner potential.

The ideal resolution of this conflict lies in the child giving up (renouncing and repressing) the oedipal wish and identifying with the same-sex parent. Identification occurs when parents neither encourage nor disparage the child's fantasies but simply accept them as a normal phase of childhood, when the same-sex parent engages the child in shared pleasurable activities and creates a collaborative relationship in which the child's instinctual energies can be redirected toward school and learning skills for adult life. When the child arrives at a resolution (identification), he seems to become more calm, more relaxed. "Most of all, he seems to be self-activated, in possession of a certain surplus of energy which permits him to forget failures quickly and to approach what seems desirable (even if it also seems dangerous) with undiminished and better aimed effort" (Erikson, 1980, pp. 78–79). The ego quality that emerges with this resolution of this conflict is a sense of purpose.

According to Erikson, hatred for a parent is one of the deepest conflicts in life. It is only when such hatred and guilt are alleviated that a person can develop a truly free sense of enterprise.

A Sense of Industry Versus Inferiority (about 7 to Puberty)   The developmental push at this stage, according to the "ground plan," is toward learning. The child wants to learn, wants to be shown how to do things, wants to observe and try to participate as his capacities and his initiative grow. While play is still important, the need now seems to be for a sense of being useful, of being able to make things and make them well—that is, for a sense of industry. A sense of industry develops when the child can engage in a task, work on it diligently, complete it, and do it well. It develops when his effort is recognized, acknowledged, and encouraged by adults whose opinion he values. Recognizing this developmental push, all cultures have some form of systematic schooling for children this age. The ego quality that emerges at the end of this stage is the sense of competence; the danger is the development of a sense of inadequacy and inferiority.

Schools and teachers have direct significance in the development and maintenance of a sense of industry (or inferiority) in the child. Crowded classrooms that permit little personal attention, inadequate books and supplies, or teachers who do not recognize, or indeed devalue the qualities and strengths the child comes with do much to create a sense of inferiority and inadequacy in the child. On the other hand, a good school environment can do much to create a sense of industry even when conditions at home are far less than optimal. With reasonably adequate teaching resources and respect from their community, good teachers can balance work and play, recognize special efforts, encourage special gifts. There are many stories of people who have been inspired by a teacher at some point in their life.

> . . . this is socially a most decisive stage: since industry involves doing things besides and with others, a first sense of *division of labor* and of *equality of opportunity* develops at this time. When a child begins to feel that it is the color of his skin, the background of his parents, or the cost of his clothes rather than his wish or will to learn which will decide his social worth, lasting harm may ensue for the *sense of identity*. . . ." (Erikson, 1980, p. 93)

A Sense of Identity Versus Identity Diffusion (Adolescence)   "One might say that personality at the first stage crystallizes around the conviction 'I am what I am given,' and that of the second 'I am what I will.' The third can be characterized by 'I am what I can imagine I will be,' and the fourth 'I am what I learn'" (Erikson, 1980, p. 87).

Following this line of logic, one might say that the fifth stage can be characterized by "I am all of the above, and more, together as one."

Adolescence is the stage when all the previous identifications, values, and qualities developed at each of the previous stages come together to form an integrated whole, giving the individual a sense of identity, of who he is. The danger of this stage is identity diffusion. Some identity diffusion is inevitable in early adolescence because of the dramatic body changes, the transitioning to sexual maturity, and anxiety about the world ahead in which the adolescent must make his own way. Identity diffusion in later adolescence can occur because of strong previous doubts about one's ethnic and sexual identity, the ego strengths and qualities that emerged (or did not emerge) at each successive stage of development, and the inability to settle on an occupational identity. To defend against a sense of identity diffusion, adolescents may overidentify with the heroes and charismatic leaders of various groups, or they may form their own groups and clans, which become very intolerant of and cruel to others who are different in any way.

Ironically, the danger of identity diffusion is also created by the very freedom and opportunity that is valued so highly in American society. The promise of "you can be anything you want to be" liberates young people from traditionally prescribed social roles and presents what seems like infinite possibilities. The young person is faced with the question, "what do I want to be?" He must choose from among a myriad of possibilities and decide for himself. Just emerging from childhood, most young people don't know what they want to be. Thus the question and the decision can be very frightening, especially when there is little meaningful guidance and structure from trusted adults at home or at school. There is, very often, a fear of making a wrong choice, which can lead to a fear of making any decisions or commitments.

> Democracy in a country like America poses special problems in that it insists on self-made identities ready to grasp many chances, and ready to adjust to changing necessities of booms and busts, of peace and war, of migration and determined sedentary life. . . . This is hard on many young Americans because their whole upbringing, and therefore the development of a healthy personality, depends on a certain degree of choice, a certain hope for an individual chance, and a certain conviction in freedom of self-determination. (Erikson, 1980, pp. 98–99)

A Sense of Intimacy and Distantiation Versus Self-Absorption (Young Adulthood)   When childhood and youth come to an end, another life begins—that of work, career, and a family of one's own. The developmental push is for intimacy with one other person, a kind of deeply satisfying emotional closeness that is different from the attachments of childhood and adolescence. Such intimacy is possible only after a reasonable sense of identity has been established. The young adult who is not sure of his identity shies away from interpersonal intimacy, but the surer he becomes of himself, the more he seeks it in the form of friendship and love. When such intimacy is not achieved, a sense of isolation and "aloneness" develops, even in the presence of other, numerous friendships.

A Sense of Generativity Versus Stagnation (Middle Adulthood)   Generativity is primarily the interest in establishing and guiding the next generation—usually one's own children. It can also take other forms of creativity and of altruistic activities that seem to create a sense of enrichment in life. Where such enrichment does not occur, a pervading sense of stagnation and interpersonal impoverishment develops. Often people compensate for this impoverishment by becoming overly self-indulgent and self-centered.

A Sense of Integrity Versus Despair (Old Age)   According to Erikson, integrity is a state of mind one arrives at after weathering the triumphs and travails of the previous stages. It is the state of acceptance of one's life the way it was, and that this is the way it had to be. This state of mind is characterized by a measure of serenity and peace with oneself. The danger here is a sense of despair, which manifests as disgust, chronic displeasure, and a fear of death—conscious or unconscious.

The Ninth Stage   In his original formulation in the 1940s and 1950s, when he was in his middle adulthood, Erikson conceptualized adulthood in terms of three stages described above. Later, when he was in his 90s, he added another stage and called it the Ninth Stage. Old age in the 80s and 90s, Erikson noted, brings with it new demands and challenges. Even the best cared-for body begins to weaken and lose autonomy. Independence and control are challenged, self-esteem and confidence weaken, hope and trust sustain no more. The dystonic quality of each of the previous stages becomes the more prominent one.

The wisest course under the circumstances, said Erikson, is to face down despair with faith and appropriate humility.

Thus Erikson's theory synthesizes psychosexual and social development.

> Personality can be said to develop according to steps predetermined in the human organism's readiness to be driven toward, to be aware of, and to interact with, a widening social radius, beginning with the dim image of a mother and ending with mankind, or at any rate that segment of mankind which "counts" in the particular individual's life. (Erikson, 1980, p. 54)

COGNITIVE THEORY

Jean Piaget (1896–1980), a Swiss psychologist, viewed development from the perspective of intellectual or cognitive growth—how children learn to think, reason, and perceive the world around them. His interest was in learning *how* the child comes to know what he knows, how intelligence develops. In pursuit of the question of *how,* Piaget and his colleagues also amassed a great deal of information about *what* the child knows, and *when* he knows it. The "what" and the "when" aspects of his work are very useful in understanding children's behavior; the "how" provides an understanding of what they need in order to realize their cognitive potential. What has come to be known as Piaget's Cognitive theory is the result of Piaget's own work (observations of his own children and numerous experiments with other children) as well as the work of many of his associates and colleagues around the world. His observations have been confirmed and validated by others in experiments with children across cultures, races, and languages.

According to Piaget, mental development occurs via the mechanism of *adaptation* that characterizes any biological organism. Adaptation occurs via the twin processes of *assimilation* and *accommodation. Assimilation* (psychological or biological) is the transformation of the external world in such a way as to make it an integral part of oneself; Piaget referred to it as "fusing a preexisting schema and a new object" (Piaget, 1977, p. 216). Biologically, it means the taking in and digesting of food; psychologically, it means taking in new knowledge and experiences (stimuli) from the environment and fusing them into the preexisting structures of the mind—the knowledge, intelligence, and the preconceived notions. *Accommodation* is the stretching of the preexisting structures in different directions and modifying them in such a way as to permit fusion of new information that could not be assimilated otherwise. That is, it is the altering of preconceived notions to interpret an event or experience in a new way. One does not necessarily accommodate to the reality of the event or experience, but to reality as it is understood and is manageable at the time.

The mental structures for the processes of assimilation and accommodation begin with the automatic reflexes an infant is born with, such as the sucking reflex and the grasping (palmar) reflex. Through these rudimentary mental structures, the infant filters in the stimuli it can manage (out of all the stimuli in the environment) and assimilates the new information (knowledge) from these stimuli (experiences) much as the body assimilates food. Just as assimilated food helps the body grow, the assimilated knowledge helps the mental structures grow and modify. Growing mental structures can take in more stimuli; more stimuli help the mental structures continue to grow. The process is repeated over and over again. Thus grow intelligence and the child's internal schema—the notions and conceptions of the world through which further experiences and events are understood and interpreted. Changes in the mental structures are reflected in the changes in the repertoire of the child's behaviors to accommodate to the demands of reality.

Adaptation thus is a continuous, spiral process of assimilation–accommodation. The first building blocks of the very early phases of cognition are the birth reflexes; intelligence begins with them and develops as a function of their adaptation to the environment.

According to Piaget, mental development of the child unfolds over three major periods—the Sensori-Motor Period between the ages of 0 to 2 years; the Period of Concrete Operations between 2 and 11 years; and the Period of Formal Operations between the ages of 11 and 16 years. Each period extends the one before, reconstructs it on a new level, and then surpasses it, taking it to the next level. The three periods are further divided into stages. These stages have a definite and constant order of succession; their sequence never varies though the average ages at which they occur and the rate of development may vary. Mental structures constructed at a given age become an integral part of the structures of the following age. Thus each structure results from the preceding one, integrating it as a subordinate structure, and prepares for the subsequent one, into which it is sooner or later integrated. At any given time, the child's behavior reflects the stage of development of his mental structures. No matter how unusual or puzzling, behavior can be understood in terms of the child's mental structures at the time—what he was born with, the nature of stimuli in his environment, and his adaptation to them.

According to Piaget, these stages of development are not entities in themselves but serve as points of reference for understanding the course of development. Nor are they absolute, a prescription for what must be achieved. They describe the *potential*—what *could* be achieved. The actual rate and degree of completion vary with each individual, depending on the individual's biology, culture, and the nature of stimuli in his environment.

The Sensori-Motor Period (0–2 Years) The first cognitive substructures— filters of the mind that take in and assimilate new information and form the first notions of the world—are constructed during the first 18 months of life.

Development in this period is a progression from spontaneous movements and reflexes to acquired habits to intelligence in six stages that flow smoothly from one to the other. It begins at birth with the sucking reflex and the palmar (grasping) reflex. These two reflexes are quickly consolidated by repeated use— what Piaget called functional exercise. For example, a newborn child doesn't quite know where the nipple is and has to be guided. After a few days, he nurses with much more assurance and finds the nipple easily (*stage 1*). Repetitive use of reflexes, supported by neurological and physical maturation, forms the beginning of learned behavior and acquired habits (*stage 2*). In about the second month, the infant can consciously repeat an action. Behavior that was an automatic reflex now becomes a deliberate response to a stimulation of a previous experience. An example is seen in the evolution of thumbsucking behavior. While it may have started accidentally, the child soon finds that sucking the thumb (or finger or toe) produces tension-relief and pleasure. This information is assimilated in the infant's schema. Now when the child needs tension-relief or pleasure, he will purposefully bring the thumb into his mouth. Next, eye–hand coordination begins to emerge (*stage 3*). At around 4½ months the baby starts grasping and manipulating everything he sees in his immediate vicinity. The grasping reflex evolves in to shaking, pulling, tugging. Now behavior is directed toward making events last; for example, grasping and holding a finger, repeatedly banging an object to produce a sound, repeatedly pulling the cord of the mobile above his crib to make it move and produce music, and the like. Imitation behavior also begins. The child will imitate gestures of the adult such as opening and closing of fingers, sticking the tongue out, and so on.

Between 8–12 months (*stage 4*), the child begins to reach for an object that is out of reach in simple ways. Around 11–12 months, the child experiments with new and increasingly more complex ways of obtaining the object and learns by trial and error (*stage 5*). Between 12 and 18 months (*stage 6*), the trial-and-error of earlier experiments begins to diminish; he can now use the information assimilated from these experiments to think before he acts, to consider new and different ways of achieving what he wants. He learns that objects out of sight have not ceased to exist and can be found (object permanency). He delights in games that involve hiding an object and finding it—games such as peek-a-boo acquire particular developmental significance.

The sixth stage marks the end of the sensori-motor period and transition to the next period. During this stage, sensori-motor experiences are slowly replaced by semi-mental functioning. Children now begin to gain the ability to recall without having to repeat an activity with their sensori-motor system. They have developed some notions of time, space, object permanence, and constancy of size and form. Imitation now proceeds with the attempt to copy either the action itself or the representative symbol of the action (for example, words). Often, when they come across something new—object, person, situation, taste, noise—they will experiment to discover the nature and quality of new experiences, then they will leave the new experience alone for a while before returning to it with a clearer notion in mind of how the experience can start to fit into an emerging understanding (schema).

Thus in this first major period of cognitive development, substructures for cognition develop via the repetitive, rhythmic exercise of sensori-motor structures—vision (looking), hearing (listening), prehension (grasping), ingesting (sucking), vocalization (crying) and the general limb movement. Intelligence develops via action; the child learns by doing. Initially the child's universe is entirely centered on his own body and action. In the course of the first 18 months, a kind of general decentering process occurs whereby the child comes to regard himself as an object among others in a universe that is made up of permanent objects. He learns that an object does not cease to exist when it disappears, and he learns where it does go.

Affect and the first affective substructures also develop from sensori-motor experiences. Early manifestations of affect (for example, smiling, crying) are related to physiological satisfactions and discomforts. In the course of stages 3 and 4, manifestations of psychological satisfactions and discomforts also begin to appear, for example, smiling and cooing in interactions with familiar people, wariness and anxiety in the presence of strangers, and so on. Noting the correlations between cognitive development and interpersonal interactions, Piaget pointed out that the developmental arrests observed in children being raised in institutions may not necessarily be due to separation from the mother per se, as believed, but due to lack of stimulating interactions. Separation from mother becomes a factor because she is the one who creates a "private mode of exchange" between herself and her child that provides the stimulating interactions (Piaget, 1969, p. 27).

The Period of Concrete Operations (Ages 2 to about 11 Years)   Toward the end of the sensori-motor period, around 1½ to 2 years of age, a new function appears that Piaget called the semiotic or symbolic function. This function consists of the ability to represent something (a signified something: object or event) by means of a signifier (language, mental image, symbolic gesture, and so on). He defined representation as "the presentation, in thought, of what is perceptually absent" (Piaget, 1977, p. 485). This ability is manifested in five kinds of behavior patterns that begin to appear almost simultaneously around the age of 2. In the order of increasing complexity, they are (1) deferred imitation—imitation that starts after the disappearance of the model, (2) symbolic play or the game of pretending, (3) drawing or graphic image—which rarely appear before the age of 2½, (4) mental images—reproductive images that evoke sights seen previously, and anticipatory images of objects not seen before, and (5) nascent language, which permits verbal evocation of events that are not occurring at the time; for example, the child saying, "Daddy go bye-bye," pointing to the door after the father has left. The latter four—symbolic play, drawing, mental images, and language—are based on imitation.

In these behavior patterns, symbolic-representational thought structures evolve from simple to increasingly complex patterns over the next eight or nine years, consolidating and coming to a state of equilibration around the age of 11.

Like the sensori-motor period, this period, too, is divided into stages.

The Preoperational Stage (2–4 Years)   At this age, the child is beginning to take a greater interest in objects and people around him. He knows the world only as he sees it, and he sees it from his own point of view. As this world is all he knows, he believes that everyone sees, thinks, and feels as he does.

This is the age of curiosity. Preschoolers are always questioning and investigating new things, looking for explanations of why things are the way they are. When they don't find explanations that fit their internal schema, they make up their own. They believe that natural phenomena are man-made, and everything has life. They may know how to count, but they count by rote; they don't have the concept of numbers. They can focus on only one idea at a time. For example, a mother can only be a mother; she cannot also be a wife, a sister, a daughter, or have any other role simultaneously. A big red ball can be either big or red. It is difficult to comprehend both qualities of the ball at the same time.

Children this age do not have the faculty of *conservation*—the ability to retain in memory the characteristics (shape, size, weight, color) of an object encountered in the past, which is not in view presently. Piaget's experiments with glasses of different sizes are commonly used to illustrate this concept. The same amount of liquid is poured into a tall, thin glass and a short, wide glass. When asked which glass has more liquid, the two-year-old will invariably point to the tall glass. The level of the liquid is higher, so, in the thinking of the child, it must be more.

Stage of Intuitive Thought (4–7 Years)   For children between the ages of 4 and 7, widening social contacts reduce egocentricity and increase social participation. Children begin to use words to express their thoughts and feelings. They begin to grasp the concept of numbers and the notion of reversibility, that what can go up can also go down, numbers that can be added can also be subtracted. Symbolic play becomes the most important developmental phenomenon. It is through symbolic play that the child assimilates new experiences. Thinking is based more on intuition than on reason or logic.

Stage of Concrete Thought (7–11 Years)   For a child around the age of 7 or 8, concepts of numbers, time, space, and speed begin to coalesce. The child begins to understand the concepts of multiplication and division. He can now group things with like characteristics (classification) and arrange them according to increasing or decreasing size (seriation). He also discovers the notion of conservation. Now when asked which glass has more liquid, he can see that it is the same amount of liquid, regardless of the shape of the glass.

Notions of morality and conscience also begin to coalesce at this stage. The overriding interest at this stage is in rules of behavior, be it in games and sports or in other aspects of life. Between the ages of 2 and 4, rules were simply accepted; now the interest is in the negotiation of rules rather than just accepting and obeying them, and in the just and fair enforcement of rules. This leads in to a sense of obligation to abide by those rules. However, formation of a sense of obligation is subject to the condition that the rules are given by a person for whom the child has both affection and fear. Affection alone is not sufficient to produce a sense of obligation; fear alone provokes only physical or self-interested submission.

The Period of Formal Operations (11 to about 15 Years)   As the child enters the age of preadolescence, new substructures of abstract thought, reason, and logic begin to evolve. The nature of thought, therefore, changes. While the child thinks largely in terms of the present, the here-and-now, the adolescent can think beyond the present, beyond his own experiences and belief systems, to the future. While still egocentric, the adolescent can hear and see things from perspectives other than his own. He can now comprehend geometric and proportional relationships, the concepts of relativity, probability, and chance, and think in terms of the hypothetical. He forms notions, ideas, and concepts about everything from the past through the present into the future; his conceptual world becomes full of ideas and theories regarding himself, life, society—what is, what ought to be, what could be. Values regarding morality, religion, social justice, and social ideals may be questioned, re-examined, and re-formed, in agreement with or in opposition to family and culture—depending also on social factors such as socialization and cultural transmission.

These new substructures of abstract thought, reason, and logic make the adolescent capable of reflective thinking.

Thus, according to Piaget, cognitive development begins with a physical world—the world of objects. It proceeds through a world of social relations and culminates in a world of ideas—the ideational world. The final mental structures of formal thought are a synthesis and a fusion of all the substructures developed in previous stages; intellectual development from here on consists not of a creation of new structures but an increase in knowledge and depth of understanding. These complex mental structures are the filters through which the mind takes in and assimilates new information; they are the mental tools for dealing logically and effectively with the complex demands of everyday life.

Attachment Theory

Attachment theory presents a different view of development. The stage model conceptualizes human development as occurring in a series of pre-set stages along a single developmental line; one could get stuck (fixated) at any stage and could regress to a previous stage along that line. Attachment theory conceptualizes development as unceasing progression along one or another of an array of potential developmental pathways. Like branches of a tree, all pathways start close together so that at conception, an individual could potentially develop along any of them. Should he encounter an obstruction or an opportunity, he can move to another pathway, like moving to another branch of the tree. Development thus is seen as neither linear nor pre-set, but dependent on the interaction between the individual as he has developed up to that time, and the environment in which he finds himself at that time.

> At conception it turns on the interaction between the newly formed genome and the intrauterine environment; at birth it turns on interaction between the biological constitution of the neonate, including the germinal mental structure, and the family, or non-family, into which he is born; and at each age successively it turns on the personality structures then present and the family and later the wider social environment then current. (Bowlby, 1988, p. 64)

A critical element in that environment, according to attachment theory, is the quality of intimate affectional bonds and attachments with other people.

Attachment theory was first introduced in the 1960s by John Bowlby (1907–1990), a child psychiatrist in London. Bowlby's ideas evolved from studies in the 1940s and 1950s of bonding behavior in birds and mammals, which showed that bird and other animal babies did not develop normally when separated from their mothers. Around the same time, other studies were beginning to show the adverse effects of institutional care on human infants. In his own practice, Bowlby was observing anxiety, grief, and depression in children separated from their mothers when hospitalized—feelings that could not be explained by the then-prevalent concepts of psychoanalytic theory. From these studies and observations, Bowlby concluded that like other animals and birds, human infants too must have such bonding behaviors, that they too must be predisposed toward some sort of relational experience, and that with them too development could go awry if separated from their mothers. Thus began the theory of Attachment and Separation. Initially introduced by Bowlby, attachment theory was advanced by his colleague Mary Ainsworth in her now-famous studies of mother–infant bonding during the first year. Much research since then by many researchers in many different countries and cultures with many different populations has contributed to the state of knowledge at this time; much research continues to date.

Attachment theory states that human infants are born with a biological instinct to become attached to a primary caregiver (usually the mother) in order to ensure their physical survival and emotional well-being. Thus they are born with a repertoire of behaviors such as clinging, sucking, smiling, babbling, looking, listening, and so on, whose goal is to elicit maternal care and keep the mother close by. Establishing and renewing proximity to the mother creates feelings of love, security, and joy; distance and separation create feelings of insecurity, anxiety, grief, and in extreme cases, depression. These relationship-seeking behaviors are enriched and developed by the responses they elicit from the environment. During the first year, the child begins to display a range of systematic behaviors indicating attachment to the mother or primary caregiver— crying at her departure, showing pleasure at her return, following her, clinging to her when frightened—which Bowlby refers to as the "attachment behavior system." The attachment behavior system leads the child to continually monitor the accessibility of the mother (attachment figure), and to flee to her as a haven of safety when alarmed, fatigued, or distressed for any other reason. The attachment behavior system is considered to be biologically-based and as essential to survival as the feeding system or the reproductive system.

While first attachment (with the primary caregiver) is formed around 7 months of age, the need for attachments and intimate emotional bonds with selected individuals persists throughout life. During infancy and childhood bonds are with parents (or parent substitutes) who are looked to for protection, comfort, and support. During adolescence and adulthood these bonds are complemented by new bonds with friends and romantic partners. Often children as well as adults develop a hierarchy of attachments with multiple figures, and although most noticeable in early childhood, attachment behavior—the propensity to monitor the accessibility of attachment figures and to seek them out, especially in stressful situations—can be observed throughout life. Attachment theory therefore does not regard the desire for comfort and support in adversity as childish dependency. Instead, it regards the capacity to make intimate emotional bonds with other individuals, sometimes in careseeking role and sometimes in the caregiving one, as a principal feature of effective personality functioning and good mental health.

According to attachment theory, personality develops in the context of close social/emotional relationships, beginning with the first attachment, in two ways. First, the child uses the mother (the primary attachment figure) as "a secure base" from which to explore the world. When the child feels secure, he explores his world more freely. When he wanders too far away in his explorations or he perceives the environment as alarming, he pulls closer to mother for protection, security, and comfort. When proximity and contact with mother create a sense of "felt security," exploration begins again. The more secure he feels, the more confidently he explores the world. Attachment behavior and exploratory behavior are thus seen as complementary.

Second, through attachment relationships with other people the child develops a sense of himself as a person and of others around him.

From the very beginning, babies are active participants in the social world in which they find themselves. They show interest in and try to engage other people in interactions. Reciprocal interactions are a source of pleasure and stimulation, but there are times interactions with people and objects can hurt. The world is not always very safe.

According to Bowlby, the relative safety or danger of a situation is not appraised afresh every time. Through continual interactions with the world of people and objects, babies begin to construct increasingly complex "internal working models" (like Piaget's cognitive structures) in order to make sense of that world, the people and objects in it, and of themselves in relation to that world. Of particular significance in infancy and childhood is the sense they make of themselves in relation to their mother or primary attachment figure. If the attachment figure gives help and comfort when needed, the child will tend to develop a working model of the parent as loving and of himself as a person worthy of such love. Conversely, if an attachment figure frequently rejects or ridicules the child's bids for comfort in stressful situations, the child may come to develop not only an internal working model of the parent as rejecting but also one of himself as not worthy of help and comfort.

Internal working models serve to appraise the relative safety or danger of a new situation and guide behavior. Operating outside consciousness, internal working models of the significant attachment figures and of the self become the templates within which subsequent relationships are interpreted and experienced.

PATTERNS OF ATTACHMENT

Ainsworth (1978) expanded upon Bowlby's primarily biological perspective through her now-famous "strange situation" experiments to study mother–infant attachment during the first year of life. These experiments involved observing children 12–18 months of age and their mothers in a series of separation and reunion sequences, in a laboratory situation and in their homes, several times over the course of a year. Ainsworth's experiments have been replicated by other researchers in different countries with different cultural groups. In the last three decades, attachment behaviors in infants, children, adolescents, and adults have been the subject of much research.

In this research, four principal patterns of attachment and the family conditions that promote them have been identified. These are the secure, insecure-ambivalent/resistant, insecure-avoidant, and insecure-disorganized/disoriented. These patterns begin to form in the first year of life, and barring a change in the attachment relationships or other outside intervention, they tend to persist through childhood, adolescence, and adulthood, and get played out in the individual's relationship with his own children.

Secure Attachment   As babies, the securely attached treat the mother as a "secure base" for exploration and exhibit little anger toward her and little anxiety regarding minor separations. Upon brief separation, they protest or cry, show pleasure at her return, are easy to console, and once consoled, they easily return to play. This secure response pattern is associated with mother's tender, careful holding, readily returning his smile, being readily available and responding sensitively to feeding and distress signals, and supporting his autonomy and exploration.

In preschool, securely attached children tend to make friends easily and are flexible and resilient under stress. On tests of self-esteem, they tend to show higher scores. This pattern continues into adolescence and adulthood. The mere knowledge that the attachment figures are available and responsive provides a strong and pervasive sense of security. Being confident that attachment figures will be available, responsive, and helpful in adverse or frightening situations, these individuals feel bold in their explorations of the world. As parents, they are more responsive to their children and promote a secure attachment pattern in their children.

The Insecure-Ambivalent/Resistant   As babies, the insecure-ambivalent/resistant tend to be clingy, anxious, afraid to explore on their own, preoccupied with their mother and her whereabouts. Upon brief separation, they become very agitated; when she returns, they seek contact with her but simultaneously arch away from her angrily and resist all efforts to be soothed. Such a pattern often appears in babies whose mothers are not rejecting but inept in holding, inconsistent, unpredictable, and sometimes belated in their sensitivity and response to their infant's cues.

The pattern of crying and clinginess continues through early childhood. In preschool, these children become fretful and easily overwhelmed with anxiety, are immature and overly dependent on the teacher, worried about mother when apart. In early and middle childhood, they have difficulty sustaining peer relations and tend to become the victims of bullies at school. As adults, they remain embroiled with anger and hurt at parents, which affects their other intimate relationships. This pattern is promoted by a parent's being available and helpful on some occasions but not on others, by separations, and by threats of abandonment used as a means of control. The ambivalent individual always remains uncertain whether his parent or other attachment figure(s) will be available or responsive or helpful when called upon. Because of this uncertainty he is always prone to separation anxiety, tends to be clinging, and is anxious about exploring the world. As a parent, such an individual is likely to be anxious and ambivalent about parenting—being available some times, unavailable at other times, unsure or inept at other times.

The Insecure-Avoidant   Even as babies, the insecure-avoidant children give the impression of independence. They explore the new environment without using their mothers as a secure base. Brief separations don't seem to affect them; upon her return they tend to avoid or snub her. This pattern is generally seen in babies of mothers who reject attachment behavior. These mothers dislike physical contact with their babies, are not sensitive to their infant's signals and cues, and are low in emotional expressiveness.

By the end of the first year, insecure-avoidant children tend to seek little physical contact with mother, are randomly angry with her, and are unresponsive to being held but often upset when put down. In preschool these children are often angry, aggressive, defiant. They are far less able to engage in fantasy play than securely attached children, and when they do, their play is more often characterized by irresolvable conflict. However, at four years of age they have been observed to seek contact with their teachers at a greater rate than securely attached children. At the same time they are also frequently sullen or oppositional and not inclined to seek help when injured or disappointed. In early and middle childhood they tend to have no close friends, or the friendships are marked by exclusivity and jealousy. Often they tend to become bullies and victimize other insecurely attached children. As adults, they dismiss the importance of love and connection. This pattern is the result of repeated rejections and constant rebuffing in the early attachment relationship. The avoidant individual has no confidence that when he seeks care he will be responded to helpfully; on the contrary, he expects to be rebuffed. Such an individual attempts to live his life without the love and support of others, tries to become emotionally self-sufficient, and may later be diagnosed as narcissistic or as having a false self. As a parent, such an individual is very likely to reject and rebuff attachment behavior in his children.

The Insecure-Disorganized/Disoriented   The behavior of the disorganized/disoriented babies is a mixture of the characteristics of the secure, the ambivalent/resistant, and the avoidant. These children seek proximity to their caregiver and avoid her at the same time, freeze in response to distress and separation from their caregiver, and also show apprehension regarding the caregiver. Attachment behavior is considered to be a child's strategy to manage stressful situations, but these children seem to have no organized strategy at all. They are disorganized, fragmented, conflicted. At age 6, disoriented/disorganized children were observed to have become controlling and parental toward their parents, being either punitive or caregiving.

This attachment style is at times observed in children who are physically abused or grossly neglected by their parents, children of mothers who are depressed, mothers who have experienced trauma of any kind (including physical/emotional/sexual abuse), and mothers who have unresolved losses of their own attachment figures. Psychologically unavailable mothers are not able to provide any emotional support to their children. Main (1990) has suggested that unresolved trauma may lead to frightened and/or frightening behavior on the part of the parent. In a stressful situation, the infant wants to approach the mother for comfort but is at the same time frightened by her, so becomes confused, disorganized, disoriented.

The insecure attachment patterns (ambivalent, avoidant, disorganized) are seen as an adaptive response to the environment—the child's strategy for dealing with his mother's inconsistency or unavailability. The ambivalent child is hooked by the fact that mother does come through and respond some times, so he constantly tries to hold on to her, influence her, or punish her for being unavailable. He cannot give up hope that some day she will give him the love he yearns for, and cannot allow himself a substitute. The avoidant child, on the other hand, having been rebuffed and rejected consistently, has no such hope. He becomes angry, distant, indifferent, or over-independent, as if saying, "I don't need you, I don't need anybody, I can do it on my own." In conjunction with this attitude, grandiose ideas can develop about the self—"I am great, I don't need anybody." In American society where individual independence and self-sufficiency is a prime cultural value, some parents promote such grandiosity in the child.

Patterns of attachment are not fixed. Because they are an adaptation to the quality of relationships with attachment figures, they can change with a change in the quality of these relationships. A mother can become more (or less) available and attuned to her child with a change in her circumstances. Cross-cultural studies have shown that in households in which fathers are significantly involved in child care, and/or in which grandparents or other multiple caregivers are available, mothers are more responsive and the children more secure. That is, the primary attachment figures can function more supportively when they themselves receive the support of others. Patterns can also change when intimate emotional bonds are formed with attachment figures other than the mother or primary caregiver—fathers, older brothers and sisters, grandparents, teachers—not only to supplement and support the mother, but as an alternative to the mother when the quality of relationship with the mother cannot be changed.

Thus according to attachment theory, the attachment relationship with the mother is not necessarily the prototype for all others. The first year's effects, though still assumed to be profound, are not necessarily indelible.

Effects of Abuse and Neglect

Abuse and neglect (maltreatment) can have significant physical and psychological effects on the child's development. Physically, maltreatment may result in death, brain/neurological damage, mental retardation, cerebral palsy, learning disorders, and sensory deficits. Psychologically, the trauma of maltreatment at any stage of development can cause fixations, regressions, developmental arrests, and a host of other psychological problems ranging from simple personality disorders to serious psychopathology and psychosis.

Effects on the development of a child depend not on single individual acts of maltreatment but on the overall pattern of care and the total environment of the family. Within the context of the total pattern of care, effects depend on the age of the child, the type of maltreatment, and other mediating factors that can serve to buffer the child from adverse consequences.

AGE AND TYPE OF MALTREATMENT

Effects are not the same for all types of treatment; in fact, neglect is potentially a lot more damaging to development than abuse. Maltreated children below the age of five have generally shown failure-to-thrive syndrome, developmental delays, low IQ, low reading and verbal scores, and impaired capacity for relationships. However, physically abused children tend to show more of low frustration tolerance and low attention span and are easily distractible. Verbally abused children tend to show more anger and avoidant behavior. Sexually abused children tend to show more fear of punishment and abandonment, guilt, shame, self-blame, disbelief, denial, and anxiety. Neglected children, on the other hand, are generally the least flexible, most clingy and whiny, most dependent on the teachers, lowest on self-esteem, and show language delays more than in any other group (Augustino, 1987; Cicchetti et al., 1989; English, 1998).

School-age children also show similar effects. Neurological impairment or brain damage begins to have an emotional overlay. The inability to adequately understand and learn in school, keep up with peers, and meet the expectations of those around them produces a great deal of frustration, anxiety, and a sense of inferiority. Physically abused children begin to manifest a strong need to control, to know what is going on. They display pervasive and severe academic and socio-emotional problems. Neglected children, on the other hand, are at extreme risk of school failure. Sexually abused children begin to manifest depression, eating disorders, sexualized behavior, suicidality and self-destructive behaviors, along with learning disorders.

Problems persist as the child grows. Longitudinal studies have found that adolescents and young adults who were physically or sexually abused as children show more depressive symptoms, anxiety, psychiatric disorders, emotional and behavioral problems, suicidal ideation and suicidal attempts, and more substance abuse and substance dependence than their non-abused counterparts (Silverman et al., 1996).

Several common characteristics have been observed in children of all ages, whether they have experienced one or more than one type of maltreatment. These include acting-out behavior; depression, anger, and self-hate; apathy or overly compliant behavior; and at times food-hoarding behavior. They show signs of low self-esteem, an inability to deal with aggression, and inability to enjoy themselves. Their sense of self and their capacity to establish relationships are profoundly impaired. They seem to display a compulsive need to provoke punishment or rejection in their encounters with people. Unable to establish satisfying relationships, some children become withdrawn, others develop skills at initiating relationships but cannot sustain them. Intellectual development is delayed even though there is no evidence of neurological impairment, particularly in the area of verbal skills. Lacking trust in their environment, maltreated children are often afraid to risk talking and thus get little practice in speech and expressive language. Thus a maltreated child often appears less competent than he really is. Barring any outside intervention, these characteristics can persist over time.

An item worthy of note: Many children living in poverty also show the same kind of behaviors and characteristics even when they have not been maltreated in the usual sense.

ADAPTING TO THE MALTREATING ENVIRONMENT

Having to adapt to a dangerous and hostile environment, maltreated children develop a variety of survival strategies.

Hypervigilance   In an attempt to stay out of harm's way, the child becomes a watcher, an observer acutely sensitive to adults and any sudden change in the environment that is inexplicable to him. This hypersensitivity extends to remarkable acuity for perceiving the slightest changes in mood, facial expressions, and the like of adults in his surroundings. The child becomes guarded, careful. This leaves little energy to explore and enjoy the world and acquire a sense of autonomy, mastery, and achievement.

Chameleon-like Nature   The child learns to change and shift his own behavior in accordance to nuances of the erratic and inconsistent environment in which he lives. Thus his behavior, too, becomes unpredictable, his life stance reactive rather than proactive.

Inhibition, Denial of One's Own Drive and Impulses, Withdrawal and Avoidance   For a child in a maltreating environment, to try a task and fail may be more dangerous than not to try at all; to be silent may be safer than talking and exposing himself to ridicule and punishment. Moving about freely, exploring his environment, or any action at all can provoke adult antagonism. In such an environment, the child can become inhibited, withdrawn, self-denying.

Passive-Aggressive Behavior, Passive Resistance   The abused child attempts to maintain some self-integrity without openly challenging the authority of adult caretakers. As direct refusal to do what is asked or expected can bring punishment, the child becomes an expert at passive resistance, of appearing to do without doing. He makes cooperative gestures and noises, says yes and states that he is doing what is told while doing quite the opposite. This is the beginning of denial and distortion of his own behaviors. He often feigns incompetence or lack of understanding.

The Parentified Child   The abused child lives in an environment where love and nurturance are not readily available. He is loved and appreciated only when he is meeting the expectations of the parent, which may be when the child is taking care of the adult. The abused child is at times seen to be taking care of his parents, physically and emotionally, far beyond what is normally expected at their age. The preschool child may do the family wash, fix breakfast, babysit an infant sibling. These behaviors keep the child safe from verbal or physical attack, but are also ways by which the child has learned to obtain attention and approval from his parents.

Precocious Islands of Ego   Some children develop extraordinary mastery in one or another area of functioning—one much beyond their years—while remaining at or below the age-appropriate functioning level in other areas. Some children become parentified; some children excel academically.

MEDIATING VARIABLES

Effects of abuse and neglect can last throughout a person's life. For some children the effects are adverse, while other children show few if any indications of adverse consequences.

Several factors appear to act as buffers, protecting the child from adverse effects or ameliorating the adverse effects of maltreatment. Among them are

1. *High IQ*. Possession of above-average intelligence appears to have protective effect as it allows children find escape in reading and validation from teachers when they excel in academic work.
2. *A cheerful personality*. Children with a cheerful personality seem to have some self-confidence and spontaneity, an ability to enjoy themselves, and an ability to form good relationships with other people. These qualities seem to shield them from some of the adverse effects of maltreatment.
3. *Availability of age-appropriate play materials* can ameliorate the effects of maltreatment. Through play children can work through their pains and frustrations and master their fears and anxieties.
4. *A stimulating environment*. Because a young child learns through action and experience, an environment that stimulates them cognitively and affectively can offer other avenues for developmental progress.
5. *Involvement of the mother in the activities of the child* has also been found to be significant. When mothers are involved in the play or a task with their children, children are more responsive, enthusiastic, alert, positive toward themselves and toward their task.
6. *Other social supports* to the child in the form of other nurturing, supportive adults such as grandparents, teachers and coaches, parents of friends and peers, a neighbor, and so on can have both a protective and an ameliorative effect.
7. Many researchers have suggested that for children, any attention is better than no attention. Even *intervention by the child welfare system* has been known to be beneficial—in protecting the child from adverse effects, in

ameliorating, and at times even reversing the adverse effects of maltreatment. Some studies show that removal from home is more beneficial, other studies show that keeping the children at home is more beneficial. However, of the children who are removed from home, those who do best developmentally are those who experience few placement changes and whose legal proceedings are resolved quickly. Study after study since the 1950s has shown that the more placement changes the child experiences, the worse the outcome.

Development thus is affected not just by the presence or absence of maltreatment. The presence or absence of maltreatment interacts with other aspects of the child's environment to determine outcome. It is possible that the more severe and frequent the neglect and abuse, the less significant other factors become in affecting developmental outcome. In less severe cases, however, these factors may be better predictors of outcome than the maltreatment itself.

Effects of Separation

Separation from the attachment figure is one of the most distressing experiences for a child. Separation produces feelings of insecurity and anxiety, which activate attachment behavior. But because the attachment figure is not there, the child is left experiencing the full impact of anxiety on his own.

Separation and loss are an inevitable part of human life. Some separations are part of the normal developmental process and occur predictably at specific developmental points in life, such as birth, death, the first day of school, going away to college, divorce, move to a new city, etc. Each of these experiences provokes a feeling of anxiety. But other separations such as the ones witnessed in the child welfare system are not universal. They present their own unique set of emotional difficulties for the child.

Bowlby and his associates had identified three stages of mourning in young children separated from their mothers. At first the child protests vigorously, often crying inconsolably. If the separation is prolonged, the child enters a stage of despair in which he becomes withdrawn, listless, apathetic, showing little interest in people or toys. Further continuation of separation results in a final phase of detachment. The child returns to play and activity, but, as Howe (1996) puts it, "Life is lived but the sparkle is missing" (p. 7). Upon eventual reunion with the attachment figure, the child responds with a mixture of crying, clinging, anger, and bursts of rejection before gradually returning to normal.

Anna Freud (1943) observed and recorded the effects of separation on children separated from their mothers during World War II. Since then, numerous other practitioners and researchers have added to this body of knowledge through their work with children of the various wars, children in foster care, and children of divorce. This accumulated body of knowledge shows that the effects of separation depend on the age and developmental stage of the child at the time of separation. It also shows that separation produces a multitude of feelings that interfere with the child's ability to master age-appropriate developmental tasks and his ability to adjust to his new living environment. However, mediating factors such as the nature of care subsequent to separation and the nature of contact with the parent during the period of separation can serve to buffer the child from adverse effects of separation.

AGE

In the first few months of life before the first attachment is formed, the infant is upset when separated from the primary caregiver, but the period of upset is short. Thereafter, he accepts care and nurturance from another primary caregiver and forms an attachment with that person.

For children between the ages of one and two years, separation is devastating. Their newly formed first attachment with the mother (primary caregiver) has all the intensity and strength of a first love. When separated, the child feels suddenly deserted by the only person he has known and loved all his life. He is stricken with grief. He yearns for his mother. He is inconsolable. The grief and yearning for the mother can be so intense that they override all other bodily sensations. Some children refuse to eat or sleep; many refuse to be handled or comforted by strangers. Many cling to any object—a toy or a blanket or anything else—that represents a material presence of their mother. Grief of such intensity may last only two or three days, but for a two-year old, it is equivalent to a year or two of intense mourning in adult terms. When they settle down after their mother returns, many children refuse to recognize her, being resentful and angry with her for having left them.

Some children, on the other hand, have a delayed reaction. At first they seem placid, dazed, more or less indifferent. Depressive symptoms appear after a few days, sometimes even after a few weeks.

In 3- to 5-year-old children, reactions of this earlier stage continue, but they are modified by growth in intelligence, which allows some understanding of the real reason for separation. They can derive comfort from memories of the past and hopes for the future. But separation at this time becomes a confirmation of their negative oedipal feelings. Separation from the same-sex parent is perceived as their oedipal wish coming true; separation from the opposite-sex parents is perceived as punishment for forbidden thoughts. Thus develop the fear of the strength of one's own wishes and feelings, along with guilt and anxiety. Many children cope with these feelings by overstressing the love. Loyalty to parents and everything connected with them becomes fierce; their commands and prohibitions are obeyed religiously.

In time, most children under the age of three tend to forget their parents or at least become apparently indifferent toward them and shift their affections to the new surroundings and new people. After the age of three, children generally do not forget. As cognitive capacities grow, they can understand better and they can rationalize. They often tend to deal with their separation feelings by idealizing the absent parent; to them the parent can do no wrong; separation must be the child's fault, the child welfare worker's fault, or somebody else's fault. They also tend to internalize the characteristics of the absent parent. The child will begin to walk like the parent, talk like the parent, and, in fact, become much like the absent parent. Some children, no matter what they are told or how much verbal preparation they are given, still remain hopeful that separation will not really occur. Consciously or unconsciously, they cling to a hope that something will happen to prevent the actual final separation. When separation does finally occur, and they can no longer hold on to their hope, they show the most severe anxiety reactions. Some children cling to a fantasy of reunion with the parent long after separation, no matter how unrealistic that fantasy might be.

FEELINGS

While the general reaction in all children is one of fear and anxiety, separation evokes a multitude of other feelings that affects their sense of self. First, regardless of the reason for separation, the child seems to experience a feeling of abandonment that contains elements of loss, rejection, humiliation, complete insignificance, worthlessness. In addition, he is flooded with a feeling of complete helplessness, of lack of control over what is happening to him, as well as anger at the parent he feels has deserted him. He deals with these feelings by denying them and by blaming himself. He is the one who is bad, not they. Along with the feeling of badness comes the fear of punishment for that badness. The younger child tends to unconsciously expect that he will be completely abandoned by his parents, and then he will die. The older child usually unconsciously anticipates that he will be physically attacked and his body harmed or mutilated. In addition, most children unconsciously fear that death will befall their parents. This fear of being hurt becomes evident in their preoccupation with injury and danger; it becomes a lens through which they begin to view their subsequent experiences.

As children cannot verbalize their feelings and fears, they manifest them in anxiety symptoms such as restlessness and hyperactivity, tenseness, vomiting, sleep disturbances, crying, eating and bowel upsets, thumbsucking, bedrocking, headbanging, masturbation, colds, sore throats, tonsillitis, toothaches, asthma, and so on. These reactions may occur along with a varying degree of resentment, withdrawal, depression, or despair.

IN NEW LIVING SITUATIONS

Separated from their parents, children come to a new living situation with apprehension, fearing rejection, disinterest, and punishment. They try to ward off these feared reactions in many different ways.

Some children become too good, trying to please their new caregivers in every way they know. Others take the opposite approach—behaving in ways they know are unacceptable, thus provoking anger and rejection. Still others adopt the "I'll do it to them before they do it to me" attitude, rebuffing and rejecting any overtures of nurturance from the new caregivers—causing them to feel hurt and rejected. Children unable to tolerate too much emotional closeness withdraw emotionally. Many children desperately want to be close to their new caregivers, but at the same time are afraid of their wish, afraid of being hurt. The provocative behavior then serves as a protective shield through which they test the caregiver's resolve to care for them. Only when the caregiver has passed the test does the child permit himself to form an attachment with this person.

For many children, however, that stage never arrives. They bounce from one placement to another—be it foster homes, institutions, or back and forth with biological parents. Bouncing from one caregiver to another, some children never get an opportunity to be with one caregiver long enough to form an attachment. For others, attachments are established and lost so many times that they give up, they don't want to establish another close relationship ever again.

These children tend to develop a pattern of nonattachment, or what is often termed "Attachment Disorder." Such children tend to be indiscriminate in their relationships; anyone seems as good as anyone else. People are interchangeable and matter only so long as they hold out the prospect of meeting some current need. Relationships tend to be superficial; marriages may be ended as quickly as they were started. There is little distress experienced when people disappear out of their lives. Feelings of frustration, impulsiveness, conflict, and anger are easily aroused, particularly if basic needs are not met or supplied. When they become parents, they find it difficult to understand and meet the emotional needs of their children.

MEDIATING FACTORS

The most significant factor that alleviates the effect of separation is the nature of care subsequent to separation. When a child is separated just once, and placed in care of other adults who provide appropriate care, nurturance, and attachment the rest of his childhood, separation can be beneficial rather than harmful. Indifferent, inadequate, and care that is worse than before makes separation even more hurtful. Repeated separations from one or more attachment figures can exacerbate the harm and can cause attachment disorders.

The pattern of relationship with parents prior to separation, and the nature of contact with parents during the time of separation, can also affect the child's adjustment in the new living situation and future development. When the prior attachment was relatively secure, or the separation relatively temporary, a regular consistent contact with the parent, however painful, can mitigate some of the effects of separation and make reunification less problematic. No contact in such a situation can foster unrealistic expectations of reunification and idealization of the absent parent. Conversely, when the prior relationship was characterized by gross abuse and/or avoidant attachment pattern, separation and no contact can create a sense of relief and freedom in the child. He can go on to form new relationships if appropriate nurturing adults become available. But for the child with an ambivalent attachment to the parent, no contact or inconsistent and unpredictable contact with the parent can exacerbate the effects of separation. Unable to give up the hope that his parent will come through, he cannot permit himself to form any new attachments.

Another mediating factor is the child's understanding of the reason for separation. When the child can understand that separation has to do with the circumstances of the parent, that neither he nor the parent has to be "bad" and nobody has to be blamed, he is better able to accept the separation and deal with his feelings of loss.

Separation from the attachment figure in childhood, without the provision of appropriate substitute caregiver(s) and attachment figure(s), can have a profound influence on the development of the child's personality and adult relationships. An experience of separation can create increased sensitivity to later separation experiences and a pattern of conscious or unconscious expectation that all future relationships will have the same consequence. In childhood, separation can create trauma that can interfere with the mastery of developmental tasks. In adolescence, the conflict between dependence and independence becomes more difficult to resolve. In adulthood, there manifests a fear of emotional closeness and commitments. In parenthood, barring intervention, the pattern can get transmitted to the children—and so the cycle gets repeated.

Integrating Theories in Practice

Each of the theoretical perspectives discussed above provides an understanding of one or another aspect of the child's development. Psychoanalytic theory provides an understanding of the feelings and emotions underlying a child's behavior, his fears and anxieties, and how he copes with them. This is useful in assessing the extent to which these issues affect the child's psychosocial functioning and the extent to which these issues will need to be addressed in intervention in order to facilitate his safety and well-being with his family. Psychosocial theory explains the child's attitudes and his family/environmental/larger societal conditions in which they developed. This is useful in assessing if these attitudes need some modification for healthier adaptation to his surroundings, and the external conditions (family, school, other social supports and resources) he will need in order to facilitate such modification. Cognitive theory elucidates what the child can understand and what he can do at what age, within his physical and genetic capabilities and constraints. It enables realistic expectations of the child's ability to learn and the ability to "understand" what is happening, and the kind of cognitive-affective stimulation the child will need in his environment. Attachment theory, on the other hand, provides critical insights into the child's way of relating with others (patterns of relationships). This is particularly useful in understanding his needs in the area of intimate relationships and bonds of affection, in anticipating behavior when the child needs to be separated from the parent or caregiver (biological or foster parent), in assessing the foster child's ability to use the positive relationships in his new placement, and in selecting an appropriate permanent family for the child.

The different aspects of the child's development, though viewed and examined separately from different theoretical perspectives, do not exist separately in any child. They are interrelated, intertwined, and overlapping. Understanding the needs of the whole child requires viewing and understanding the child from all theoretical perspectives, and synthesizing the different views to engender an integrated, comprehensive picture of the child as a multifaceted human being.

Understanding the Language of the Child—The Need for Cultural Sensitivity and Cultural Competence

Children usually cannot express their feelings and their needs in words; they express them in their behavior, in the themes of their play and games, and in their symptoms. Depending on their age, developmental stage, and familial/cultural norms and practices, children convey their psychological distress in different ways. These include *disturbances related to bodily functions* (for example, eating, sleeping, bowel and bladder functions, speech and motor functions), *disturbances related to cognitive functions* (for example, precocity, learning failures, disturbances in thinking, memory, awareness), *disturbances related to affective behavior* (for example, fearful and anxious behavior, depressive symptoms, hyperactivity, hypochondriacal behavior, uncontrollable crying, separation anxiety), and *disturbances in social behavior* (for example, aggressive behavior, antisocial behavior, oppositional behavior, withdrawn behavior).

Behavior, play, and symptoms are thus the language of the child. This is the way children express their feelings, fears, anxieties, and ways of coping with the myriad frustrating, confusing, and distressing things in their life. In child welfare practice, the onus is upon the child welfare worker to understand the language of the child.

Theories provide a way of understanding children's language, but theories cannot and must not be applied rigidly. Any child's behavior, play, and symptoms have to be interpreted in the context of the norms, practices, values, and beliefs of that child's family and culture. In many cultures weaning, toilet training, sexual curiosity, and masturbation are not major issues; hence a child may not have the kind of conflicts that psychoanalytic theory speaks of. Even if the conflict exists, it may be manifested in very different forms of behavior. Some cultures value obedience more than independence, so desire for independence and autonomy would be considered inappropriate and unacceptable. In many cultures the latency-age child derives a sense of group identity not in relation to peer group but in relation to his place in the family and his culture. In cultures where individualism and personal possessions are valued, early narcissism is considered healthy and cute; in cultures that value collectivism, duty and responsibility to family and society before personal pleasures, behavioral expressions of feelings of grandiosity, entitlement, omnipotence, and self-centeredness are discouraged. In a child from a historically oppressed group living in a neighborhood/city/society that is perceived as hostile or unfriendly, mistrust rather than trust might be a more healthy adaptation. For many children and families, of any culture or ethnicity, the helping systems (including the child welfare system) have often been hostile. Their mistrust of the system and of any worker in the system, regardless of the individual personality of the worker, is the most adaptive, healthy response.

Culturally competent practice requires knowledge, and nonjudgmental acceptance, of the client's cultural beliefs and child-rearing practices, and with what is considered respectful (or disrespectful) behavior between parents and children, between family and non-family, in formal and informal relationships. As no worker can know all the details and subtleties of all the different cultures, competence lies in beginning with a general knowledge and familiarity with the client's culture and then (1) seeking appropriate consultation from people more familiar with the culture, and (2) asking the client what his cultural practices are, to what extent he believes in and uses his traditional practices, and what they mean to him.

ASSESSMENT: WHAT DOES THIS CHILD NEED?

Within the context of cultural competence, assessment of the child's needs begins with the following questions in mind: Is this child functioning at an age-appropriate level in all aspects of development? If not, what level or stage of development does this child's behavior indicate, emotionally and cognitively? What are his dominant attitudes, coping mechanisms, and patterns of relating with others? Are there any fixations, regressions, developmental arrests? Why? How do his current behavior patterns and level of functioning affect his safety and well-being?

Answers to these questions are derived from two sources of information. One is the child himself, the other is the adults in the child's life—parents and caregivers, teachers, and any other adult who may have meaningful knowledge of and interactions with the child.

Information from the child is obtained by observing the child's behavior in his normal everyday life activities such as at home and school, and interacting with him in specially set-up play interviews, which may be structured or unstructured or semi-structured (Samantrai, 1999). The task of the worker is to observe, listen, and understand the language of the child—what he is saying in his behavior and in the themes of his play.

Information from parents and caregivers is obtained by taking as thorough a developmental history of the child as possible, from the time of conception to present. This involves asking the parents or caregivers how they handled the developmental task at each stage (for example, weaning, toilet training, starting school, other separations, and so on)—how the child behaved and what their response was to that behavior. This also involves asking what their usual disciplinary practices are, and the nature of child's close relationship with them and attachments with others—be they people, animals, or toys.

Information from both sources (personal observations and history), organized, examined, and analyzed through different theoretical lenses, singly or in any combination, produces a clear, focused picture of where the child is at, physically and developmentally, in the different areas of psychosocial functioning. Comparing it to where he would be if he were developing age-appropriately (in view of his family's culture as well as in the view of the dominant culture) reveals lags (or culture conflicts), if any, possible reasons for these developmental lags, and their effect on the safety and well-being of the child. The worker can then identify what the child's needs are at this time—physical needs in terms of safety, food, shelter, clothing, health care, and so on; and developmental needs in terms of nurturance, stability, opportunities for educational and social growth, and so on—needs that must be met in order to promote his safety, well-being, and age-appropriate psychosocial functioning.

ASSESSMENT: FAMILY'S ABILITY TO MEET THE NEEDS OF THE CHILD

The McMaster model of family functioning (Epstein et al., 1993) provides a useful conceptual framework for assessing the "goodness-of-fit" between the child's needs and the parents' ability to meet those needs. This model is based on systems approach, which views the family as "a system of interacting individuals, being acted upon and in turn acting on a number of other systems at obvious levels such as surrounding subculture, culture, economic domain, and biological substrates of the individual concerned" (Epstein et al., 1993, p. 138). The assumptions of systems theory underlying this model are (1) the parts of the family are interrelated, (2) one part of the family cannot be understood in isolation from the rest of the system, (3) family functioning cannot be fully understood by simply understanding each of the parts, (4) a family's structure and organization are important factors determining the behavior of family members, and (5) transactional patterns of the family system are amongst the most important variables that shape the behavior of family members (Epstein et al., 1993, p. 140).

This model starts with the assumption that the primary function of families is to provide a setting for the development and maintenance of family members on the social, psychological, and biological levels. In the course of fulfilling this function, families have to deal with a variety of issues and tasks, which can be grouped into three areas—the Basic Task Area, the Developmental Task Area, and the Hazardous Task Area. The Basic Task Area includes the meeting of basic physical needs such as food, shelter, clothing, physical protection, health care, and so on. The Developmental Task Area entails life-cycle issues— issues that arise as a result of individual and family development over time. The Hazardous Task Area involves the handling of crises that arise as a result of illness, accident, loss of income, job change, and the like.

Family functioning in these three task areas depends upon the structure, organization, and habitual transactional patterns of the family. This model focuses on six dimensions: (1) problem-solving—the way the family's resolves problems; (2) communication—the manner in which the exchange of information occurs within the family; (3) role functioning—the patterns of behavior by which family members fulfill family functions of physical survival, emotional nurturance and support, decision-making, and so on; (4) affective responsiveness—the quality, quantity, and range of feelings in response to any situation, and the usual patterns of expressing these feelings; (5) affective involvement—the extent to which the family demonstrates interest in and values the particular activities and interests of individual family members—the amount of interest as well as the manner in which they express and demonstrate it—the extent to which they get involved with one another; and (6) behavior control—the pattern a family adopts for handling behavior in three areas: physically dangerous situations; situations that involve the meeting and expressing of psychobiological needs and drives; and situations involving interpersonal socializing behavior both between family members and with people outside the family.

Using this model, assessment of the family becomes a three-step process. Step one involves the question *What* the family's problems and the family's strengths are. This involves identifying the Task Area(s) (basic, developmental, hazardous) in which the family is experiencing the difficulty that brings them in contact with the child welfare system, and Task Area(s) in which the family is functioning well, or at least adequately. Step two involves the question *How Long*—how long has this family been experiencing this difficulty in this task area, and how long has the family functioned well or adequately in another task area. Step three involves the question *Why*—why the family is experiencing this difficulty at this time. The question *why* involves assessment along the six dimensions of problem-solving, communication, role functioning, affective responsiveness, affective involvement, and behavior control—the degree to which each of these dimensions contributes to the situation that brings this family to the attention of the child welfare system at this time, and the degree to which each of them contributes to family strengths.

However, the ability of families to function adequately in the three task areas is also affected by other factors that are not mentioned in this model. These include (but are not limited to) developmental delays, substance abuse, domestic violence, any mental health issues, parents' own history of trauma, limited coping mechanisms, lack of knowledge and/or opportunity, societal conditions such as oppression, discrimination, poverty, violent neighborhoods, learned helplessness, and so on. Child welfare workers need to expand upon the six dimensions of this model and include these other factors in their assessment.

Such an assessment can be made by taking a thorough history of the family and its functioning in the three task areas since its inception.

GOODNESS-OF-FIT BETWEEN THE CHILD'S NEEDS AND THE FAMILY'S ABILITY TO MEET THOSE NEEDS

Putting together an assessment of the child's physical needs and developmental needs (from the developmental history and current functioning of the child) and an assessment of the family's functioning in the three task areas (basic, developmental, hazardous) reveals the goodness-of-fit between the needs of the child and the ability of the parents or caregivers to meet those needs. Gaps between the two, and the extent of risk of harm posed by these gaps, can be identified. At the same time, ways of filling these gaps—be they the strengths and resources within the family or outside resources including the child welfare system—can be identified so as to reduce the risk of harm to the child.

This is the assessment that forms the basis of the agency's service plan for the client, the case plan.

The next four chapters illustrate the use of the goodness-of-fit model of practice in Emergency Response, Family Maintenance, Family Reunification, and Long-Term Care. These illustrations come with a word of caution. One needs to be flexible in the use of this or any other model of practice. Concepts of "health," "normality," and "appropriate behavior" are value-based and culturally defined. In making any assessment of any family, the family's cultural norms and values always have to be considered and respected, even when they violate the worker's personal values and sensibilities. When they conflict with the dominant culture's norms and laws, the task of the child welfare worker is not to pathologize the family but to help the family understand, adapt to, and live by the laws of the land.

The cases here reflect situations commonly encountered in child welfare practice anywhere in the country; they do not describe any specific family or client. All names are fictional. Discussion of the case material is intended to stimulate reader's own thinking; hence by design, it is neither complete nor comprehensive.

INVESTIGATING
THE FIRST REPORT:
ASSESSMENT
IN EMERGENCY
RESPONSE

Child welfare practice begins with the first report of suspected abuse or neglect. At this point the task of the worker is to assess, by phone and/or in person, the seriousness of risk of physical harm to the child and decide whether or not to accept the referral. Should the case be accepted, the worker's task is to do a more thorough assessment of the risk of harm and decide whether or not to remove the child from the home and what services need to be provided immediately to ensure the child's physical safety. Several standardized instruments to measure the child's relative risk or safety have evolved over the last two decades. Currently, several states have developed and adopted their own standardized instruments (tools) and other procedures for risk-assessment. Workers are expected to use their agency's prescribed assessment tools and protocols to guide their decisions. (For description and discussion of several assessment tools, please refer to American Humane Association, 1998, in the bibliography.)

Another component of assessment, one that is often overlooked, is the risk of emotional harm to the child from the trauma of separation should the child be separated from the family. In situations where the risk of physical harm is clearly high or clearly low, the decision to remove or not remove the child from that situation is clear. However, many situations are ambiguous; the decision is not so clear. In such situations workers must exercise their own professional judgment to decide whether or not to separate the child from the family. In such situations the risk of physical harm must be weighed against the risk of emotional harm to the child from the trauma of separation. This involves an assessment of the developmental effects of separation on the child, how the child and other members of the family might react to and cope with the separation (constructively or destructively), how their reactions and coping methods might impact the safety and well-being of the child in question, the child's adjustment in the new living situation, and his eventual return to the family. The framework for assessment in emergency response, therefore, has two components: (1) imminent risk of physical harm to the child; and (2) risk of emotional harm, to the child and to other members of the family, from the trauma of separation. Not attending skillfully to separation issues causes enormous emotional damage to the child, as the case in this chapter will illustrate.

Framework for Assessment

1. Risk of (imminent) physical harm to the child.
2. Risk of emotional harm to the child from the trauma of separation.

Question: Can this family stay together safely?

CASE ILLUSTRATION—THE CASE OF JENNY

Jenny, a Caucasian girl now 9 years old, was 4 at the time of initial referral. At that time, her parents had been divorced for two years, and Jenny visited her father every other weekend. This was a middle-class family; Jenny and her mother, Vicky (age 38), lived in a suburban middle-class neighborhood. Father, Ed (age 40), lived in another county, about 50 miles away.

The divorce had not been amicable. Vicky became concerned when Jenny, at age 3, started saying things like, "Daddy wants you to die," "Daddy says you are bad," and "Daddy says not to talk to you," and so took her to a therapist for counseling. During the year of therapy, the therapist became increasingly concerned about Jenny's sexual behaviors—fondling herself, pulling her panties down and masturbating throughout the day, attempting to get her dog to lick her vaginal area. She also started saying to her mother "Daddy puts things in me," "Daddy does things," and so forth. These behaviors were said to be especially prevalent after Jenny came back from her visit with father. The therapist suspected sexual abuse by the father and therefore made a referral to the local Child Protective Services Agency (CPS). Vicky was very upset about the referral. She said Ed had connections with the law enforcement people in his county. She was afraid that he might lose his job, that he might kidnap Jenny, or that he might become violent toward her (Vicky).

Since Jenny and her father lived in two different counties, the matter of legal jurisdiction had to be addressed. An agreement was made between the two Child Protective Services (CPS) agencies; CPS in Jenny's county would investigate the report and send the findings to CPS in the father's county for follow-up.

A male worker interviewed Jenny and her mother. Jenny was found to be an active, intelligent, developmentally appropriate 4-year-old child. She would not discuss her father, avoiding the subject by insisting on showing her various pets and toys to the worker. Another visit a week later did not reveal anything more. A medical examination did not show any physical signs of sexual molestation. So the case was closed.

However, the sexual behaviors persisted and Jenny's preschool teacher became concerned about her effect on other children. So she made another referral a few months later, and the earlier agreement between the two CPSs was revived. This time, a female worker conducted the investigation. In the two interviews with Jenny in her home, the worker used special coloring books and markers, gearing her interviews to Jenny's developmental level. The mother was not present in the room. In these interviews, Jenny could correctly identify the 10 colors. She understood the concepts of "in," "under," "beside," and "on top of." She could also identify body parts and discriminate between (and describe) good, bad, and secret touch. She made spontaneous conflicting statements like "nobody did that to me, my dad didn't do that to me," "Daddy had a ball that went inside me," "I don't want to talk about that any more." Jenny liked visiting her father, but wanted the "bothering stuff" to stop. And she didn't want him to get in trouble.

In interviews with the mother, the worker obtained the parents' marital history and the history of their divorce. According to Vicky, Ed had a history of alcohol abuse and was prone to outbursts of violence. However, this did not seem to affect his performance at his (professional) job. Divorce was at her initiation. Written reports were also obtained from Jenny's preschool teacher and therapist. A medical examination again revealed no physical evidence of sexual abuse.

Based on this information, the worker and her supervisor concluded that the possibility of sexual abuse did exist. To ensure the safety of the child, they recommended that Vicky have her attorney file in court for Jenny's visits with father to be supervised, which she did. Vicky also had Jenny continue in therapy.

The child was thus protected from further physical harm. Mother was protecting the child, so there was no need to remove her from her home, nor did there seem to be any other reason for CPS to continue its involvement with this family. So the case was closed. CPS in Jenny's county sent the report to CPS in Ed's county, but they decided that because the child was protected, there was no need for any follow-up. Because sexual abuse had not been legally proven, no criminal charges could be filed.

But Ed did not accept the outcome—supervised visitations. He denied the allegations. He claimed that Vicky was trying to take his daughter away from him. He was very bitter that nobody had talked to him during the process of investigation, that he was simply handed the decision on the day of the visit. He just could not accept that he could not see his daughter without somebody watching over him all the time, he said, so he has not had any visits in the last five years. He wrote letters of complaint to CPS supervisors and administrators in both counties and to his state legislators. A state hearing was granted, but he did not come because he felt he would not be "heard." CPS referred him to counseling; he did not accept that either.

So Jenny has not seen her father for the last five years. They occasionally talk on the phone. Jenny asks him why he won't visit her, and he tells her that he can't because he has been accused unfairly. He continues his action in court against CPS in an effort to gain the right of unsupervised visits with his daughter.

At 9, Jenny is doing very well academically, but her interpersonal relationships are problematic. She does not seem to have many friends, and she has few interests outside of books. With adults, especially adult males, she either clings inappropriately or becomes very distant and hostile.

Discussion

THE CHILD'S NEEDS

At age 4, Jenny, like any child of that age, had basic physical needs for food, shelter, clothing, medical care, and so on. Developmentally she needed the love and nurturance of both her parents. According to the developmental theories discussed in Chapter 3, children at this age and stage (oedipal stage) of development become curious about sex and seem particularly to want the love and attention of the opposite-sex parent. Oedipal strivings can produce a tremendous amount of conflict resulting in anxiety, guilt, fear, and ambivalence about the same-sex parent. Successful resolution of these issues leads to the development of a healthy identity, a healthy sense of self, positive self-esteem, and healthy relationships; problems at this time generally lead to problems with identity, feelings of guilt and rejection, thus affecting self-esteem and interpersonal relationships in adulthood.

Now, at age 9, theoretically Jenny should be at the latency stage of development, when the developmental task is to acquire a sense of competence and mastery in relationships with peers. However, her way of relating with people generally and with adult males particularly suggests unfinished resolution of the oedipal conflict, and she appears to be having difficulty with latency-age tasks as indicated by her few friendships or activities with her peers. Perhaps she will acquire a sense of competence and mastery through excelling in academic work; on the other hand, books might become her way of avoiding human relationships.

THE FAMILY'S ABILITY

Using the framework of family functioning in the three task areas, it seems this family was able to provide for the basic physical needs and was also able to meet most of the developmental needs of this child. Even with the bitter divorce, the parents made arrangements for Jenny to continue her relationship with her father.

The problem this family experienced was in the hazardous task area, in this case dealing with possible sexual abuse. Jenny's sexual behavior was more than the usual, what might be considered "normal," sexual curiosity of most children at this age and stage of development, and was beginning to affect her relationship with peers in her preschool. Child Protective Services did their job of protecting the child from physical harm very skillfully. What they did not attend to just as skillfully is what CPS usually does not attend to, the risk of emotional harm of separation. That is, the reaction of other family members, how they will cope, and how their (constructive or destructive) methods of coping affect the safety and well-being of this child. In this case it was the father, who, even though he was the one suspected of hurting the child, was nonetheless a very significant person to Jenny particularly at that developmental stage of her life. Not attending to Ed's possible reaction (even though Vicky had expressed fear and alarm) resulted in first the abrupt, perhaps traumatic separation and then essentially the severing of the father–daughter relationship. That the relationship wasn't quite severed left Jenny in limbo, perhaps with an increased sense of guilt and rejection. According to cognitive theory, children at age 4 cannot always "understand" what is happening and why. Not having satisfactory explanation of events, they tend to make up their own.

Ed's biggest complaint was that he was not heard in this matter. CPS workers who did the investigation interviewed Jenny and her mother and spoke to other adults involved, but not to Ed because Ed was in a different county and under the jurisdiction of another county's child welfare system. Even if he was in the same county, the worker probably would not have spoken to the father because most county procedures do not call for engaging the father, especially if he is the alleged perpetrator, as an ally in a problem-solving process. Ed's county's CPS did not see a need for alerting Ed that such an investigation was being conducted, nor did they see the need to speak to him afterwards, because the child was not at risk anymore.

Would Ed have reacted differently if somebody had indeed spoken to him at the beginning, and engaged him in the process of planning for the safety and well-being of his daughter, even though he was the alleged perpetrator? Would he have responded to an appeal to his sense of himself as a good father concerned about the well-being of his child, despite his feelings about his former wife, Vicky? Or would he have kidnapped Jenny, as Vicky feared?

Situations of sexual abuse where a close family member is involved always pose such dilemmas to child welfare workers. When it happens in the context of an acrimonious divorce, the situation gets more complicated. In this case, an additional complication arose from the jurisdictional issues of two different counties. The "system" protected the child from physical harm. It did not protect the child from emotional harm; in fact, it might have even exacerbated it.

SUGGESTED EXERCISE

Assume that you are the social worker on this case at the time of the second referral and Jenny is about 4 years old. Your task is to assess (1) risk of physical harm to the child, (2) risk of emotional harm from the trauma of separation, (3) the level of risk to decide whether or not the child should be separated from the family, (4) the goodness-of-fit between the child's needs and the family's ability to meet those needs adequately so as to reduce the risk of harm to the child, and (5) to formulate a case plan that would reduce the risk of harm to the child and increase the child's safety and well-being.

Organize the information given above as follows:

1. The child—name, age, gender, race/ethnicity/culture, educational status.
2. The family—for each member of the family—name, age, gender, race/ethnicity/culture, brief overview of the living and working conditions, the general nature of relationship between the members of the family, with each other and with the child.
3. Other people (or institutions) who might be of significance to the child and the family.
4. Reason for referral/presenting problem:
    a. Initial presenting problem/first referral: Who referred the client to the agency? When? Why? What has been done since the first referral until the time the case was assigned to you?
    b. Current presenting problem: Why was this client assigned to you?
5. Relevant history:
    *   History of the presenting problem, from the beginning, in chronological order. When did it first start? What has been done about it so far, by the client, family, or anybody else? With what success? What is the current status of this problem?
    *   Child's developmental history, from conception to present.
    *   History of the family, from the beginning, in chronological order. How they have functioned in the three task areas from beginning to now; how they have dealt with any major life events, the nature of their relationships? Relate the family's history to child's age—for example, when the child was __ years old, the family was __. Note the child's behaviors and parents' or caregivers' response to the child's behaviors at these times.

Analyze the information above from different theoretical lenses and your knowledge of the cultural norms of this child and family. Use the theories discussed in Chapter 3 and any other theories you know well and wish to use. Answer the following questions:

1. The child:
    a. Is this child functioning at an age-appropriate level, "age-appropriate" as defined by theories, by the norms of the child's culture, and by the norms of the mainstream culture? If not, at what developmental level is this child functioning? Why? (Consider biological, psychological, social, cultural, and any other possible factors that might have contributed to this.)
    b. What is the nature of the child's attachments?
    c. What effects, if any, do you see in this child's behavior of the suspected abuse or neglect?

    d.   If the child were to be separated from the family or other significant people, what effects might it have on the child?

2.   The family:

    a.   In which task area(s) is this family experiencing difficulty? In which task areas do they function well? For how long have they been functioning well, or been having difficulty, in these task areas? Why? (Consider the possible contribution of biological, psychological, social, cultural, and any other factors.)

    b.   What are the family members' strengths, resources, limitations, and social supports? Their motivation for or resistance to change?

    c.   If the child were to be separated, what effects might it have on each member of the family, and on other significant figures? How are they likely to deal with it? How might that affect the child's safety and well-being?

Assessment: Based on your analysis above,

1.   What does this child need physically, emotionally, socially, cognitively, and in terms of attachment with significant people in her life?

2.   Which of these needs can the family meet adequately? Which of these needs can they not meet adequately? (That is, what is the goodness-of-fit between the child's needs and the family's ability to meet those needs adequately?) Where do you see gaps?

3.   What kind of risk of harm do the gaps pose for the child's safety and well-being? (Consider risk of physical harm *and* the risk of emotional harm of separation from significant people in her life.)

Do you need more information to make this assessment? If so, exactly what information do you need, and where will you get it from?

Case plan: Based on the assessment above, the case plan should include:

1.   How the identified gaps will be filled, to reduce the risk of harm.

2.   How the family's own strengths and resources will be developed and mobilized.

3.   How the family will be helped to utilize outside services.

4.   How their progress toward well-being will be monitored.

CULTURAL COMPETENCE:
APPLYING PRINCIPLES IN PRACTICE

This family has been identified as Caucasian, middle-class, suburban, and as having a professional father.

1.   In your culture, how are people of the client's culture generally viewed? What are the usual stereotypes, negative or positive? And vice versa, how are people of your culture generally viewed in the culture of the client?

Consider how these cultural views of each group might enter into your work with this client.

2. What other cultural factors, of your culture and of the client's culture, might enter into how you engage this family, and how you conduct your investigation? In your analysis, assessment, and case planning for this case?

3. How might you adapt your methods of investigation and engagement of this family in the investigative and case planning process if (a) this was a family of color—African-American, Latino, Asian-American, or Native-American? or (b) this family (regardless of color) was not middle-class or lived in the inner city or in a rural area?

MAINTAINING FAMILIES: WHEN RISK EXISTS, BUT NOT ENOUGH TO REMOVE THE CHILD FROM HOME

There are times when parents or caregivers are not able to attend to all the needs of their children, and while the risk of harm—physical and/or emotional—does exist, the risk is not serious enough to warrant removal of children from the home. With some outside help, this risk can be reduced so that the family can remain together safely.

In such a situation, the central question for assessment and case planning is: What does this family need to stay together safely? To find the answer to this question, one has to ask three additional questions. First, what does this child/these children need? This involves an assessment of each child's physical, developmental, and social/emotional needs, including the effects of the conditions that pose harm or the risk of harm. Second, which of these needs can these parents or caregivers meet adequately on their own, and with which of these needs will they need outside help? This involves an assessment of the parents' or caregivers' level of functioning in the Basic Task Area, Developmental Task Area, and Hazardous Task Area, taking into account their own physical, developmental, social/emotional states as well as the external, societal conditions that affect their functioning in these task areas. And third, what strengths and resources does this family have, internal and external, that could be developed and mobilized?

Based on this assessment, the case plan would consist of a plan to reduce the risk of harm to the children by helping the family use the outside services and programs needed as well as develop and mobilize its own strengths and resources.

Framework for Assessment and Case Planning

Question: What does this family need to stay together safely?
Assessment should include:

1. Each child's needs—physical and developmental; effects of abuse/neglect.
2. Parents'/caregivers' functioning in Basic Task Area, Developmental Task Area, Hazardous Task Area.
3. The goodness-of-fit between children's needs, and parents'/caregivers' functioning in the three task areas. Identify any gaps.
4. Level of risk of harm: Is the risk of harm serious enough to warrant removal of children at this time, weighing the protection of children by removal against the harm caused by separation? If not,
   a. What outside services will the family need in order to reduce the risk of harm?
   b. What are the family's strengths and resources that could be developed and mobilized?

Case plan, based on the assessment above, should include:

1. How the identified gaps will be filled, to reduce the risk of harm.
2. How the family's own strengths and resources will be developed and mobilized.
3. How the family will be helped to utilize outside services.
4. How their progress toward well-being will be monitored.

CASE ILLUSTRATION: THE S. FAMILY

The Agency is a multi-service Community Center (referred to as the Center) in an ethnically diverse working-class neighborhood. The Center houses, under one roof, staff from several different county services—Social Services (Eligibility, Child Protective Services, Adult Protective Services), Health, Mental Health, Drug and Alcohol Services, and Employment Services. Each department functions independently; they also often work together collaboratively with families that need services across programs.

The S. family first came to the attention of Child Protective Services (CPS) five years ago. At that time this family consisted of Mr. S. (age 33), Mrs. S. (age 26), and four children—Amy (age 8), Rosie (age 6), Michael (age 3), and Patty (age 1).

Over the two years prior to the first CPS referral, neighbors had called the police several times reporting fighting in the family and Mr. S. beating his wife.

When the police had gone to investigate, Mrs. S. didn't seem to have much bruising or injury, and she didn't want to press charges, so the police officers felt they could do nothing more than warn Mr. S. Five years ago, at one such investigation, Rosie disclosed that her father had sexually abused both her sister Amy and herself. Police arrested Mr. S. and made a referral to CPS. The Emergency Response (ER) worker investigated and decided that with Mr. S. away in jail, there was no imminent risk of further abuse of the children, so there was no need to remove the children from the home immediately. The ER worker referred the family to the Family Maintenance (FM) worker for continuing assessment and services.

Mrs. S. was a tall, overweight, disheveled-looking woman, with short, stringy hair and a somewhat slurred speech. She told the FM worker that she is developmentally delayed and has been on SSI since birth. She was an only child in an alcoholic family. When she was about 8, her father left the family and never came back. When she was 16, she moved in with Mr. S., who lived in the same apartment complex and had just finished trade school. They were never married legally. Over the course of the next two years, Mr. S. started drinking and beating her. At one point he was arrested and sent to jail for a couple of months. When he came back, he moved the family to this town, about 500 miles away. She did not know what kind of work Mr. S. did, but according to her he traveled a lot and came and went as he pleased. Financially, sometimes they did very well, other times when he didn't have much work it was hard. Mrs. S. could not give any information about Mr. S. or his family: she had never met any of his family, he never mentioned any. She herself had not had any contact with her mother since they moved to this town.

The FM worker was not sure at this time if Mrs. S. would be able to care for the four children by herself. However, the house looked clean enough and the children looked reasonably healthy. If Mr. S. was an inconsistent and unpredictable presence in the home—the worker reasoned—very likely Mrs. S. had been taking care of her children by herself, and therefore, possibly with some help, she could continue to do so. So the worker decided to take a chance and try to keep the family together.

The FM worker worked with this family for about a year at that time. First she connected Mrs. S. with the eligibility worker so Mrs. S. could get AFDC for the children, then connected her to a financial counselor to help her manage her bills. The worker also helped Mrs. S. file a restraining order against Mr. S. so he would not be able to come back to the house after he got out of jail. At first Mrs. S. was not willing to do this. However, when told that her children might have to go to foster care if she let him come back, she agreed to the restraining order; she did not want to lose her children. While there was concern about whether she would resist Mr. S's visits if he wished to come back, the worker decided to take a chance. The family was referred for counseling at the Center. They went for about four weeks, then stopped because Mrs. S. said talking did not help her, it only made her more sad.

The worker also arranged for Mrs. S. to be tested for the extent of her developmental delay, which the worker found was relatively mild. She also found that Mrs. S. was "educable." The local Regional Center for the Developmentally Delayed agreed to work with Mrs. S. on her speech. After about six months, Mrs. S. expressed interest in a job; the worker connected her with the Employment Services at the Center, which helped her get a part-time job as a yard-guard at the elementary school. After about a year, the case was closed. Amy and Rosie were going to school and seemed to be doing okay. Michael was enrolled in the Headstart program. Mrs. S. seemed to be managing okay. She would come to the Center for routine health care for the children and sometimes to see the financial counselor when she had difficulty with her bills.

Three years ago, the family experienced another crisis. Rosie, then 8, was killed by a hit-and-run driver right outside her school. Mrs. S. was in the school yard and saw the accident. At that time, Mrs. S. seemed to fall apart—becoming very depressed, unable to do any of her housework or attend to the children. Amy stopped going to school; Michael started bedwetting and having nightmares, Patty cried constantly. The worker tried to locate Mr. S., but he was nowhere to be found. Since Mrs. S. had no other family, the worker arranged for a parent-aide (hired with emergency funds) to come in for a few hours every day and help Mrs. S. do her household chores, which seemed to calm her down. The family was again referred for counseling at the Center. Again Mrs. S. went a couple of times, then stopped. She said talking did not help her, she felt better when she kept busy with work. The Center did not have a child therapist, so the children were referred to another Center some distance away. However, Mrs. S. took them only a couple of times, then stopped. She did not have a car, and the public transportation system was too confusing for her.

In about six months the family appeared to be stabilized. Amy and Michael seemed to be doing okay in school and Mrs. S. seemed to be managing her household and her part-time job. Physically she looked better, her speech was much better. She did not want to enroll Patty in the Headstart program at this time, so the school permitted her to bring Patty with her to work. The case was then closed.

Now this family has been referred again. Michael (now almost 9 years old) was caught shoplifting at the mall. Apparently he has become involved with a group of 12- to 13-year-old boys who threatened to beat him up if he did not steal for them. All the boys were caught and charged; but charges against Michael were likely to be dropped because of his age. Mrs. S. was awaiting a decision for a fine.

A visit with Mrs. S. at this time revealed that she was having difficulty with all her children. Amy, now 13, argues with her mother constantly, refuses to do whatever her mother tells her to do, tells her mother she hates her and never wants to be like her, resents the fact that she looks like her mother. She is beginning to get involved with boys, which worries Mrs. S. Michael also argues and yells at her, makes comments like "You don't love me, you just love Patty . . . maybe I should call the police and have them take me away from you . . . you can't take care of us. . . ." Patty, now 6, is fearful, clingy, cries easily. Mrs. S. feels totally overwhelmed. She yells at them mostly, but when she can't stand it any more, she has slapped them, which frightens her and makes her feel very bad, she says.

All the children are reasonably healthy physically and average students in school, academically and socially. In the past year, Mrs. S. has acquired a male friend who visits her from time to time. She met him at the local supermarket and does not seem to know much about him.

Discussion

Assuming that the goal is still to keep the family together, assessment begins with the question, What does this family need to stay together safely?

THE CHILDREN'S NEEDS

Amy (13), at the beginning of adolescence, is manifesting behavior that seems to be somewhat age-appropriate (in this family's culture as in the mainstream American culture)—arguing with mother, not doing what mother says, not wanting to be like mother, beginning interest in boys. However, as Amy's mother is developmentally delayed, Amy's wish not to be like her mother and resentment about looking like her mother may be not just a normal developmental need to separate from mother but an expression of real fear on Amy's part that she will become like her mother. Amy also has a history of sexual abuse. The developmental task during adolescence is identity development; both her sexual abuse and her fear of becoming like her mother could have a significant impact on Amy's identity development. There is little information on what feelings Amy might have and how she copes with them, constructively or destructively, hence it is difficult to identify what her specific emotional needs might be. Generally, Amy needs what all adolescents need—the guidance of a trusted adult to help her through the trials and travails of adolescence.

Michael, age 9 (latency stage), also appears to be functioning at an age-appropriate level in some ways, doing okay in school academically and socially. However, he clearly expresses feeling of being unloved, uncared for, and unprotected by his mother. The developmental task during latency is to acquire a sense of industry and competence in relation to one's peers; it is important to belong to, and identify with, a group of peers. Michael at this time seems to have become affiliated with a group of boys older than him. Either he is being bullied by them into unwilling action, or he is seeking their approval. In either case, this affiliation is of concern. Emotionally, he needs a sense of being loved, cared for, and protected by a trusted adult.

Patty, at age 6, theoretically should be finishing up the oedipal stage and at the point of moving into the latency stage. However, the person critical in the developmental tasks of oedipal stage—the father (or any other male figure)—has been absent in Patty's life. Fearful and clingy behavior is not age-appropriate; it will very likely affect her ability to relate with her peers.

All three children have had a life filled with many traumatic events—their father's violence and sexual abuse and subsequent arrest and total disappearance, their sister's violent death. On the other hand, they have also had some measure of stability in their lives, a home and a neighborhood in which they have lived almost all their lives, a mother who has been there despite all her limitations. At this time, it is possible that the entry of a male friend in their mother's life is raising their anxiety.

All three children need a sense of safety and security. Developmentally, Amy and Michael need adults they can look up to, idealize, and identify with. Very likely, Patty does too.

MOTHER'S ABILITY

Mrs. S., now 31, appears to function reasonably adequately in the Basic Task Area. The house is clean and well-kept, children are fed and healthy, they are doing okay in school. However, she could not protect either herself or her daughters from their father's abuse. In the Developmental Task Area, it is possible that when the children were young she could meet their need for nurturance through taking care of them physically. But as they are growing older and developmental needs get more complex, she is having a hard time. In the Hazardous Task Area her functioning is minimal. However, in times of crisis she has been able to stabilize herself and her family with the help of services from the Center.

Mrs. S. is developmentally delayed, that is, her cognitive abilities are somewhat limited. She finds comfort in structure and concrete activities; the talking, reflection, and understanding through counseling are not helpful to her. She was born and raised in an alcoholic home, went into an alcoholic, abusive relationship, abandoned by father, abandoned by husband. It is possible that she herself experienced little sense of safety and security. On the other hand, she is a likable, "educable" person, she can apparently hold a part-time job along with taking care of her home and family. She appears to be attached to the children. Despite all her limitations and adverse circumstances, she has made a reasonably stable life for herself and her children.

GOODNESS-OF-FIT, AND LEVEL OF RISK

In this family, Mrs. S. can meet the basic needs of her children. However, she will need help in meeting their developmental needs. Having experienced little sense of safety and security herself, she is not able to provide such a sense to her children. Both Amy and Michael are vulnerable to, and at risk of problems with the law, drugs, early sexuality with all its dangers, exploitation by unscrupulous adults . . . the myriad dangers adolescents encounter in the outside world. Mrs. S. will not be able to guide them through the potential pitfalls of adolescence.

SUGGESTED EXERCISE

Assume that this case has now been assigned to you. Your task is to assess what this family needs to stay together safely. Can this family stay together safely? In the information given above the race and ethnicity of this family have not been identified; you may assign any race/ethnicity you wish—Caucasian or African-American or Latino or Asian-American or Native-American, or any other.

Organize the information given above as follows:

1. The family:
   a. Children: For each child—name, age, gender, race/ethnicity/culture, educational status.
   b. Adults: For each adult in the family—name, age, gender, education, race/ethnicity/culture, role in the family, brief overview of the living and working conditions. Identify the primary caregiver.
   c. The general nature of relationships and attachments between family members.
   d. Other people (or institutions) of significance to family members individually and collectively.
2. Reason for referral/presenting problem:
   a. Initial presenting problem/first referral: Who referred the client to the agency? When? Why? What has been done since the first referral until the time the case was assigned to you?
   b. Current presenting problem: Why was this client assigned to you?
3. Relevant history:
   a. History of the presenting problem, from the beginning, in chronological order. When did it first start? What has been done about it so far, by the client, family, or anybody else? With what success? What is the current status of this problem?
   b. Each child's developmental history, from conception to present.
   c. History of the family, from the beginning, in chronological order. How they have functioned in the three task areas from beginning to now; how they have dealt with any major life events, the nature of their relationships. Relate the family's history to child's age—for example, when the child was __ years old, the family was __. Note each child's behaviors and parents' and caregivers' response to the child's behaviors at these times.

Analyze the (organized) information above from different theoretical lenses and your knowledge of the cultural norms of this family. Use the theories discussed in Chapter 3 and any other theories you know well and wish to use. Answer the following questions:

1. For each child:
   a. Is this child functioning at an age-appropriate level, "age-appropriate" as defined by theories, by the norms of the child's culture, and by the norms of the mainstream culture? If not, at what developmental level is this child functioning? Why? (Consider biological, psychological, social, cultural, and any other possible factors that might have contributed to this.)
   b. What is the nature of the child's attachments?
   c. What effects, if any, do you see in this child's behavior of the suspected abuse or neglect?

   d. If the child were to be separated from the family or other significant figures, what effects might that have on the child?
2. The parent/caregiver:
   a. In which task area(s) is this caregiver experiencing difficulty? In which task areas does she function well? For how long has she been functioning well, or having difficulty, in these task areas? Why? (Consider the possible contribution of biological, psychological, social, cultural, and any other factors.)
   b. What are the family strengths, resources, limitations, and social supports? Motivation for or resistance to change?
   c. If a child were to be separated, what effects might it have on each member of the family, on other significant figures? How are they likely to deal with it? How might that affect the child's safety and well-being?

Assessment: Based on your analysis above, this should include:

1. Each child's needs—physical and developmental; effects of abuse/neglect.
2. Parents'/caregivers' functioning in Basic Task Area, Developmental Task Area, Hazardous Task Area.
3. The goodness-of-fit between children's needs and parents'/caregivers' functioning in the three task areas—identify gaps.
4. Level of risk of harm: Is the risk of harm serious enough to warrant removal of children at this time, weighing the protection of children by removal against the harm caused by separation? If not,
   a. What outside services will the family need in order to reduce the risk of harm?
   b. What are the family's strengths and resources that could be developed and mobilized?

Case plan: Based on the assessment above, this should include:

1. How the identified gaps will be filled, to reduce the risk of harm.
2. How the family's own strengths and resources will be developed and mobilized.
3. How the family will be helped to utilize outside services.
4. How their progress toward well-being will be monitored.

   Do you need more information to make this assessment? If so, exactly what information do you need, and where will you get it from?

CULTURAL COMPETENCE:
APPLYING PRINCIPLES IN PRACTICE

1. In your culture, how are people of the client's culture generally viewed? What are the usual stereotypes, negative or positive? And vice versa, how are people of your culture generally viewed in the culture of the client? Consider how these cultural views of each group might enter into your work with this client.

2. (a) Are there any cultural values, beliefs, practices, etc. that might have contributed to the difficulties that brought this family to the attention of the child welfare system? (b) Are there any cultural values, beliefs, practices, etc. that might contribute to the resolution of these difficulties?
3. What other cultural factors, of the client's culture and your culture, might be relevant to your work with this family?
4. How might you integrate your cultural knowledge and your clinical knowledge in your practice methods (a) to engage this family in the helping process; (b) in your analysis, assessment, and intervention plan in this case?

6

CHAPTER

REUNIFYING FAMILIES: BRINGING THE CHILD BACK AFTER AN OUT-OF-HOME PLACEMENT

There are times when harm or the risk of harm is sufficient to warrant removal of children from the home. However, the family may seem to have enough strengths so that given help, the risk of harm could be reduced to the point at which the family could stay together safely. The children would then be placed in out-of-home care (foster home) temporarily, and the worker would work with the family to reduce the risk of harm. The intention is to bring the children back to their home, to reunify the family.

In such a situation, case planning becomes a little more complex. The worker must work with the family to alleviate the (harmful) conditions that prompted the removal of the child from the home. The worker must also work with the child while the child is in foster placement to mitigate the effects of these conditions *and* the effects of the separation from the family; with the foster family so that they are able to meet the needs of the child, who has been hurt by adults and is likely to be very demanding and trying; and with all three—the child, the biological family, the foster family—to maintain consistent regular contact between the child and the family so that the bond between them is not broken, their attachment is maintained, and hopefully the patterns of interactions improved, so that the child can return home and the family can live together safely without reverting back to harmful conditions and interactions. The framework for assessment and case planning therefore has to include consideration of the child, the biological family, and the foster family, at the time of initial placement, during the period of placement, and at the time of return of the child to the family.

Framework for Assessment and Case Planning

Question: What does this family need, first to reunify, and then to stay together safely?
Assessment should include:

1. *During the period of out-of-home placement:*
   a. *The child:*
      i.   Needs—physical; developmental, emotional; any special needs and personality characteristics that might contribute to parental stress.
      ii. Effects of abuse/neglect and other conditions that prompted removal from home.
      iii. Effects of separation and out-of home placement.
      iv. Coping mechanisms.
      v.   Expectations of reunification.
   b. *The parent/caregiver:*
      i.   Functioning in Basic Task Area, Developmental Task Area, Hazardous Task Area.
      ii. Coping mechanisms—before the child was removed from home and during the time of separation.
      iii. The personal (psychological) meaning of the removal (loss) of children.
      iv. Expectations of reunification.
   c. *The foster family:*
      Goodness-of-fit between the (abused/neglected) child's needs and foster parents' ability to meet those needs adequately. Which of those needs could they meet adequately on their own, with which needs will they need outside help (including the child's need to maintain attachment with the parent)?
2. *At the time of return of the child to the family:*
   a. Factors/conditions (internal and external) that prompted the removal of children—to what extent do they still exist?
   b. The return of the child to the family will inevitably increase stress in the family. How is the parent likely to manage and cope with this increased stress?
   c. What is the goodness-of-fit, at this time, between the child's needs and the parent's ability to meet those needs? Where are the gaps?
   d. What kind of help and services will the family need to fill these gaps, in order to reduce the risk of recurrence of harm?
   e. What are the family's strengths and resources that could be developed and mobilized?

(continues)

> *Case plan,* based on the assessment above, should include:
>
> 1. How the identified gaps will be filled.
> 2. How the family will be helped to utilize outside services.
> 3. How the family's own strengths and resources will be developed and mobilized.
> 4. How their progress toward well-being will be monitored, to make sure that the family manages the new, additional stresses inherent in the return of a child to the family after an out-of-home placement, without reverting back to harmful conditions and interactions.

CASE ILLUSTRATION: THE G. FAMILY

The G. family consists of Andrea, age 21, and her two children—Adam, age 27 months, and Missy, age 7 months. Missy lives with Andrea, while Adam is in a foster home where he has been living since he was 9 months old. Andrea currently receives AFDC/TANF for her daughter; occasionally she earns some extra money by cleaning apartments in her apartment complex. She shares an apartment with a female roommate who is employed and shares household expenses.

Adam was made a dependent of the court at age 9 months and placed in the foster home because a local hospital diagnosed him with "Psychosocial Failure to Thrive." During the last year Andrea has maintained a fairly consistent regular visiting schedule with him. His paternal grandparents also visit him frequently. His father has seen him twice at the grandparents' home but shows little interest in the child or in Andrea.

Missy is healthy and is rated in the 90th percentile on the national growth chart. Her father (different from Adam's father) has not had any contact with either Missy or Andrea since Missy's birth because of a restraining order against him; he has a history of threatening violence against Andrea and has threatened to kidnap the child.

At the time of Adam's placement, the court's intention was to help Andrea become a better parent and return Adam to her care. The court mandated parenting classes, individual counseling, and drug and alcohol treatment. Andrea had 18 months to demonstrate to the court that she could maintain a safe and healthy home for her child. In the first 12 months Andrea completed parenting classes and started personal counseling, but did not follow through on referrals for drug and alcohol treatment; she did, however, take the drug test, albeit inconsistently. She was very angry with the Child Welfare Agency for taking her child, so twice during this period she refused the services of the Family Reunification (FR) worker. At the 12-month Court Hearing, she was told that she had 6 months left to complete the court mandate and that Adam would be returned to her only if the FR worker so recommended. So she reluctantly agreed to accept the services of the FR worker.

Andrea comes from a middle-class Mormon family and is the second of six children—four brothers now ages 22, 19, and 17, and 11, and a sister, age 15. Her parents have been married 23 years; they have lived and raised their children in a middle-class, mostly Caucasian neighborhood.

Andrea says her mother "gave her away" to her paternal grandmother during the first year of her life; she feels very resentful about it. All during her childhood she and her older brother lived frequently with their grandparents. Her father was a strict disciplinarian who believed in physical/corporal punishment, especially with the older three children. She describes her mother as critical and disapproving.

Andrea's elementary school years were uneventful, but in junior high she started acting out—dressing in extreme fashion, drinking, experimenting with drugs, cutting school. When she was 17, her parents "kicked her out of the house." Andrea then lived with a variety of acquaintances, both male and female. During this time she met Adam's father and became pregnant. He left her before Adam was born; she has had no contact with him since. Shortly after Adam's birth she married a man she had known for less than three months. He used alcohol and drugs heavily and was violent toward her and the baby. The apartment was often full of other drug and alcohol users, at times people neither of them knew. It was during this period that Adam was taken from her. She is very angry about this, because, she says, she had taken Adam to the hospital because she was worried about his health and was looking for help, but instead of helping her, social workers took her baby away from her. She maintained a fairly regular visiting schedule with Adam, developed a positive relationship with the foster mother, followed the court mandates, but rejected any help from child welfare workers. She also began to binge on alcohol and drugs (marijuana, amphetamines, methamphetamines). During one of these times, she was raped at the mall.

At the time she conceived Missy, she was involved with two men, so she was unsure of who the father was. The father was identified via a blood test after Missy's birth. Once Andrea realized she was pregnant, she gave up drug and alcohol use. During this pregnancy, she started and completed (the court-mandated) parenting classes and started personal counseling. Missy was born healthy and drug-free.

When she brought Missy home, Andrea told the worker that she had two male roommates. On check, it was found that one of these men had a court order not to be in the presence of children under 18. Advised of the possible implications, Andrea had the men move out immediately. Andrea then found her current female roommate, who has a clean, middle-class background.

At this time, Andrea looks like a young adolescent. Her hair is currently burgundy; she has numerous body piercings, which include multiple earrings, nose rings, rings through the eyebrows and belly button, and a pierced tongue. She frequently wears short shorts and low-cut t-shirts regardless of the temperature outside. In the presence of young men she has been observed to engage in flirtatious, inviting behavior. Sometimes she gets into careless sexual encounters with questionable men.

Andrea has maintained a positive relationship with Adam's foster mother; she often seeks her advice in caring for Missy. Her relationship with Adam's paternal grandparents is unclear. Her own parents and three younger siblings live in the vicinity, but they rarely visit her or the children. She calls her mother frequently, seeking attention and advice; however, these calls usually end with exchanges of anger as her mother does not approve of her lifestyle. The two older brothers are out of the house, unemployed and homeless; she has no contact with them. While Andrea does not subscribe to the doctrines of her church or attend services, she has received food, clothing, and diapers from the church.

In terms of her parenting, Andrea is very defensive. She continually watches Missy's weight and makes sure Missy is well-fed. However, she has rather unrealistic developmental expectations (despite her parenting class), such as Missy being able to stand and walk by now and understand and obey commands. All involved adults have been concerned about the excessive use of the infant swing.

Adam, according to the foster mother, was very difficult to care for in the first three months in her home. He was underweight and undernourished in every way. He cried incessantly for hours at a time, was inconsolable, and sucked his thumb until the thumb was raw. Now he is a happy, chubby toddler, entertains himself, and also listens well to directions. His favorite games are banging pots and pans, removing lids from containers and replacing them repeatedly, trying to fit keys into locks, and pushing buttons on the TV remote. He speaks one- and two-word sentences and other words such as "mama," "baby," "go bye-bye," etc. At nap time he often indicates he is ready to go to sleep by standing next to his crib. He has just started toilet training. He is still slow to warm up to strangers and tends to clings to his foster mother when in doubt. He also has asthma, which turns into bronchitis at times, so he needs watching and medical care.

Working with the FR worker the last six months, Andrea has complied with all of the court's requirements. Despite her concerns about Andrea's parenting, the worker plans to recommend reunification, along with a case plan for how this reunification should occur.

Discussion

What does this family need, first to reunify and then to stay together safely? Following the goodness-of-fit model, the question is, what are the needs of the children? To what extent can Andrea meet those needs? What kind of help will she need?

THE CHILDREN'S NEEDS

Adam, 27 months old, is developing age-appropriately as indicated by his behavior and his play. He is attached to his foster mother. He has asthma and recurrent bronchitis for which he needs continuing medical care. He also has a history of early failure-to-thrive, and inconsistent care at best during the first nine months of life. When placed in foster care at 9 months, his inconsolable crying suggests that he might have formed an attachment with Andrea despite the inconsistent care and that he was reacting to separation from her. A separation from an attachment figure at age 27 months is likely to be very traumatic for him and could precipitate a regression in his development.

Missy, age 7 months, seems like a normal, healthy infant and so does not appear to have any special needs at the moment. She will soon transition to the next (anal) stage of development—of budding autonomy, toilet training, getting into everything.

Developmentally, both children will need consistent nurturing along with firm limit-setting in order to develop a healthy sense of trust, autonomy, and self-control. Adam is likely to regress. Missy, so far, has had her mother to herself. Adam's return will mean less attention for Missy; therefore, it is likely that Missy too will react in some way.

MOTHER'S ABILITY, GOODNESS-OF-FIT, AND LEVEL OF RISK

Andrea, at age 21, seems to be functioning as a young adolescent in many ways. In other ways she is also trying to function as a parent. With Adam, she was concerned enough to take him to the hospital, seeking help. She has maintained fairly regular visitations with him, despite all the ups and downs in her own life, and has been trying to get him back. She has made sure that Missy stays physically healthy; she is perhaps too preoccupied with Missy's health. Obviously, Adam's removal from her care has had some psychological meaning to her, though the nature of this meaning is not known at this time.

In the Basic Task Area, Andrea is resourceful. Having had the experience of losing Adam, she has been more careful about her living arrangements after Missy's birth and has found an acceptable roommate. She has sought and received help from her church.

In the Developmental Task Area, Andrea is likely to need much help. She has had parenting classes, but seems to need more personal guidance, as observed in advice-seeking from Adam's foster mother as well as from her own mother. Raising two toddlers is difficult for anybody. Andrea's own family experience has been one of strict discipline and disapproval. She herself appears to be at the adolescent stage developmentally, struggling with her own issues of dependence/independence, sexuality, and relationships with men. She has little confidence in herself as a mother, especially as the child welfare system has told her she is not competent. Her strength is that she relates to parental figures well (for example, Adam's foster mother) and accepts help from non-punitive adults.

There is little on which to base assessment of her functioning as a parent in time of crisis (Hazardous Task Area). From her history, it seems likely that she will seek help from her church and other trusted adults, but not from the hospital or the child welfare system. In the past, she has resorted to drugs and alcohol, but she says she has not used any since she became pregnant with Missy.

Without adequate, appropriate help to Andrea, the risk of neglect is high.

SUGGESTED EXERCISE

Assume that you are the social worker working with this family the last six months. At this time, your task is to formulate a case plan for reunification. The question you need to address is, what does this family need, first to reunify and then to stay together safely?

The information above identifies Andrea as Caucasian from a middle-class Mormon family, but does not identify the cultural backgrounds of the two fathers. For the purpose of this exercise, assume that both fathers are *not* Caucasian and *not* Mormon. You may assign them any race/ethnicity (African-American, Latino, Asian-American, Native-American, or any other), any social class, and any religious orientation you wish.

Organize the information given above as follows:

1. The family:
    a. The biological family (to be reunited):
        • Children: For each child—name, age, gender, race/ethnicity/culture, brief overview of their current living situation.
        • Parent/caregiver—name, age, gender, race/ethnicity/culture, brief overview of the living and working conditions.
        • The general nature of relationships and attachments between family members.
    b. The foster family: Composition of the family; brief description of each family member. Identify the primary caregiver (to the child to be reunited).
    c. Other people or institutions who might be significant to the biological family to be reunited.
2. Reason for referral/presenting problem:
    a. Initial: Conditions and factors that prompted the removal of the child from the biological family. That is, when and why was the child removed from the biological family? What has been done since the first referral until the time the case was assigned to you? With what success?
    b. Status of these conditions and factors at the time the case was assigned to you. Actions and interventions (by you or by anybody else) since that time. Current status of these conditions and factors.
3. Relevant history:
    a. History of the presenting problem, from the beginning, in chronological order. When did it first start? What has been done about it so far, by the client, family, or anybody else? With what success?
    b. Each child's developmental history, from conception to present.
    c. History of the family, from the beginning, in chronological order. How they have functioned in the three task areas from beginning to now; how they have dealt with any major life events, the nature of their relationships? Relate the family's history to child's age—for example, when the child was __ years old, the family was __. Note the child's be-

haviors and parents'/caregivers' response to the child's behaviors at these times.

Analyze the information above from different theoretical lenses and your knowledge of the cultural norms of this family. Use the theories discussed in Chapter 3 and any other theories you know well and wish to use. Answer the following questions:

1. *For each child:*
   a. Is this child functioning at an age-appropriate level, "age-appropriate" as defined by theories, by the norms of the child's culture, and by the norms of the mainstream culture? If not, at what developmental level is this child functioning? Why? (Consider biological, psychological, social, cultural, and any other possible factors that might have contributed to this.)
   b. What is the nature of the child's attachments?
   c. What effects, if any, do you see in this child's behavior of the suspected abuse/neglect? And of the separation from the biological mother?
   d. If Adam were to be removed from his present foster home now, how might this separation affect his physical safety, emotional/cognitive development, and his ability to adjust to the new life with his biological mother?
   e. How might a change in Missy's living environment affect her physical safety and emotional/cognitive development?
2. *The parent/caregiver:*
   a. In which task area(s) is this parent experiencing difficulty? In which task areas does she function well? For how long has she been functioning well, or having difficulty, in these task areas? Why? (Consider the possible contribution of biological, psychological, social, cultural, and any other factors.)
   b. What are the family strengths, resources, limitations, and social supports? Motivation for or resistance to change?

Assessment, based on the analysis above, should include:

1. *During the period of out-of-home placement:*
   a. *The child:*
      • Needs—physical, developmental, emotional; any special needs and personality characteristics that might contribute to parental stress.
      • Effects of abuse/neglect and other conditions that prompted removal from home.
      • Effects of separation and out-of-home placement.
      • Coping mechanisms.
   b. *The biological parent/caregiver:*
      • Functioning in Basic Task Area, Developmental Task Area, Hazardous Task Area.

- Coping mechanisms—before the child was removed from home and during the time of separation.
- The personal (psychological) meaning of the removal (loss) of the child.
- Expectations of reunification.

   c. *The foster family members:*
- Goodness-of-fit between the (abused/neglected) child's needs and foster parents' ability to meet those needs adequately (including the child's need to maintain attachment with the parent).
- The nature of their attachment to the child and their relationship with the biological mother.
- Their motivation for, or resistance to, reunification.

   d. *Other significant people:*
- Nature of their attachment to the child; their relationship with the biological mother.

2. *At the time of return of the child to the family:*
   a. Factors/conditions (internal and external) that prompted the removal of the children—to what extent do they still exist?
   b. The return of the child to the family will inevitably increase stress in the family. How is the parent likely to manage and cope with this increased stress?
   c. What is the goodness-of-fit, at this time, between the child's needs and parent's ability to meet those needs? Where are the gaps?
   d. What kind of help and services will the family need to fill these gaps, in order to reduce the risk of recurrence of harm?
   e. What are the family's strengths, resources, and social supports that could be developed and mobilized?
   f. What might the reaction of the foster family and the other significant people be to the reunification of the biological family? How might their expectations of reunification support, oppose, or sabotage successful reunification?

Case plan, based on the assessment above, should include:

1. How the identified gaps will be filled.
2. How the family will be helped to utilize outside services.
3. How the family's own strengths, resources, and social supports will be developed and mobilized.
4. How their progress toward well-being will be monitored to make sure that the family manages the new, additional stresses inherent in the return of a child to the family after an out-of-home placement, without reverting back to harmful conditions and interactions.
5. What kind of attention and intervention might be necessary with the foster family and other significant people?

CULTURAL COMPETENCE:
APPLYING PRINCIPLES IN PRACTICE

1. In your culture, how are people of the cultures of this mother and these fathers generally viewed? What are the usual stereotypes, negative or positive? And vice versa, how are people of your culture generally viewed in the cultures of these parents? Consider how these cultural views of each group might enter into your work with this client.
2. (a) Are there any cultural values, beliefs, practices, etc. that might have contributed to the difficulties that brought this family to the attention of the child welfare system? (b) Are there any cultural values, beliefs, practices, etc. that might contribute to the resolution of these difficulties?
3. What other cultural factors, of the client's culture and your culture, might be relevant to your work with this family?
4. How might you integrate your cultural knowledge and your clinical knowledge in your practice methods (a) to engage this family in the helping process; (b) in your analysis, assessment, and intervention plan in this case?

CHAPTER

WHEN THERE IS
NO GOING BACK:
FINDING AN
ALTERNATE
PERMANENT FAMILY

On occasion, there are times when a family is not able to care for its children safely, despite help. In such a situation, the interest of the child is best served by placing the child with an alternate permanent family, via adoption, legal guardianship, or long-term foster placement. In this situation, assessment begins with the same general question, what does this child need—physically, emotionally, developmentally? However, since in this situation the very first need of the child is a stable, permanent home and family, the question in case planning for long-term care starts with its own unique question— where should this child live? What is the best long-term legal arrangement— adoption, legal guardianship, or long-term foster placement—with a family, or in a group home/residential care home? And, in selecting an alternate permanent home, what is the goodness-of-fit between the child's needs, current and over time, and the alternate family's ability to meet those needs over time? Which of those needs will they be able to meet on their own, which of those needs will they need outside help with? In the case of adoption, issues of separation and attachment acquire a particularly critical significance, as adoption signifies a giving up of hope of reunification, letting go of the attachment with the biological parent, and beginning new attachments with other adults who take on the role of parents. As in the case of reunification, assessment has to be made about how the process of adoption should be facilitated and then about the kind of post-adoption services the child and the family will need so that the adoption is not disrupted. Because each child and each family is unique, the plan for pre- and post-adoption services has to be individualized.

Case planning for long-term care, therefore, requires a somewhat different assessment.

Framework for Assessment and Case Planning

Question: If not with the biological family, where should this child live? What is the best long-term legal arrangement—adoption, legal guardianship, or long-term foster placement—with a family, or in a group home/residential care home?
Assessment should include:

1. *The child:*
   a. Needs—physical; developmental, emotional; any special needs and personality characteristics.
   b. Effects of abuse/neglect, separations, number and duration of previous placements, and any other conditions that bring the child to this point of long-term care.
   c. Habitual coping mechanisms.
   d. The nature and patterns of attachment relationships.
   e. Readiness to accept an alternate permanent family.
   f. Expectations of the new family.
2. *The biological parent:*
   Readiness to give up the child, how the parent is likely to cope, and how the parent might facilitate (or hinder) the child's adaptation to the new family.
3. *The permanent family:*
   a. Functioning in Basic Task Area, Developmental Task Area, Hazardous Task Area.
   b. Habitual coping mechanisms.
   c. The reason for adoption, its psychological meaning to them.
   d. Expectations of the adopted child.
4. *Goodness-of-fit* between the child's needs, and the family's ability to meet those needs adequately. Where are the gaps?
5. *Level of risk* of disruption?

Case plan, based on this assessment, should specify:

1. Pre- and post-adoption services to be provided in order to ensure successful adoption and reduce the risk of disruption.
2. How the identified gaps will be filled.
3. How the family will be helped to utilize outside services.
4. How the family's own strengths and resources will be developed and mobilized.
5. Any services to the biological parents.

CASE ILLUSTRATION: THE J. FAMILY

The J. family consists of Mr. and Mrs. J, an interracial couple in their late 30s, and their three children: Janie, age 7; Joanie, age 5; and Jimmy, age 3.

This family first came to the attention of the child welfare system when their oldest child, Janie, was an infant. A report came in claiming Janie was being left unsupervised and being abused. An investigation showed no signs of physical abuse, so the case was closed. About six months later, the county hospital reported that the mother had given birth to a child (Joanie) with a positive tox screen. Again an investigation was made, the mother was referred to a drug treatment program, and the case was closed. About six months later, another report came in claiming neglect and abuse of both girls. An investigation showed minimal food supplies in the house. The family was poor, and the house seemed not so well-kept but not particularly dangerous to the children. However, given the history of drug use, there was some risk, so the investigating worker referred the family to the Family Maintenance (FM) worker for continuing services. The FM worker helped them apply for food stamps, referred them to the local Food Bank and to another Substance Abuse Treatment Program, monitored their attendance for three months, and then closed the case. About a year later, another report came in to CPS from the hospital; the mother had given birth to another child (Jimmy) with a positive tox screen, this time for cocaine and opiates. The child had to be kept in the hospital for three weeks for treatment of withdrawal symptoms, but during this time neither parent came to visit the child. An investigation at this time revealed that the father had outstanding arrest warrants for possession of drug paraphernalia. Both parents were arrested—father for his failure to appear in court on previous charges of possession, mother for neglect/abuse of children. Jimmy (who looked like his father) was placed with his paternal uncle, who lived in the same town. This uncle would not take the girls because the girls looked like their mother, of a different race. Besides, in the uncle's culture male children are valued more, and the uncle blamed the mother for getting the father addicted to drugs. The girls were therefore sent to live with their maternal grandmother in another state some distance away.

In the last three years, the father has been in and out of jail, and the mother has been in and out of drug treatment programs. Twice the children were returned to the parents when it seemed they were stabilized, but each time the mother's drug use returned, and the children were sent back to their relatives, Jimmy with his uncle, Janie and Joanie with their grandmother. The mother calls the girls occasionally, tells them she will soon be well and then they will all be together again. The father takes no interest in the girls.

Last month the grandmother died. Janie and Joanie are currently in a temporary shelter; they need long-term, permanent placement. The paternal uncle is still not interested in taking them. The mother is still in and out of drug treatment programs and seems to have no visible means of support. It is not clear where the father is. The mother has two brothers and a sister, but it seems they are all involved with drugs and the law; they all have unstable lives. The older girl, Janie, desperately wants to go back to her mother; she is sure she can take care of her mother and make her mother well. She is also very attached to her younger sister Joanie.

Discussion

Where should Janie and Joanie live? Should they be sent back to their mother, or should they be placed in an alternate permanent home? In the latter case, should it be via adoption, legal guardianship, or long-term foster placement? How will the interest of these two sisters be best served?

As usual, case planning begins with assessment. What do these children need—physically, emotionally, developmentally?

The material here gives little indication of the girls' level of functioning and their methods of coping with the various events in their lives. In the absence of developmental information, a preliminary assessment of their needs can be made based on the knowledge of developmental theories and the girls' known history. Chronologically, the girls are 7 and 5 years old, respectively. Developmentally, Janie (7) should be in the early latency stage, having finished the tasks of the oedipal stage. Joanie (5) should be in the oedipal stage. However, for these two girls the critical figure during the oedipal stage—their father—has been missing; indeed their father and his side of the family have rejected them. Their history indicates chronic neglect, very likely inconsistent care, several moves back and forth between their mother and their grandmother in two different states—implying disrupted attachments and many separations from attachment figures. It is very likely that this history will have affected their mastery of the developmental tasks of each of the earlier stages of development—the development of trust, a sense of initiative (or guilt), a sense of autonomy (or powerlessness), and self-esteem. In addition, Joanie was positive for drugs at birth. This may have had some effect on her physiological and psychological development. The family was poor; chances are the grandmother was poor, too. Poverty, too, could have added to the effects of neglect they experienced.

Janie's desperate wish to be returned to her mother suggests an attachment with the mother and unresolved feelings about separations. This attachment is likely to interfere with her ability to give up (the wish for) her mother and form a new attachment with any other person taking her mother's place. Her comments about her taking care of her mother and making her mother well suggest a possibly parentified child with very unrealistic expectations of reunification with the mother. Joanie's attachment to her mother, her grandmother, and her older sister is not known, but we do know that the two sisters have always been together. Having experienced as many losses as they have, their grandmother's death, their move to a temporary shelter, and an uncertain future, the girls very likely have a great deal of anxiety.

Developmentally, identity is likely to be an issue with both girls. They are biracial, and rejected by their father's side of the family very likely for both their gender and their racial features. Again, in the absence of information about how the mother and the grandmother, the two principal caregivers, addressed the issue of identity with the girls, workers will need to be alert to any verbal and behavioral indicators.

So what do these girls need? Generally speaking, they need a permanent family and adults they can form attachments with. However, their experiences of separations and especially Janie's wish for reunification with her mother are likely to make it difficult for Janie particularly, and perhaps also for Joanie, to form new attachments and accept the nurturing of other parental figures. The risk of failed placement exists. Janie and Joanie need a permanent family that will tolerate behaviors that may not be age-appropriate and that may be testy and provocative, and allow them to work through possibly myriad unresolved developmental issues such as trust, identity, and self-esteem. A legal guardianship or long-term foster placement could be less threatening to Janie than adoption, as the new caregiving adult does not need to be accepted as a new parent replacing the original parent, but that could reinforce her fantasy of reunification with mother some day, further jeopardizing her chances of forming new attachments. Furthermore, even though the two sisters have always been together, at this time they could possibly have different, and perhaps even conflicting, needs.

SUGGESTED EXERCISE

Assume that you are the social worker assigned to this case now. Your task is to formulate a case plan for permanent placement for these two girls. The questions you need to address are: Where should these girls live—with their biological mother, or in an alternative placement (family home or group home/institution)? Together or separately? With what kind of legal arrangement—adoption, legal guardianship, or long-term foster placement?

In the case material given above, the girls are identified as biracial, but the races of their parents are not identified. For the purpose of this exercise, you may assign them any race you wish, keeping in mind that the material above indicates that in the father's culture male children are valued more.

Information given above on this case is quite brief and sketchy. In the process of organizing and analyzing this information and formulating your assessment, if you think you need more information, please write down what that information might be, why you need it, where you would obtain it, and how you would obtain it.

Starting with the information you have at this time, *organize* the information as follows:

1. The client:
    a. For each child: Name, age, gender, race/ethnicity/culture, education, current living situation.
    b. Biological parents: Name, age, gender, race/ethnicity/culture, education, current living and work situations. Nature of relationship with the child.

    c.   Other significant people (or institutions): Name, age, gender, race/ethnicity/culture, education, current living situation. Nature of relationship with the child and with the biological parents.

2.   Relevant history:
    a.   For each child: Life history and developmental history (physical, emotional, social, cognitive), from conception to present, chronologically. Include reasons for and duration of all previous placements. Pay particular attention to their *behaviors* in the different situations in their life, their academic performance in schools, their manner of relating with others—children and adults, and the nature of their current relationship (attachment) with their biological parents and/or with any other person or object.
    b.   Life history of each biological parent and other primary caregiver(s), as much as possible, particularly relating to their functioning in the three task areas.

Analyze the (organized) information above from different theoretical lenses and your knowledge of the cultures of the biological parents and issues of biracial children. Use the theories discussed in Chapter 3 and any other theories you know well and wish to use. Answer the following questions for each child:

1.   Is this child functioning at an age-appropriate level, "age-appropriate" as defined by theories, by the norms of the child's culture, and by the norms of the mainstream culture? If not, what developmental level is this child functioning at? Why? (Consider biological, psychological, social, cultural, and any other possible factors that might have contributed to this.)
2.   What is the nature of the child's attachments?
3.   What effects, if any, do you see in this child's behavior of abuse, neglect, and separations?

Assessment, based on the analysis above, should include:

1.   For each child:
    a.   Needs—physical, emotional, social, cognitive. Any special needs and personality characteristics.
    b.   Effects of abuse/neglect, separations, and any other conditions that bring the child to this point of long-term care.
    c.   Habitual coping mechanisms.
    d.   The nature and patterns of attachment relationships.
    e.   Expectations of return to the biological parent/s.
    f.   Expectations of the new family/placement.
    g.   Readiness to accept an alternate permanent family.
2.   For each biological parent:
    a.   Readiness to take the child back and parent the child adequately, with or without help.
    b.   Readiness to give up the child. How is the parent likely to cope with the loss, and how might the parent facilitate (or hinder) the child's adaptation to the new family?

3. Other significant people: Readiness to give up the child; how they are likely to react, and how their reaction might help or hinder the child's adaptation to the new placement.

    Case plan, based on this assessment, should specify:

1. Where should these children live? With the biological mother or in an alternate permanent placement? If alternate placement, with a family or in a group home/residential care home? What is the best long-term legal arrangement—adoption, legal guardianship, or long-term foster placement? Should the placement and the legal arrangement be the same for both girls, or not?
2. What pre- and post-placement services need to be provided—to the children, to the permanent family/caregiver(s), and to the biological parents and other previously significant people—in order to ensure success of the permanent placement and reduce the risk of disruption?

    Point to ponder: If this was your case in any of the earlier referrals, what might your case plan have been at that time?

CULTURAL COMPETENCE:
APPLYING PRINCIPLES IN PRACTICE

1. In your culture, how are people of the mother's culture and the father's culture generally viewed? What are the usual stereotypes, negative or positive? And vice versa, how are people of your culture generally viewed in their cultures? Consider how these cultural views of each group might enter into your work with Janie and Joanie.
2. What other cultural factors, of the girls' culture and your culture, might be relevant to your work with this family?
3. How might you integrate your cultural knowledge in your clinical knowledge and practice methods to engage this family (including the girls) in the assessment and case planning process?

INTERVENTION

Intervention, according to the *American Heritage Dictionary,* means "to come in or between so as to hinder or modify." In child welfare practice it refers to the actions the child welfare worker (or the agency) takes to hinder harm to children, to modify the goodness-of-fit between parents/caregivers and children to ensure children's safety and well-being. To achieve its desired goal, intervention has to be based on an accurate assessment of the client and the client's situation.

Like assessment, intervention has two components—method(s) of practice, and program(s) of service. Methods of practice refer to what the worker does—the manner in which the worker uses his or her knowledge and skills in working with the client. Programs refer to the nature of services for the client and the manner in which they are organized and delivered. This chapter describes two methods of practice used predominantly in the field of child welfare—Case Management and Crisis Intervention. It then describes four (culturally responsive) programs that started evolving in the last decade— Family Preservation and Family Support, Kinship Foster Care and Family Group Decision-Making, and Shared Family Foster Care/Whole Family Foster Care.

CASE MANAGEMENT

Case management is a method of practice for providing coordinated services to clients who have multiple concurrent needs requiring help from several service providers simultaneously. It gained popularity in the early 1980s when social workers' long-standing concerns about fragmentation in services met the emerging political reality of draconian cuts in federal social service budgets.

The problem of fragmentation—the phenomenon of families with multiple problems having to deal with multiple agencies and service delivery systems in order to meet the needs of all their members—had been observed since the early days of professional social work. In the 1950s, it became a subject of much research and concern. It was noted that multiple agencies serving the same client family often worked at cross-purposes and made conflicting rules and demands. Each agency addressed a narrowly defined problem or target population and assumed responsibility for its own service, but nobody took responsibility for the entire gestalt of services for the family—whether and how the multiple services came together for the family. Often some services were duplicated while some needs did not get addressed at all. Already overwhelmed and overburdened families encountered significant difficulties in negotiating with many service providers to bring services together for them in a compatible, coherent way. And it was observed that although multi-problem families formed a small proportion of the total client population, they used up a large proportion of the total social service resources. These problems were noted and acknowledged and a solution (case coordination) was proposed, but no significant change occurred in practice.

The dominant issue in the 1950s was the quality of service to clients—a social service issue. In the 1980s, the issue that became dominant was a political/economic one, that is, the drastic cuts in federal funds. These cuts made it critical for the social service system to rethink its methods of practice.

Case management was conceived as a method of reducing fragmentation, which, it was believed, would improve the quality of services to the clients and at the same time reduce the cost of services to the government. Case management places responsibility on one person (the case manager) who works with the client in an ongoing relationship to develop an appropriate service plan, to assure access to services, to monitor service delivery, to advocate for the client, and to ensure that services across a cluster of service delivery systems are integrated and coordinated and that services continue over time as client needs change. Case management has a dual emphasis. On the one hand, it is directed toward developing and enhancing a resource network for the client and increasing the capacities of the resource network to meet the needs of the client. On the other, it is directed toward developing and enhancing the personal knowledge, skills, and abilities of the client so the client can use the resource network effectively. It thus attends to both sides of the person–environment fit.

The Process and Functions of Case Management

Case management has been defined as "a set of logical steps and a process of interaction within a service network which assures that a client receives needed services in a supportive, effective, and cost-effective manner" (Weil, 1985, p. 2); "a process of helping people whose lives are unsatisfying or unproductive due to the presence of many problems which require assistance from several helpers at once" (Ballew & Mink, 1986, p. 3); and "a client-level strategy for promoting the coordination of human services, opportunities, or benefits" (Moxley, 1989, p. 11).

However defined, case management has some key functions that the case manager undertakes sequentially and may repeat when necessary. These functions are (1) assessment and intervention planning, (2) intervention, (3) monitoring and coordination, and (4) advocacy.

ASSESSMENT AND INTERVENTION PLANNING

Assessment—the process of finding out what the client needs—involves engaging the client in identifying and prioritizing client's needs, goals, and type of help needed, and identifying a network of formal and informal helpers (the resource network/service delivery network, including the worker) who can meet these needs. It also involves exploring and identifying any barriers that may impede the client's use of the resources and help, for example, external barriers such as lack of transportation and child care, or internal barriers such as psychological resistance due to beliefs, attitudes, values, and experiences; or other inherent barriers such as disabilities of any kind.

After the needs, goals, resource network, and barriers are identified, intervention planning involves developing an action plan to meet the needs and achieve the goals. This includes clarifying and negotiating roles and expectations of each person or system in the client's resource network—who will do what—including the client and the worker. The concrete product of assessment and intervention planning is the case plan or service plan. This written document delineates the specific goals that both the client and the worker have agreed upon, the methods, strategies, and services to be used for reaching those goals, actions that the worker and the client are to take, timelines for these actions, and procedures for measuring progress and success of the plan. The case plan is the blueprint for intervention.

INTERVENTION

Intervention means implementing the service plan, delivering services as planned. In keeping with its dual emphasis, intervention in case management is a two-pronged approach, working directly with the client on one hand, and on the other, working with the service delivery network on behalf of the client.

Direct work with the client involves maintaining an ongoing positive working relationship with the client, connecting the client with appropriate resources and services in the community, and ensuring that the client can make use of the services offered. This involves giving information to the client and making referrals as well as removing the external and internal barriers to the client's access and utilization of services. Case managers often need to arrange for very practical matters such as child care and transportation. Case managers often also need to do counseling/therapy in order to help clients overcome their internal psychological resistances that prevent them from accepting and using the help of their resource network. Often they also need to be teachers and role models in order to help clients develop new life skills and new ways of coping.

The other side of intervention involves working with the network of formal and informal systems from which the client is receiving services. This may mean negotiating with different service providers and advocating if needed for responsiveness to client needs, facilitating communication among the service providers to reduce conflicts, and gaining agreement to common goals.

MONITORING AND COORDINATION

Monitoring the implementation and the effectiveness of the service plan involves maintaining links and connections with the client, with the service providers, and between clients and service providers to ensure that the client is getting and using needed services. It also involves modifying assessment and intervention plans as client needs change, and coordinating all the services so that they come together for the client as a coherent whole. Through monitoring activities, the worker evaluates the impact of services on the client, judging whether and to what extent the client is experiencing any benefits and whether the service plan is meeting its goal of improving the functioning and well-being of the client as intended.

ADVOCACY

Advocacy focuses on the bureaucratic, systemic barriers clients encounter. At times needed services are denied or withheld or delayed for the client, or the client encounters problems related to a service provider's policies and procedures, waiting lists, or other systemic issues. The case manager intercedes on behalf of the client to enable the client to receive services. At times the family, employer, or other social institutions make demands that are too overwhelming for the client. The case manager intercedes with the family and other systems to reduce the demands or at least reduce the cost of not meeting those demands. And at times some needed services simply do not exist in the community. The case manager then advocates for the creation of new programs and services.

Advocacy is particularly important in case management. Clients are often very vulnerable; they may have neither the power nor the capacities to assert themselves. Much too often they have not had fair access to services or have been poorly served in both policy and programs. Advocacy can be carried out at the case level, when the case manager presses for the needs and interest of the individual client. Advocacy can also be carried out at the system level, when the case manager lobbies, negotiates, mediates, and works with other individuals and organizations to change the system of policies, programs, and/or procedures to benefit an entire class of people who have the same problem.

Case and class advocacy are an integral part of case management process. The case manager has to be able to move back and forth between them, advocating for an individual client (for example, a maltreated child) as well as advocating for all people who face a similar problem (for example, all maltreated children).

The Strengths Perspective in Case Management

Most helping approaches generally tend to focus on the client's problems. The helping process consists of identifying and treating the deficiencies, inadequacies, and pathologies that cause the problem, be they within the individual's psyche, or in the family, or in the environment. Even though client strengths are identified, the predominant emphasis of work remains on the deficiencies. In contrast, the strengths approach attempts to understand clients in terms of their strengths. Though problems are acknowledged, this approach focuses predominantly on the strengths of the client, on what the client can do and has done successfully. Focusing on strengths turns attention from blaming the client to discovering how the client has managed to survive, even in difficult circumstances. The helping process consists of assisting the client to build on his strengths rather than on treating him for his deficiencies.

The strengths perspective is based on the following beliefs and principles: First,

> . . . every person has inherent power that may be characterized as life force, transformational capacity, life energy, spirituality, regenerative potential, and healing power. These and other terms point to an inexplicable, probably biologically grounded, but vibrant quality that is an irrevocable aspect of being human. The act of empowering reawakens or stimulates someone's own natural powers. (Cousins, 1989, as cited in Saleebey, 1992. p. 24)

Second, people with problems are more than just the problem. Every person has a range of experience, characteristics, and roles that contribute to who that person is. Similarly, families also have histories and experiences that make them who they are. Individuals and families possess knowledge that is important in defining both the problematic aspects of their situation and the potential solutions for it. They also possess innate strength that helps them deal with the many challenges of life, as well as un-used or under-used competencies and resources that can be brought forth with help.

Third, people are resilient; they have the capacity to overcome even the harshest experiences of life. Research in the last few decades has shown that many children who grew up under the most horrifying conditions of poverty, severe maltreatment, war and dislocation, racism and other forms of social oppression and other harsh conditions have developed into fine, successful adults.

Fourth, like individuals and families, all communities—rich or poor, urban or rural, diverse or homogenous, young or old—have a wealth of strengths, capacities, skills, and assets. These strengths are embedded in the individuals, families and households, and formal and informal groups and organizations that comprise that community. Once identified, these community strengths can be mobilized to improve clients' lives. The identification and use of community strengths and assets are just as critical as the identification of individual strengths.

Fifth, a person's behavior and well-being are in large part determined by the resources available and the expectations of others toward that person.

Given necessary appropriate environmental resources and opportunities, individuals and families can improve their psychosocial functioning and can live up to their full potential.

With these guiding principles, assessment from the strengths perspective consists of the worker and client working together to identify what the client has achieved so far, what he knows, the capabilities he possesses, the resources and opportunities that have been or are currently available to him, what his hopes, aspirations, and dreams might be, and how he has managed and survived the challenges of his life so far. The case plan is based on the client's (not worker's) perception of his needs, strengths, goals, and vision for his future. The specific activities to achieve the goals are flexible and tailored to each client's individual strengths.

The strengths-based approach is thus an empowerment approach. The key method in this approach is the use of a collaborative relationship between social worker and client, a relationship that conveys respect, courtesy, and a sense of cooperation and partnership in culturally appropriate ways. The worker and the client form a partnership in assessment—in defining problems, goals, strategies, and success. Clients are also partners in the intervention in that they participate in decision-making about what actions are to be taken and act on their own behalf to the extent that they can. Collaboration begins as clients share their understanding of the situation, the outcomes desired and ideas about how to achieve that outcome; and the worker listens, helps them discover their vision, and builds a case plan based on their vision. A worker who listens to clients' stories patiently in the way they can best tell, affirms their perceptions, recognizes their survival efforts and successes, acknowledges their resourcefulness and perseverance in managing adversity, and bases case plans on their perception of their needs, strengths, and goals helps clients achieve a sense of personal efficacy and power.

Contact between the worker and client is not office-bound or talk-bound. The worker meets the client in the client's normal environment, where the client is, literally and figuratively. The worker joins the client in the activities of the client's everyday life such as doing the dishes or folding laundry or teaching how to fix the plumbing or fix the bike or playing basketball or accompanying the client to an appointment at another agency. In the context of seemingly innocuous mundane activities of the client's everyday life, the worker builds trust with the client as the client tests the worker's intent and sincerity. As confidence and trust build, communication between them becomes more open and a partnership begins to form.

Other methods are environmental modification and advocacy. The environment is both a resource and a target of intervention. Environmental modification involves generating resources, options, and opportunities for the client; the worker fosters client links to contexts where client strengths can develop and flourish. It may also take the form of educating other people in the client's environment.

The strengths perspective in case management is a shift in paradigm from a pathology orientation to a strengths and resilience orientation. It allows for a different way of thinking about clients and provides a framework for helping that uncovers strengths and the power within clients. It "allows us to see possibilities rather than problems, options rather than constraints, wellness rather than sickness. And once seen, achievement can occur" (Rapp, 1998, p. 24).

Clinical Social Work in Case Management

Clinical social work is an integral and essential component of effective case management (Roberts-DeGennaro, 1987; Siu and Hogan, 1989; Samantrai, 1991). However, because it occurs in the informal context of the client's everyday life rather than in the formal context of "talk therapy" in a therapist's office, the fact that it occurs, and its critical significance in working with child welfare clients, is often overlooked and devalued.

Clinical social work is about using clinical knowledge and skills in the context of a professional relationship to promote the client's healing, growth, and empowerment. It involves addressing clinical themes—"aspects of psychological or emotional functioning that are intense and recurring issues for clients, expressed nonverbally or verbally, that require some degree of resolution for the client to function at an adequate level" (Siu and Hogan, 1989, p. 339). It has been defined as

> . . . the professional application of social work theory and methods to the treatment and prevention of psychosocial dysfunction, disability, or impairment, including emotional and mental disorders. . . . Clinical social work includes interventions directed to interpersonal interactions, intrapsychic dynamics, and life-support and management issues . . . (National Association of Social Workers, 1989).

In child welfare practice, clinical themes abound. Clients, both children and adults, experience numerous intense emotions and present clinical issues that, if not recognized, addressed, and worked through by the case manager, obstruct an accurate assessment of client needs (therefore the formulation of an appropriate case plan) and client's use of the help and resources offered. They contribute to unnecessary separation of children and families, failure of placements, and bouncing of children from one foster home to another.

Separation: The overarching, intensely emotional, recurring theme is the theme of separation. In all aspects of child welfare practice there is either actual separation or the threat of separation of the child from birth-parents or other attachment figures or from accustomed surroundings and routines. Inherent in and intertwined with separation are the themes of loss, grief and mourning, rejection, abandonment, ambivalence, guilt, shame, blame, sense of failure, and depression. Feelings and behaviors reflecting these themes exist to varying degrees in all child welfare clients—children, biological parents, foster parents, adoptive parents, families and extended families—influencing individual and family functioning profoundly. These feelings affect the client–worker relationship and the ability of the family to use help offered. They also affect the child's adjustment in foster care or adoptive placement, often resulting in disruptions and multiple placements. They contribute to biological parents' reluctance to relinquish the child for adoption when that becomes necessary, often causing the need for court action, which prolongs impermanence for the child.

Identity: For children who have had multiple foster placements and children being prepared for adoption, identity becomes a major issue. Children who are moved around frequently cannot develop a sense of belonging anywhere, which is developmentally essential for the formation of an integrated identity. In the situation of adoption, it is not only the biological parent who has to relinquish the child; the child also has to relinquish the biological parent and the identity that comes with being a child of that parent before he is able to fully accept a new parent, a new family, and a new identity.

Two other clinical themes that are particularly salient in child welfare practice are the themes of resistance and countertransference (Samantrai, 1991).

Resistance: Resistance is encountered in clients in any social work setting; however, it is a particularly salient theme in public child welfare practice, as a majority of child welfare clients are involuntary and perceive the child welfare system as a foe rather than a friend. Resistance manifests in a myriad of ways—from superficial compliance to evasive, passive-aggressive, hostile, aggressive, and sometimes even threatening behavior—in the beginning stages of client–worker contact or at any time during the course of their work together. In case management, if resistance is not recognized and addressed, it would be easy for the worker to become authoritative and misuse the legal authority inherent in the child welfare worker role. Given the usually high caseloads, it would also be easy for the worker to avoid resistant clients until there is a crisis. Any of these actions on the part of the worker subvert the goal of public child welfare practice—protecting children while preventing unnecessary separation from families. Any of these actions can also reinforce clients' feelings of rejection, abandonment, guilt, or anger and hostility toward the system that is supposed to help.

Countertransference: Intense recurring psychological and emotional issues are inherent and recurrent not only for the client but also for the worker in the field of child welfare. If left unacknowledged and unresolved, worker issues can interfere with the resolution of client issues.

   Child welfare workers encounter some of the most horrendous, heart-rending family situations, which can easily evoke feelings of anger and pain. These situations can also evoke feelings of fear, inadequacy, overidentification with the child or with parent(s), and the desire to rescue the child or the parent from untenable living conditions. Sometimes, as a result of the child welfare worker's (unresolved) countertransference, children may be removed from the home unnecessarily, or conversely, they may be forced to live with parents who cannot provide continuity and consistency of care.

The function of clinical social work in case management is not to treat mental illnesses but to enable children and families to establish and maintain bonds with their informal and formal resource networks, bonds that sustain and nurture them so they can be "good-enough" families. This requires knowing when, how, and to what extent clinical issues need to be addressed with each member of the family. It also requires sufficient knowledge of psychopathology. With mental health services usually never being sufficient, many emotionally troubled and mentally ill parents and children are funneled into the child welfare system. A worker who does not have sufficient theoretical knowledge of psychopathology may not recognize illness-related behaviors, may not know of the effects of illness on psychosocial functioning, and therefore may not make appropriate case plans. Not knowing, the case manager may not recognize mental illness when it does exist or, on the other hand, may misperceive (and mislabel) normal behaviors as psychopathology and therefore falsely pathologize the client.

Case management was conceptualized as a method of coordinating services in a fragmented service delivery system so as to make them less costly for the government and more appropriate for the clients. The belief was that enough services do in fact exist, but because they are delivered in a haphazard, fragmented manner they are not being utilized efficiently and effectively, and that if service providers would only work together there would be enough resources. This belief has proven to be a fallacy. Services were never sufficient before; under the guise of case management they were reduced even further. The "less-costly-for-the-government" objective appears to have completely overshadowed the other objective of "more-appropriate-for-clients." In many jurisdictions, case management tasks have become restricted to information, referral, and monitoring (like a "watchdog," according to Cimmarusti, 1992, p. 244) a client's compliance with standardized case plans that may or may not be relevant to the client's individual needs.

Case management cannot coordinate services when services don't exist. It has been asserted that lacking adequate societal resources and programs, case management has become a cover-up for a non-system, an attempt to cope with a chaotic service environment.

A major debate in case management has been about the role of clinical social work in case management, specifically whether therapy should be considered a case management task. Some contend a case manager's role is limited to only brokering services, that case management should be done by paraprofessionals. Others argue that case management and therapy go hand in hand, be it in the child welfare system or in health/mental health systems or the school systems or whatever other system that works with people with multiple, concurrent needs. Case managers can acquire the in-depth knowledge of the client adequately to assess needs and facilitate the processes for meeting them only through therapeutic involvement. And therapists in community care of the mentally ill find themselves "acting as both a therapeutic agent and a participant in their clients' daily lives, becoming involved in a communal relationship that may involve profound interpretations on one day and the most mundane tasks on another" (Kanter, 2000, p. 398). It has been suggested that the dichotomy between therapy and case management is a false dichotomy, that people who perform these functions should be referred to as case-manager/therapist or therapist/ case-manager (Lamb, 1980; Roberts-DeGennaro, 1987; Kanter, 2000).

Case management is not simply an administrative function designed to process clients more efficiently. Nor is it a panacea for the numerous problems of contemporary human services. However, given an adequate service network in the community and adequate professional training and time to case managers so that they can establish an ongoing relationship with their clients, it can be a humane, responsive, and cost-effective method of providing services to people with multiple, concurrent needs.

CRISIS INTERVENTION

The other method child welfare workers are most frequently called upon to practice is crisis intervention. A discussion of crisis intervention theory and practice, however, needs to begin with a review of the concept of "functioning."

The Concept of Functioning

From the moment of birth, each individual begins to have multiple social roles in different spheres of life. In the family, an individual is a child to the parents, a sibling to other siblings, a spouse or partner, and a parent to one's own children, as well as possibly a grandparent, aunt, uncle, cousin, and so on. In other spheres of life, one is a student (or a teacher), friend, employee, colleague, perhaps a boss, a member of a religious or social or recreational or other civic organizations. In each role, one is expected to behave in a certain way, do certain things, perform certain tasks, measure up to certain standards. Family expectations are defined by the family's culture, values, and beliefs. Workplace expectations are defined by the norms and standards of the workplace. Similarly, expectations in other organizations are defined by the norms and standards of the organization, and in friendships and other social relationships expectations depend on both the norms of the culture as well as the personal expectations of the friend. And most of all, expectations are also defined by one's own self. Functioning simply means how well one meets the demand and expectations of his or her various roles, as defined by others and as defined by oneself.

People who can meet the demands of their various roles very well are considered to be very high functioning. However, there is hardly anybody who can meet all the demands of all their roles perfectly. On the other hand, there are few people who cannot meet any demands of any of their roles. If functioning is visualized as a continuum from "perfect functioning" at one end to "totally non-functioning" at the other, most people are likely to place themselves somewhere along the middle range of that continuum. That is their usual, normal *level* of functioning.

Functioning is affected by the stress one experiences at any given time. Stress can be caused by simple physiological factors such as hunger or fatigue or lack of sleep. Such stress is usually temporary and can be relieved by a simple coping mechanism such as eating, resting, sleeping. Other stresses, which may not be quite so temporary, are caused by the sheer number of demands of their various roles, high expectations, and societal conditions such as poor economy, violent neighborhoods, and lack of needed services and resources. In the course of growing up, people develop a repertoire of coping mechanisms that become habitual, a part of their personality. When they experience stress, their functioning goes down. Habitual coping mechanisms come forth more or less automatically and relieve the stress; functioning is restored to its normal level again. Thus, functioning at any level goes up and down constantly, affected by the amount of stress experienced at any given moment and the effectiveness of the coping mechanisms utilized to relieve that stress. "Functioning then can be visualized not as a straight line but as a wavy zigzag line—going down when there is stress, going up again when habitual coping mechanisms reduce or eliminate the stress" (Samantrai, 1996, p. 49).

This up-and-down process occurs several times a day, day after day. In the process of growing up, each person develops a steady, predictable *pattern* of this wavy zigzag manner of functioning which becomes a part of his personality. Some people have a very calm personality; nothing disturbs them too much. Others have a very labile personality—they react quickly to everything. And there are numerous variations in between. Whatever the pattern of functioning and the level at which a person functions, what is significant is that that level and pattern are his usual, typical way of functioning, his normal "steady state." Other terms such as "dynamic homeostasis" and "equilibrium" are also used to express the concept of steady state.

Like individuals, families also have to meet certain expectations such as providing children with food, shelter, clothing, and protection from harm. Some expectations are imposed by the society in which they live and are determined by the family's and the dominant culture's beliefs, values, norms, standards and laws; others are imposed by themselves and their own beliefs, values, and standards. Like the individual, each family also develops its own habitual coping mechanisms and its own "steady state" of functioning, which is its typical, normal way of being, its normal state of equilibrium.

The State of Crisis

Crisis in individuals or in a family occurs when stress upsets their steady state, and habitual coping mechanisms fail to restore them to their normal level and pattern of functioning rapidly. They go into a state of flux, a state of disequilibrium.

While often the terms "crisis" and "stress" are used interchangeably, the two in fact are not the same. Stress is the state in which the habitual coping mechanisms do restore the normal steady state. In crisis, they don't; the state of crisis requires new coping mechanisms. In addition, "stress" is a sort of load or burden on a person's being. Crisis, on the other hand, while posing a danger of breakdown, can also be an opportunity for change. Making old habits ineffective, it serves as a catalyst for developing new strengths and new ways of being that would not have developed had the crisis not occurred.

Crisis is a reaction to a stressor event or situation, not the event itself. All individuals and families faced with the same event do not experience it in the same way; an event or a situation that precipitates a crisis for one individual or family may or may not be experienced as a crisis by another individual or family. On the other hand, there are certain common situations such as natural or man-made disasters in which most people will be in a state of crisis to a greater or lesser extent.

Three factors interacting with each other create a state of crisis: (1) the stressor event; (2) the person (or family); and (3) the meaning of the event to the individual or family. The stressor event is a situation for which the individual/family has little or no prior preparation. It demands competencies the individual /family does not have—either they never had these competencies or the competencies are, for some reason, not available now. The event may be internal/maturational (such as reaching a particular birthday, birth of a child, a death in the family—any milestone that is a normal part of an individual's or family's life cycle); or external, such as disaster, illness or accident, job loss, a change in social status, etc. A person or family with many internal coping mechanisms and external supports and resources can weather such stressor events without experiencing them as crises. However, individuals and families who have few internal and external resources and supports are more vulnerable. They experience stressor events with greater frequency and greater severity, and they define these events more frequently as crises. Often such individuals and families come to be known as "crisis-prone."

Whether or not an event is experienced as a crisis also depends on the meaning that event has for that person or family, as the same event may not have the same meaning to all people. Generally, a stressor event can be perceived as a threat to survival, or as a loss, or as a challenge. When an event is perceived as a threat to survival—threat to one's life, body, or loss of control over one's impulses—the response is enormous anxiety. In the child welfare system, telephone calls from frantic parents saying, "I am afraid I am going to hurt my children" are not unknown. On the other hand, the very appearance of a child welfare worker on the door can be perceived as a threat to the survival and the integrity of the family, as child welfare workers often take the children away from their families. When an event is perceived as a loss of something or someone loved and valued, or loss of self-esteem, the response is usually depression. And, if the event is perceived as a challenge, it can mobilize the person's energy into purposeful problem-solving and searching for new ways of coping and being. Herein lies the potential for growth.

Characteristics of the State of Crisis

The state of crisis has some distinctive defining characteristics. One, it is *time-limited,* usually lasting no more than about six weeks. Human nature is such that it cannot remain in flux for very long. It seeks to restore some sort of equilibrium, and in doing so it finds a way of coping, be it adaptive or maladaptive. If the original normal level cannot be restored rapidly, it stabilizes at a different (usually lower) level of functioning.

Two, it has certain *typical phases*. In the initial phase, there is a rise in tension in response to the initial impact of stress. During this period habitual problem-solving mechanisms are called forth, that is, the individual/family attempts to resolve the problem as it has always resolved problems in the past. If the first effort fails, there is an increase in the level of tension and distress. This tension acts as a powerful internal stimulus for the individual/family to mobilize its internal and external resources and utilize other problem-solving approaches that may not have been tried before. If the problem still cannot be resolved by any of these means, a state of crisis ensues.

Three, some *disorganization* always occurs with some effect on functioning. There is a general feeling of bewilderment, helplessness, anxiety, desperation and sometimes apathy, often accompanied by a state of cognitive confusion in which the individual literally does not know how to think of his problem, how to evaluate reality, and how to go about considering, planning, and deciding upon alternative problem-solving possibilities. The mind is muddled. Such a state of disorganization may last from a few minutes to several hours, days, or weeks.

Four, people are more *open to change* and more susceptible to the influence of significant others in the environment when they are in a state of crisis than at any other time. Therefore, at this time, a little help that is purposefully directed and strategically focused is more effective than more extensive help given at any other time.

Five, a crisis usually evokes memories/feelings of previous similar experiences, and therefore is an *opportunity* to resolve previously unresolved issues. And six, *successful experience* with crisis strengthens the individual/family; failure and defeat further weaken them.

Crisis Intervention

The goal of crisis intervention is to stabilize the individual/family and restore them to their pre-crisis level of functioning. In doing so, the worker helps the individual/family develop different ways of perceiving the situation, new ways of coping, and new problem-solving strategies so they can face future stresses in a more effective way. So while the goal is restoration of a pre-crisis level of functioning, crisis intervention can often set the client on the path of a level of functioning that is higher than before.

As the state of crisis is time limited, crisis intervention also has to be time-limited. It also has to be fast-paced; it cannot be limited to the traditional one-hour-a-week model. Because the client is, by definition, in a state of disorganization, the worker has to take a much more active and directive approach.

The process of crisis intervention has been conceptualized as occurring in four steps (Aguilera, 1998), seven steps (Puryear, 1979), or nine steps (Dixon, 1987). Regardless of the number of steps conceptualized, the substance in each conceptualization is the same, involving the processes of assessment, intervention, and termination.

ASSESSMENT

Assessment of the person and the problem involves exploration of the three factors that created the crisis—(1) the stressor event that precipitated the crisis; (2) the person/family experiencing the crisis, and (3) the meaning of the event to the person/family. Exploration is done by asking appropriate questions and observing non-verbal behavior—the appropriateness of client's and family's affect and manner to the situation (which may be culturally defined and may or may not be what is considered "appropriate" in the worker's culture and training or the dominant culture); orientation to time, place, person (mental status); their cognitive functioning (memory, capacity to give and take in information, speak coherently, capacity to think, plan, and engage in problem-solving).

The questions to elicit information about the event are: What happened? What precipitated this crisis? When did it occur? Whether the situation is acute or chronic, and what was the last straw? Why a referral came in at this time, rather than sooner, or later? In assessing the person/family who is the client, the issues to explore are: Who is in the family? How is each one affected? What was their pre-crisis level of functioning? What can they still do, and what capacities have been lost? What is the level of stress and role-demands? What are their habitual coping mechanisms—what do they usually tend to do in stressful situations? What crisis meeting resources do they have, within themselves or in their support system or in the community? Are they being used now? If yes, with what success? If not, can they be mobilized?

A most immediate and critical component of assessment in any crisis situation is risk assessment—risk of suicide and homicide (or hurting without necessarily killing), risk of physical or emotional harm to the children, risk of break with reality (psychosis), and risk of the client physically fleeing the situation. In child welfare, there are several standardized risk assessment tools to assess the relative safety or danger of a situation to the children; many states and counties have adopted one or the other for use by their child welfare workers (American Humane Association, 1998). Generally, risk assessment is done by asking questions in the interview about (1) history—personal and familial, of risk-behavior, (2) any means and plans the client may have about carrying out the risk-behavior, (3) controls—internal and external—that are stopping the client from undertaking the risk-behavior. Questions in the interview are supplemented with observations of client's level of anxiety, desperation, despair, sense of hopelessness, and contact with reality. If it is determined that the child is not safe in the home, then the worker must attend to the child's safety first by either removing the child or removing the source of danger from the home.

The skill and technique most essential at this stage is that of focusing while allowing the client to ventilate and express the sometimes overwhelming flood of emotions. Because the client is usually in a state of disorganization, the worker's focusing technique can elicit more coherent information for assessment as well as help the client pull himself together cognitively and emotionally. Thus a gently focused initial interview can serve as an instrument of both assessment and intervention.

INTERVENTION

Intervention planning occurs simultaneously as assessment is made about how much time has elapsed between the occurrence of the stressor event and this initial interview; how much the crisis has disrupted the person's life and the effect of this disruption on others in the family; what his level of functioning was before, what has been lost and what he can still do; and what supports and resources can be mobilized. The goal of intervention at this time is not to bring about major changes in the client's personality but to restore the client to a pre-crisis level of equilibrium. Intervention involves mobilizing the client's internal and external resources, with the worker viewing her/himself as part of the network of the client's resources and relationships. The exact nature of intervention will depend on the client's pre-existing strengths and supports that can be mobilized, as well as the personal and cultural norms and expectations. It will also depend on the worker's professional knowledge and orientation, personal beliefs and values, and the level of creativity and flexibility.

Generally, there are three approaches to intervention. The *affective* approach involves expression and management of feelings and may involve techniques such as ventilation, psychological support, emotional catharsis. The *cognitive* approach involves helping the client understand the connections between the stressor event and his response. Often, because of cognitive confusion, the individual sees no relationship between the stressor event and his state of disequilibrium. Clarifying the problem, identifying and isolating the factors involved, and helping the client gain an intellectual understanding of his crisis all restore cognitive restructuring, which in itself may be enough to restore the previous level of functioning and emotional equilibrium. The cognitive approach also involves giving information, discussing alternative coping mechanisms, and changing perceptions; for example, helping the client see the situation not as a threat to survival or a loss but as a gain, a challenge, an opportunity to do something different.

The third approach is *environmental modification*. It involves pulling together needed external, environmental resources, be they within the client's familial and social network or from formal helping systems such as public and private social services, health (physical and mental) services, etc.

Any or all of these approaches may be used with a client at any time, sometimes even within the same interview, depending on where the client is, emotionally and cognitively, at that moment. A client flooded with emotion needs time to express those emotions. Giving information at this time is likely to be quite useless as the client will not be able to absorb it. Conversely, to a client coming from a culture where verbal expression of feelings is not acceptable, pressure to talk about feelings would be frustrating to both the client and the worker. The client's (cultural) reluctance to talk about feelings can easily be misconstrued as denial or resistance. To such a client perhaps a more cognitive approach is more useful. With a client who is at the point of needing resources rather than talking, the most suitable approach would be environmental modification, focusing on mobilizing external, environmental resources.

Thus, the nature of intervention and the techniques used at any moment are highly dependent on the worker's assessment of where the client is, emotionally and cognitively, at that moment, what the client needs to restore stability and pre-crisis level of functioning, and what the client's cultural norms are. There is much danger here of misunderstanding the client's nonverbal behavior as well as spoken word, be it due to cultural differences or the client's state of disorganization. Therefore, it becomes imperative for the worker not to assume that he or she understands what the client means by his spoken word or non-verbal behavior or that the client understands what the worker means. It is best to clarify and make sure.

TERMINATION—RESOLUTION OF CRISIS AND ANTICIPATORY PLANNING

The last step involves a summation of the work done. The worker and client together consciously acknowledge, recount, and reconfirm the progress made and the change accomplished. The worker reinforces the adaptive coping mechanisms the client has used successfully to reduce stress and anxiety and discusses ways in which the present experience may help in future crisis. The worker also assists the client in making realistic plans for the future and in connecting with any services and resources needed after their contact is terminated.

A crisis is a critical turning point in life. A little strategic help at this time, delivered skillfully, can lead an individual/family to a higher level of functioning than before. If appropriate help is not available, the individual/family may become totally immobilized or resort to destructive and maladaptive behaviors. A skillful crisis worker is one who is creative and flexible, involves the entire family in problem-solving process, reinforces the family's ability and strengths, and conveys a sense of hope to the family. If the family senses that the worker believes a positive resolution to the crisis is possible, family members also begin to feel confident in their ability to bring about change.

FAMILY PRESERVATION AND SUPPORT

The Adoption Assistance and Child Welfare Act of 1980 (P.L. 96-272) emphasized prevention of unnecessary out-of-home placement of children and preservation of families by providing services to families. In practice during the 1980s, however, emphasis remained on the removal of children from their homes. Neither the public child welfare service delivery system, nor its funding, nor its practice methods were geared toward prevention of out-of-home placement. Services were often more focused on managing crises (such as investigation of alleged abuse or neglect, removing children from their homes) and less focused on prevention and treatment. At the same time, the larger social problems of a poor economy, an enormous increase in the number of families living in poverty and homeless families, and the spread of drug abuse were leading to an alarming increase in the number of children coming into care, putting the

INTERVENTION   133

child welfare system in crisis. Hard-pressed not only to achieve the intent of the law but also to deal with the rising tide of children in care and children at risk, state child welfare officials looked for other, different program models that would permit them to do some early intervention work with families. In the context of these circumstances, two new program models evolved as part of public child welfare services—Family Preservation and Family Support.

Initially, a few states started with a few small programs using their own or other non-federal funds. However, with the need being high and their own economic resources being severely constrained, they pressed for federal support and funding. In response to states' pressure the federal government incorporated some funds for financial assistance to low-income families and early intervention service systems for children and families in the Family Support Act of 1988 (P.L.100-485). In 1993, federal support was expanded by adding a new subpart to The Omnibus Budget Reconciliation Act (P.L. 103-66)—the Family Preservation and Support Services provisions—under which $930 million was authorized in funding to states over a five-year period to initiate or expand family preservation services and community-based family support services. Congress reauthorized Family Preservation and Support Services in 1997. Now, all states offer such services in a variety of forms.

Family Support services are generally community-based primary prevention services designed to promote the well-being of children and their families. Their goal is to increase the strength and stability of families and prevent child and family problems from escalating to the point of crisis where out-of-home placement may have to be considered. While available to all children and families, they are usually targeted toward at-risk populations—those identified as being in increased danger of becoming abusive. They can include a range of social, health and mental health, and educational or other services according to the needs of the community. Usually no time limits are imposed; people can use the services they need for as long as they need.

Family Preservation services, on the other hand, are short-term, intensive services for families in crisis who are at the point of imminent out-of-home placement of children. Their purpose is to restore adequate family functioning, reduce the risk of harm to the children, and thereby avert the need for the imminent removal of children from their home. Family preservation services are often employed only after all other assistance has failed or has been judged inappropriate. Services are generally delivered in the client's home.

Family Preservation is based on the principle of crisis intervention theory that people are more amenable to help and change when they are in crisis. It therefore uses the crisis intervention method. Originally conceived as a service delivery model to prevent the imminent removal of children from their homes, Family Preservation is now also being increasingly used when reunifying children in foster care with their families and in averting disruption of foster and adoptive placements. Some states are implementing family preservation services with high-risk families even before child maltreatment has been confirmed. Used for these purposes, it approaches the family from a family treatment/family therapy orientation rather than a crisis intervention orientation.

Common Characteristics

Many different designs of Family Preservation programs have evolved in different communities. However, they all share some common characteristics. These are:

1. *Immediate response to referrals.* The worker sees the family as soon as possible after a referral is made, within no more than 24 hours.
2. *Continuous availability of services.* Services (that is, the family's worker) are available 24 hours a day, 7 days a week.
3. *Intensive, short-term intervention.* The worker's contact with family may be as much as 5–20 hours per week, depending on family need. However, the duration of services is short, anywhere between one to six months.
4. *Small caseloads.* Because the work with each family is so intensive, workers carry a much smaller caseload of two to six families at a time. Many programs use a team approach. The primary worker maintains a supportive, nurturing relationship with the family; one or more colleagues are designated as team members or back-up for the primary worker.
5. *Family focus.* Although problems of individual members are addressed, the focus is on the functioning of the family as a whole. Families are also viewed as part of a larger social environment that can weaken or support them. Interaction among family members and the associated behaviors are one point of change; the family's interaction with and use of the formal and informal supports in their social environment is another point of change.
6. *Range of services.* Family preservation provides a mix of clinical and concrete services—counseling, education, skill-building, information and referral, concrete assistance, advocacy, and, of course, crisis intervention. Workers may provide some services themselves; for others they may connect the family with other service providers.
7. *Limited treatment objectives.* Though intensive and comprehensive, services are targeted to only those issues and behaviors that precipitated the placement crisis, not to all the problems of the family. Service objectives are specific and measurable, not vague or general; they are determined by clients in consultation with the worker, not unilaterally conceived by the worker and announced to the family.
8. *Client's home and community as the locus of all services.* Family preservation services are delivered where the family lives. The worker sees families at home and makes frequent visits convenient to the family's schedule. Many services are also provided in school and neighborhood settings. The worker may also accompany and bolster family members who visit other helpers such as the schools, courts, doctors, and public assistance offices.
9. *Assessment and intervention are based on the family's strengths.* Services are provided to the family in the context of the family's values, beliefs, and culture. They are tailored to the family's needs.

Effective Intervention Techniques—What Works

A growing body of research on the effectiveness of Family Preservation programs has identified some successful intervention techniques that improve the overall functioning of the family and protect children at the same time. These are empowerment and enabling techniques, repairing family relationships, and multisystemic interventions (Nelson, 1997).

Empowerment techniques such as those described in the strengths approach—a relationship that conveys respect and partnership in culturally appropriate ways, allowing the locus of decision-making to rest clearly with the family so that the family takes the primary role in identifying and prioritizing its needs, determining its goals, and the ways of achieving them—have been found to be related to placement prevention in several studies. *Enabling interventions* that emphasize skill and self-esteem building, creating opportunities for the family to acquire pro-social, self-sustaining, self-efficacious, and other adaptive behaviors, and actively assisting families to identify and access community services and support on their own have been found to be more effective than simply providing concrete services. These strategies empower the families to gain mastery over their affairs and manage their life events more effectively.

Attention to the repair of family relationships has been found to be very significant. De-escalating parent–child or marital conflict is essential in cases involving physical abuse. In cases involving neglect, repairing relationship with extended family members and other sources of support was found to be of critical importance. Without repair of relationships, parent education—a frequently used intervention—was found to have limited ability to improve parenting.

The most encouraging results were found in programs that combined *interventions at several levels simultaneously*. Multisystemic family therapy, which provided individual and family therapy, worked with parents to improve relationships with the school, and promote peer activities for children, was found in carefully controlled studies to significantly reduce placement and recidivism among youthful offenders over as much as a four-year follow-up period. Multisystemic therapy has also been found to be effective with delinquent, substance abusing, and sexually offending teenagers (Brunk et al., 1987; Cimmarusti, 1992; Henggeler et al., 1993).

Family Preservation programs are intended to remove the risk rather than the child from the home. They present a model of service delivery that is flexible, accessible, coordinated, and culturally relevant. However, they have come under attack for questionable cost-effectiveness and for not living up to their promise of dramatic reduction of out-of-home placements. Supporters of the program argue that such an expectation is unrealistic, that short-term interventions, no matter how intensive, should not be expected to solve long-term family problems, and that reduction of out-of-home placement should not be the only criterion of this program's success. They point out that Family Preservation programs are not for all families and they are not a panacea, but they are useful when used as part of a continuum of child welfare services.

KINSHIP CARE

Kinship care—the care of children by relatives—is one of the oldest traditions in many cultures. Its evolution as a formal child welfare policy and service, however, is very recent. It was the basis of the Indian Child Welfare Act of 1978; in 1996, it became a formal federal policy for all children in need of out-of-home placement, codified in the Personal Responsibility and Work Opportunity Act of 1996. Now, all states require that workers give priority consideration to relatives when making decisions about a child's out-of-home placement.

The term "kin" generally refers to any person related by blood or marriage or any person who has close family ties. Kinship care has been defined as "the full-time nurturing and protection of children who must be separated from their parents by relatives, members of their tribes or clans, godparents, stepparents, or other adults who have a kinship bond with a child" (Child Welfare League of America, 1994, p. 2). In child welfare practice, it is understood as the out-of-home care provided by relatives to children who have entered the custody of the state child welfare agency because of abuse, neglect, or abandonment.

Issues Affecting Practice

Kinship care grew very quickly in the last decade. While it has been observed that practice issues are much more complex in kinship foster care than in the non-relative foster care, the issues are still in the process of being identified and innovative methods are still in the process of being developed.

Kinship foster care differs from non-relative foster care in several ways. The family system with which the worker must work consists not only of the child and the biological parent(s), but also of the kinship parents and other extended family members who might be important to the well-being of the child. Established relationships already exist between the child and the kinship parents, and between the kinship parents and biological parents. The extended family dynamics affect the family's relationship with the worker, the agency's case plan, reunification of the child with the biological parent, and other permanency options such as adoption or guardianship.

In addition to the greater complexity of the larger family system, assessment and intervention in kinship care become more complex due to three policy issues. One, the purpose for which relative placement is being considered—as a diversion from out-of-home care or as a type of formal foster care. Two, who holds legal and physical custody of the child—the biological parent, the relative caregiver, or the state? And three, the source and level of financial support given by the state to the relative caregiver. These policy issues can impinge upon the worker–family relationship and affect the nature and duration of services provided by the child welfare agency.

DIVERSION, FORMAL FOSTER CARE, CUSTODY

Kinship care is used as a diversion program (to keep children out of formal foster care) as well as part of the formal foster care program. The decision about whether diversion from foster care or formal foster care is more appropriate for a particular child and family is based on the child's and the family's needs, risk and safety factors, and issues of physical environment, permanency planning, and preservation of the family. If the extended family circumstances are such that there are no risk factors involved but the family needs some income support, then a diversion program is considered more appropriate. If, however, risk factors exist, then a more formal foster care is considered more appropriate. In diversion, the child is placed with a relative by court order. The relative takes custody of the child, but the state retains jurisdiction. If deemed necessary, the state provides protective supervision in the form of regular visits by the child welfare worker to oversee the child's well-being and safety and may provide other supportive services to ensure stability and continuity. Once the worker is assured that the relative will look after the needs of the child, the formal child welfare involvement is discontinued; the kinship family continues to receive income support through TANF. If, however, the worker determines that the relative is not meeting the needs of the child, the state assumes custody and brings the child into the formal foster care system.

In formal foster care, the child is in the custody of the state but in the care of a relative. More often than not the relative home is not a pre-existing licensed foster home; they may choose to go through the licensing process at the time of placement of their kin-child. Some states do not differentiate between relative and non-relative homes and use the same licensing criteria and procedures for both. Other states do not require kinship homes to meet the standard foster home licensing requirements; they vary on the criteria they alter for relative homes. In practically all states, when some kinship families cannot meet the state's licensing standards and requirements but can otherwise provide a safe, nurturing home environment for the child, they are assessed for risk of abuse and neglect but licensing requirements are waived.

FINANCIAL SUPPORT

Kinship care is supported by either TANF (former AFDC) funds or by federal foster care funds. The level of payment is significantly lower under TANF. Even when foster care funds are used, the level of payment for homes not licensed by the state is lower than those that are. Different levels of financial support to kinship families may be accompanied by different levels of other supportive services from the agency and different standards and expectations. Differential payment rates can also become an issue to be addressed in the client–worker relationship.

Assessment

Assessment in kinship care changes from a dyadic assessment of the child and the biological parents (that is, the nuclear family) to a triadic assessment of the child, the nuclear family, and the extended family, which may include everybody the family defines as kin. It requires attention to the intergenerational, multidimensional family systems and their interpersonal dynamics, their relationship with the environmental/societal systems, and an understanding of the kinship family's culture, community, and child-rearing practices. In addition, factors requiring focus in assessment can be different at different times. When the caregiver home is being approved for temporary placement, issues of safety, protection, and the willingness of the relative caregiver to meet the immediate health, educational, developmental, and emotional needs of the child are of high priority. At the time of permanency planning, however, issues of attachment, permanence, and continuity also become very significant. At this time, a more in-depth assessment has to be made on the kinship parents' ability to meet the ongoing needs of the child and engage in working with the agency on long-range planning for the child.

Whether for temporary or long-term or permanent placement, assessment in kinship care includes consideration of the following factors: (1) the nature and quality of relationship between the child and the relative as well as between the birth-parents and the relative, and the effect of these relationships on the safety and well-being of the child; (2) the birth-parent's preference about the placement of the child with the relative; (3) any potential risk factors in the relative home—for example, an intergenerational history of abuse/neglect, the presence of alcohol and drugs, and the possibility that family members will pressure the child to recant the disclosure of abuse; (4) the ability of the kinship parent to protect the child from further abuse or other maltreatment; (5) the ability of the kinship parent to meet the developmental needs of the child (This includes the age and health of kinship parents, other existing demands on the kinship parents, and existing supports to which the kinship family has access.); and (6) the kinship family's willingness and ability to cooperate with the agency.

Intervention

Children's and birth-parents' service needs are more or less the same in kinship care as in non-relative foster care. But kinship parents are not similar to non-relative foster parents; their motivation for becoming foster parents and their service needs are very different. Research has shown that most kinship parents are grandparents, usually grandmothers. They tend to have limited incomes and less formal education than non-related foster parents. Unlike non-related foster parents, when they take on the parenting role, it is usually unplanned. They come forward to care for children because of family ties and/or a sense of obligation to care for their own. They become foster parents to foster their own kin child only and do not generally take in any other, unrelated foster children.

Caring for children often places financial stress on kin as they take on full-time parenting roles. It can also bring enormous emotional stress as it evokes unresolved past issues and feelings about the birth-parents that get juxtaposed with current issues and feelings. Kin parents may feel responsible for creating or contributing to birth-parents' current problems. They may also feel responsible for helping birth-parents or the child and holding the family together, guilty because of the child's abuse or neglect by other family members, doubtful about the quality of their own parenting, or frustrated with the birth-parents and unwilling to continue any involvement with them. The need for working through these extended family relationships is much more paramount in kinship care. This is best met by multisystemic counseling—simultaneous individual and family counseling with all and/or different combinations of family members involved. The need for concrete services such as child care, respite care, home-maker service, and help in accessing services from other formal service providers as well as informal support networks is often also greater. Most of all, kinship parents need to be viewed not only as providers of services but as members of the family, to be involved in case planning and implementation as part of the team of service providers.

Benefits and Concerns

Kinship care grew because of an increasing number of children in care (especially children of color), not enough foster families (especially families of color), and the concern about alienation of children from their families and their ethnic and racial heritage. Kinship care offers many benefits; it has also raised a host of other issues of concern.

From a child-centered perspective, kinship care offers children familiar caregivers in a time of family crisis. Kinship caregivers express a commitment to the children in their care and are willing to care for them as long as needed. They provide the most family-like and least restrictive home environment as well as continuity of family identity and knowledge, access to other relatives, and ongoing life within the ethnic, religious, and/or racial community of origin, thus preserving the child's cultural identity. Kinship placements have also been found to be significantly more stable than other foster placements.

From a cost perspective also there are many benefits. There are no costs for recruiting and training foster parents, and their turnover rate is much lower. The monthly cost of care is much less as caregivers who are not licensed foster homes are paid at significantly lower rates than the licensed foster homes. In addition, often the cost of supervision and other support services is also much lower.

On the other hand, because kinship placements are more stable, often much less effort is devoted to reunifying children with their birth-parents, and there are fewer adoptions. Children therefore stay in foster care longer (U.S. GAO, 1999). Kinship care overburdens the caregivers with the demands of children with special needs. Even though children in kinship care experience as many medical, educational, and emotional problems and needs as children in non-relative foster care, they and their families receive much less support and far fewer services from the state.

Thus, cost-saving may occur at the expense of child's well-being and may exploit people's sense of family responsibility. These possibilities raise the question: Is kinship care a way of empowering families, or is it an excuse for spending fewer public resources on children at risk?

FAMILY GROUP DECISION-MAKING

The evolution of kinship care has spawned a new innovative model of intervention—Family Group Decision-Making (FGDM). FDGM was first instituted by law in New Zealand in 1989 in response to their concerns about foster care such as alienation of children from their ethnic, racial or tribal heritage, instability of placements, the failure to include family members' perspective in decisions about placement, and the many minority children in the care and custody of the state. Since then, it has been adapted for use in several communities in the United States, England, and Canada.

FDGM is based on the value that families, broadly defined, have the knowledge, expertise, and ability to be responsible for the safety and well-being of their children and that allowing families to make decisions about the care and protection of their children empowers them. It also obligates extended families to take responsibility for the care and well-being of their children—a value set in the early English poor laws. Ernst (1999) describes the process of FDGM in New Zealand as follows:

The process begins with the child welfare worker substantiating risk to the child and determining that the child is in need of the state's protection and care. The worker, in cooperation with the family, identifies as many "kin" as possible and makes a referral to the coordinator of the FDGM Project.

The coordinator organizes a family conference in consultation with family group members and the involved service providers. The coordinator invites family members who are currently involved with the child or who could potentially play a role in the child's life [the child's parent(s), godparents, extended family members, close friends, and others whom the family defines as family, even if they are at some distance], arranges a comfortable, neutral place for the family conference, and makes all the practical arrangements for their travel and stay.

The conference is convened with the family [including the child(ren) in question] and the service providers such as the child welfare worker, the teacher, psychologist, and other professionals working with the family. However, service providers do not outnumber family members. The conference begins with an opening that is consistent with the culture of the family group (greeting, prayer, etc.). The coordinator reviews the purpose of the conference, the process, and ground rules (for example, confidentiality, no violence). Then the service providers give information, which includes the reason for the conference and the needs to be addressed in the family's deliberations about a care plan for the child. The family is also given (educational) information, sometimes by guest speakers, on the dynamics of the issues that put this child at risk (for example, abuse/neglect/sexual abuse, addictions, mental illness). After all the information is provided, the professionals, including the coordinator, leave the room so that the family group can have private time to brainstorm about options and develop a plan for the care and protection of the child. Sometimes the worker who is expected to continue working with the family stays. The family can take as much time as it needs—even if it is several days. When the family group formulates a plan, they invite the coordinator back. Together, they review the plan to ensure that it is clear, comprehensive, and acceptable to everybody. The plan may include a decision about where the child will live (with the child's input), what services will be needed (for example, income support, counseling, addictions treatment, in-home supports, child care, transportation), and what kind of supports the family members will provide to each other. In essence, the plan for the care and protection of the child is developed primarily by the extended family, and it reflects a collaboration between the child welfare system and the extended family. It may be formalized by a court order if necessary, or it may remain a less formal agreement between the family and the child welfare agency.

The final stage involves implementation of the plan. An ongoing worker (case manager) works with the family and oversees the implementation of the plan. If at any time, the plan needs to be changed or modified, the case manager can call another family meeting.

In use in other countries and other communities, family meetings have been found to reduce out-of-home placement of children and to increase the frequency with which children are placed within their own ethnic, racial, and/or religious group. They have also been found to be an effective intervention with families where children's well-being is jeopardized because of domestic violence, such as abuse of the mother (Penell and Burford, 2000). However, the immediate cost of bringing family groups together for family meetings can run high.

SHARED FAMILY FOSTER CARE/
WHOLE FAMILY FOSTER CARE

The term "Shared Family Foster Care" refers to the situation in which the whole family—parents and children together—are placed in the home of a specially trained foster family. Foster parents share the care and nurturing of the children with the biological parents; at the same time they also care for, nurture, and mentor the biological parents as parents work on their own personal issues while simultaneously learning to be good-enough parents. Shared Family Care is an age-old practice in the African-American community. It is also widely used as a formal child welfare service in Western Europe, but in the United States, it is a very new concept for child welfare services.

In traditional foster care, parents are expected to work on their personal and parenting issues while the children are not living with them. Separated from each other, both parents and children miss the chance to adjust to the continual changes they experience as individuals in relation to each other. Visits, no matter how regular, do not teach family members how to interact with each other on a day-to-day basis. Thus, even though parents may be functioning quite adequately on their own, when reunited they are not always prepared to resume care of their children 24 hours a day and deal with the stresses and frustrations that are a normal part of parenting. This can often result in re-abuse/neglect and in children's re-entry into care.

In addition, many times parents may themselves have been abused or neglected and may be isolated from their own families and from other community supports. Many adults have had limited role models for good parenting; they must learn for the first time how to be effective parents while struggling with their own personal issues. Shared Family Care "re-parents the parent." It ensures that parents and children have adequate housing, a structured and safe environment and models of successful living, and that children are protected while parents learn the parenting and living skills necessary to care for their children and maintain a household while concurrently dealing with their own personal issues and establishing positive connections with community resources.

Shared Family Care thus provides a sort of living laboratory in which families can learn to handle typical day-to-day stresses, to make better decisions, and to live together as a family. It allows parents to receive feedback about their parenting styles and skills on a 24-hour basis and across many and diverse parenting tasks. It also provides an opportunity for evaluating a parent's skills through direct daily observation. Thus, although the primary objective is to keep families together, it can also help some parents come to the realization that parenting is not for them. Their decision to terminate their parental rights and free the children for adoption is then made voluntarily, without coercion from the child welfare system. In these situations, the children can remain with the foster family until a permanent placement is arranged.

Shared Family Care has been used to prevent separation of parents from their children and to reunify families by providing a safe environment in which to bring together families and children who have been separated. It has been used for teen parents as well as for adult parents, for single mothers, for single fathers, as well as for two-parent families. It has been used for families with diverse issues such as poverty and homelessness, substance abuse, mental illness, and low IQ. It has also been used with parents coming out of prisons, chemical dependency treatment programs, and battered relationships (Barth and Price, 1999; Nelson, 1992; Gibson and Noble, 1991).

Shared Family Foster Care offers many advantages. By simultaneously ensuring children's safety and preserving a family's ability to live together, Shared Family Care prevents unnecessary separation of families and can decrease the number of children re-entering the child welfare system. It can also expedite permanency planning by helping parents make the choice to terminate their parental rights, thus preventing the enormous trauma to both parents and children and the cost of lengthy, extended court hearings. It provides stability for children while alternative permanency plans are being made. Costwise, it is less expensive than therapeutic foster homes, group homes, and institutional care.

SELECTING AN APPROPRIATE INTERVENTION MODALITY

The ultimate purpose of intervention in child welfare is to ensure the physical safety and emotional well-being of children and their families. There are no simple formulae or decision-trees for selecting appropriate intervention modalities, but there are time-tested and research-based guiding principles that should guide professional practice. Among the most fundamental of these principles is that intervention must be based on assessment—assessment of how good (or not good) the fit is between the child's needs and the parents' ability to meet those needs adequately, and what kind of risk of harm it poses for the child. Such an assessment points out the areas in the parent–child fit that need modification so as to reduce the risk of harm to the child, where the focus of intervention needs to be. Selecting an appropriate intervention modality then becomes a process of logically deducing what services, from where, and for how long will best facilitate the needed modification in the parent–child fit in a culturally sensitive and culturally responsive manner. An appropriate intervention modality is one that directly targets the areas identified.

Research over the last 50 years has shown that for children, emotional well-being means stability and continuity of relationships and attachments with significant adults, a sense of belonging with a family and community, along with the societal resources and opportunities for age-appropriate physical, cognitive, and social development. For the purpose of ensuring children's well-being, therefore, interventions have to be selected with these needs in mind. Research has also shown that for clients of child welfare agencies—adults, children, and families—interventions that have been found to have best results include (1) long-term (positive) relationship with the same helping person, (2) comprehensive (multisystemic) services—a mixture of concrete services, counseling, education, advocacy, etc. as needed, (3) enabling and empowering practices and techniques that build on client strengths and promote self-efficacy, and (4) attention to improving interpersonal relationships and meaningful connections with other people. Thus, an appropriate intervention modality would be one that includes these practices and techniques, tailored to the needs of the client.

And finally, any intervention modality must be based on the principles of acceptance and nonjudgmental attitude, and the belief that families matter. Intervention is not simply a matter of whether or not family needs are met, but of the *manner* in which they are met.

SUGGESTED EXERCISE

Please reread each of the four cases presented in Chapters 4–7, and review your earlier assessment and case plan. If you wish to make any modifications in any of them at this time, you may do so. Then,

1. Formulate what you think would be an *ideal* intervention plan for the client in each case. Assume that there are no constraints on resources, your time, or anything else.
2. Compare the ideal case plan with the one you had formulated earlier. How close (or not) is the ideal plan to your earlier case plan? Thinking over it again, could you incorporate some of the elements of the ideal plan into your case plan in actual practice, if this was your case, given the reality of your agency environment, policies, practices, etc.? If yes, how? If not, why not?

THE ORGANIZATIONAL
CONTEXT OF PRACTICE

PART 3

THE ORGANIZATIONAL
CONTEXT OF
PRACTICE

Child welfare practice is influenced not only by the federal and state laws, but also by the way in which the service delivery system is organized and administered. Agency policies, rules, and its organizational structure define who the clients are, how the "problem" is defined, the nature of assessment and intervention, the size of caseloads, procedures for worker accountability and the amount of paperwork, and the level of autonomy and authority a worker can have. Almost all practice decisions reflect some agency policy or requirement. The overall agency culture and climate affect workers' morale, their professional practice, and their view of themselves.

THE SERVICE DELIVERY SYSTEM

Most public child welfare agencies are organized as large bureaucracies. Developing mostly in the 1930s and 1940s, organizing delivery of public child welfare services on bureaucratic principles—then the modern state-of-the-art knowledge in use by business and industry—seemed to be the most appropriate way of serving large numbers of people in the most efficient and equitable manner. It was also a way of addressing the earlier practices of public benefits being distributed haphazardly by those in power at their will and fancy, with no accountability, which meant inherent and rampant bossism, favoritism, paternalism, racism, sexism, and other forms of discrimination in the system.

The fundamental element of a bureaucracy is management by rules—rules that are more or less stable, more or less exhaustive, made not with any one individual in mind or based on personal feelings and likes or dislikes, but made objectively for a situation in general. Rules apply equally to all people in that situation so that all people have equal access and equal treatment; they cannot be changed at whim by any one person in authority. According to Weber (1958),

> The 'objective' discharge of business primarily means a discharge of business according to *calculable rules* and 'without regard to person' . . . the more the bureaucracy is 'dehumanized', the more completely it succeeds in eliminating from official business love, hatred, and all purely personal, irrational, and emotional elements which escape calculation. This is the specific nature of bureaucracy and it is appraised as its special virtue. . . ." (pp. 215, 216)

Authority is not vested in any one person and is not absolute. Weber (1958) conceptualized a bureaucracy as a pyramid, with one (or few) people at the top, a large number of people at the bottom, and layers of people in between at different levels of hierarchy. People at each level have a certain, well-defined, narrow task and function. People at the top do the thinking, planning, and decision-making about the mission and goal of the organization, what is to be produced, and how it is to be produced. People at the bottom carry out the decision (supposedly without thinking or questioning) and produce it. In the middle, the function of each layer of hierarchy is to supervise the one below to make sure that it carries out its task efficiently and reports to the one above. People at each level get only that information and authority necessary to carry out their function, no more. Accountability is built in through requirements of detailed record-keeping by each person to make sure that rules are followed accurately. Weber saw this functional, hierarchically graded authority as the most effective way of preventing the abuse of power and authority by any one person.

Appointment to each position is made based on a person's qualifications and training to do the job, not as a personal favor. Each person does a small, narrowly defined task that is a part of the whole; by doing the same small, narrowly defined task repetitively, the person becomes a specialist in that task and therefore can do it more efficiently. With a rational division of labor based on narrow specializations, the final product, be it a commercial product or a service, is produced most efficiently.

To Weber, a bureaucratic organization was technically superior over any other form of organization in terms of precision, speed, and smooth functioning. A well-functioning bureaucracy was like a well-oiled machine in which the individual was "only a single cog in an ever-moving mechanism which prescribes to him an essentially fixed route of march . . ." (Weber, 1958, p. 228). Bureaucracy was also a way of leveling economic and social differences and bringing democracy to the masses, as the abstract regulation and execution of authority ensured "equality before the law" and potentially eliminated the benefits of privilege and the practice of doing business from case to case.

"Mass democracy makes a clean sweep of the feudal, patrimonial, and at least in intent—the plutocratic privileges in administration . . ." (Weber, 1958, pp. 224, 225).

The Problems of Bureaucracy

The bureaucratic model was developed as a reaction against the abuses and capricious judgments of earlier days. However, the virtues of bureaucracy, while addressing the abuses of the past, have created other problems and dilemmas in the delivery of human services.

The blind application of rules to everybody equally "without regard to person" indeed assures equality before the law; however, in not permitting any consideration of individual or cultural differences, it makes the system impersonal, insensitive, inhumane. Every person and every situation are not, in fact, the same; in the delivery of services to troubled children and families, what is needed is not dehumanization but treatment of clients as unique human beings with dignity and respect.

Division of labor by narrow specializations may make the worker more knowledgeable and therefore more competent and efficient. On the other hand, it is a major contributing factor to the problem of fragmentation of services. There are numerous examples of several agencies and several workers (sometimes from the same agency) being involved with one family, each worker attending to the client's need that falls within the worker's (or agency's) narrow area of service, without regard to any other aspects of the client's life or how the various services come together as a whole for the client. This has been found to be neither helpful for the client nor cost-efficient for the service delivery system.

Rules cannot be changed easily. This was intended to assure stability and predictability in the delivery of services and to prevent rapid, unpredictable changes due to individual whim or caprice. The effect, however, is a rigidity in the structure, an inability of the system to be flexible and adapt to changes in the external environment. It was effective and efficient in a stable, predictable external environment, but in the rapidly changing social environment of the 1980s, it has proven to be completely dysfunctional. Flooded with increasing numbers of children coming into care, along with societal demands for permanency planning, cultural sensitivity, and accountability in a political environment of drastic funding cutbacks, the system could not change rapidly enough to manage the new realities effectively. It responded generally by targeting services on the most critical cases, requiring people to wait until a child was seriously injured or neglected before families could get any help. Public child welfare agencies have sought to protect themselves from scandal—a child suffering from further abuse (or worse, death!) despite being known to the child welfare agency—by making more rules, prescribing more exactly what procedures the worker must follow, and by demanding more paperwork to ensure accountability, thereby curtailing workers' professional judgment. The result is that workers have to spend much more time on doing paperwork than on helping people. Much too often they have to make practice decisions that defy both common sense and sound professional practice.

Nor is the bureaucracy the smooth-functioning, well-oiled machine it was conceived to be. The flow of communication is not smooth along the tightly controlled hierarchical chain of command; information often gets lost, diverted, or distorted as it moves from one level to another. Without direct input from workers, people at the top often make decisions based on inaccurate or incomplete information about the realities of the practice environment, and the tightly controlled decision-making structure does not leave room for individual workers to make decisions regarding their individual clients or take initiative for creative solutions. In the field of child welfare where responding appropriately and efficiently to complex family situations requires the worker's creativity and ability to make quick decisions, having to wait for approval of something that is outside the prescribed rules gums up the works. Workers are caught between the demands of bureaucracy and the demands of professional practice. Moreover, supervisors do not necessarily possess greater knowledge or competence than their subordinates, but they do possess the authority to enforce rules. Supervision, intended to facilitate worker efficiency through increasing worker knowledge, often ends up as a ritual of monitoring conformity to rules and procedures rather than increasing the efficiency of the worker.

Bureaucracy, by its very nature and structure, has proven to be a dysfunctional system for the delivery of public child welfare services that are professionally and culturally competent; it cannot fulfill its mandate of protecting children while preserving families and promoting the well-being of all children and families. Clients experience bureaucracy as inhuman, unresponsive, inaccessible when really needed. To them, bureaucracy usually means filling out forms, coping with red tape, and being made to feel powerless.

Burnout and Vicarious Traumatization

Nor does a bureaucracy benefit its staff, as is commonly believed. Worker burnout and high turnover rates are well-known major systemic problems for almost all public child welfare agencies.

Burnout is "a state of physical, emotional, and mental exhaustion marked by physical depletion and chronic fatigue, a feeling of helplessness and hopelessness, and the development of a negative self-concept and negative attitude towards work, life, and other people" (Maslach, 1982b, p. 30). It is also described as characterized by "emotional exhaustion—the sense that one's emotional resources are so depleted that there is little left to give; depersonalization—a negative, cynical, callous, dehumanized view of one's work; and reduced personal accomplishment—feeling unhappy and dissatisfied with what one can do successfully" (Maslach and Jackson, 1986, as cited in Zunz, 1998, p. 41).

Burnout in child welfare as in all human services occurs in response to the chronic emotional strain of working with troubled clients in stress-inducing workplace conditions. Burned-out workers exhibit a low level of energy and recurrent bouts of physical illnesses such as the flu, headaches, gastrointestinal problems, fatigue, difficulty in concentration, and insomnia. Becoming callous and cynical, many develop an intolerance toward their clients and a tendency to blame clients for their own problems. Many take to adhering to rules rigidly. Burnout inevitably affects their work with their clients as well as their personal and professional relationships.

The nature of child welfare work is emotionally stressful. Child welfare workers are constantly exposed to trauma and its effects as they directly intervene, observe the effects of abuse and neglect, and hear the painful traumatic experiences of clients. Recent research in the field of trauma and victimization shows that people who work with trauma victims and survivors become the victims of "secondary trauma." Even though they have not been directly traumatized, they may begin to show signs and symptoms of traumatization similar to those of the victim. First observed in mental health professionals working with Vietnam combat veterans, this phenomenon has been observed in people who work with victims and survivors of any kind of trauma, including war, physical torture, physical and sexual abuse, and rape. Mental health workers and child welfare workers (as well as emergency and disaster aid workers) have reported intense and overwhelming feelings such as sorrow, grief, horror, rage, fear, vulnerability, and numbness. They have also reported experiencing intrusive thoughts and images of client's traumatic material, flashbacks, and nightmares (McCann and Pearlman, 1990; Dane, 2000).

Exposure to trauma material over time alters workers' cognitive schema—their beliefs, expectations, and assumptions about the world—and their sense of themselves. Each client's story reinforces their gradually changing schema; the gradual erosion of their beliefs and frame of reference leads to a decreased sense of energy, increased disconnection from loved ones, increased sensitivity to violence, threat, or fear—or the opposite, decreased sensitivity, cynicism, generalized despair and hopelessness. McCann and Pearlman (1990) call this process "vicarious traumatization." Vicarious traumatization is not the same as countertransference in that it is not a reactivation of one's own unresolved or unconscious conflicts but a response to the experiences and memories of the client. It is an occupational hazard for those who work with trauma survivors.

Supervisors and managers burn out too. Supervisors are accountable for not only their own work but the work of their subordinates as well, over which they have only limited control. Their job performance depends on the job performance of their staff. Managers are faced with the challenge of overseeing programs for difficult populations who often have little public support and sympathy. They are under increased pressure for accountability, efficiency, and quality control under increasing budgetary constraints. Both supervisors and managers speak of experiencing a sense of loneliness and isolation; of not being understood or appreciated by either their superiors or their subordinates; and of the need to maneuver for a powerful position in order to survive in the organization. ". . . [M]anagerial burnout can be a 'contagious disease' that spreads throughout the organizations, creating a dysfunctional climate for both staff and clients" (Harvey and Raider, 1984, as cited in Zunz, 1998, p. 40).

Given the nature of child welfare work, organizational factors acquire even more significance in creating staff burnout. For workers, among the factors identified are unmanageably high caseloads that do not permit professionally competent practice and therefore a sense of accomplishment; paperwork and other policies and practices that are workload-driven and not client-driven, that often seem to make no sense; bureaucratic rigidity; professional isolation; and the nature of their relationship with their immediate supervisor. Even the physical layout of offices and workspace arrangements that permit neither privacy nor a moment of quiet thought add to the level of workers' stress (Samantrai, 1992a; Wagner et al., 2001).

Though organizational factors are by far the most significant cause of worker burnout, the emphasis and focus of organizational response remain directed toward the individual characteristics of the workers, not the system. Progressive child welfare agencies offer their workers professional development and training, exercise programs, dietary awareness programs, stop-smoking options, stress-management workshops, and psychological services. However, these organizational responses do not improve the working environment; dysfunctional organizations do not turn into functional ones by one or more of their workers attending training or holding formal qualifications or learning to manage their stress.

The working environment and workplace ecology of child welfare agencies are important to the quality of their service. The organizational, systemic sources of burnout constrain and limit workers' practice and their ability to bring about change in their clients' lives.

CHANGING THE SYSTEM

The 1980s were a time of crisis for the child welfare system. Passage of P.L. 96-272 (the permanency planning legislation) completely changed and expanded its mission and goal from child protection to preventing unnecessary out-of-home placement and assuring the well-being of all families. Economic recession, the spread of substances such as crack and cocaine, and the spread of AIDS brought an influx of children with problems never seen before. At the same time, a large number of refugees from other countries were resettled in the United States. The effects of trauma of war and the process of migration, and conflict between their normal cultural child-rearing practices and the definition of "child abuse and neglect" according to U.S. laws and customs, brought many suffering families into the child welfare system. Child welfare workers' inability to communicate with non-English-speaking people and understanding their different cultural practices compounded the system's problems further. The system was overwhelmed, stretched beyond capacity.

In 1988, The National Association of Public Child Welfare Administrators concluded that the system needed an overhaul. This group called for a new three-tier system comprising a more narrowly focused CPS, an expanded voluntary/preventive family support system, and an adequately funded child well-being system. Between 1988 and 1993, calls for the need to reform the system came from the American Bar Association, the American Public Welfare Association, researchers based in universities and in public policy institutes, as well as from the U.S. Advisory Board on Child Abuse and Neglect. The increasing calls for change led to proposals, recommendations, and experimentation.

Reconceptualize the Problem

Many social work practitioners and researchers felt that there was an inherent conflict in the two roles of the child welfare system—investigator of suspected child abuse and neglect, and helper responsible for preserving families. They argued that under this system the initial contact between the agency and the family begins with the agency in its investigatory role, investigating report of suspected child abuse and neglect, with parents (or other primary caretakers) already under a cloud of suspicion. Parents, feeling the agency's suspicion and knowing that the agency has legal power to remove their children, naturally become defensive, cautious, resistant, and perhaps hostile. Parental resistance is interpreted by the agency as noncooperation and noncompliance, which sets the stage for the use of coercion. Such a relationship is completely antithetical to the relationship of mutual trust necessary for the agency to perform its helping role effectively. Overcoming initial mistrust and hostility to establish a helping relationship can often become an insurmountable task. Thus, given the mandate to investigate suspected child abuse and neglect and the always-limited resources, when an agency has both roles, its investigatory/coercive role becomes dominant and takes precedence over the helping role. They argued that the two roles should be separated.

Pelton (1991) also argued that framing child welfare issues as "child abuse and neglect" is too simplistic. While there are some extreme cases of child abuse and neglect in which the parents' responsibility is clearly paramount in causing severe harm or risk of harm to the children, most harm or risk of harm is accidental and attributable to configurations of multiple causes over which neither the parents nor the child welfare agency may have much control. For example, there is evidence that higher risk of severe accidental injury is strongly related to low socioeconomic status, that for children from low-income families the physical environment of the home and the neighborhood itself can be dangerous. Financial hardship, single-parent status, physical and emotional problems of children and parents, family tensions, and social isolation can decrease parents' ability to maintain proper supervision necessary to maintain the children's safety. While all these factors are likely to increase the risk of nonintentional injury to children, framing the issue as child abuse and neglect puts the focus on parents only. With this overfixation on the parents, the child welfare system tends to do more blaming than helping. Blaming does not help any child or family; instead of focusing on who is to blame, the child welfare system should focus on what it can do to prevent dangerous conditions and circumstances.

Restructure the System

Pelton (1991) proposed restructuring the system. In his restructured system, the investigative/coercive role would be shifted to law enforcement agencies and the child placement/foster care role would be shifted to the family court. The public child welfare agency would then concentrate on its role of helping families and preventing harm to children. Child welfare workers would garner, provide, and advocate for supportive services for their clients while counseling and educating them on issues of parent–child relationships and other aspects of family life. The child welfare agency would advocate for children and families on community and statewide levels in such areas as health and welfare benefits aimed at protecting children from harm and preserving families. In addition, state child abuse and neglect laws would be narrowed to focus on severe harm to the child, and they would specify that such harm or danger must be due to clearly deliberate harmful acts or gross abdication of responsibility by the primary caretakers. Much of the previously defined child maltreatment would be reconceptualized as nonintentional injury and excluded from the laws. Reporting laws would be narrowed accordingly and clearly state what should *not* be reported along with what is to be reported.

The repeated calls for change also led to the convening of an Executive Session on Child Protective Services (CPS) at Harvard University's Kennedy School of Government in 1994. This Executive Session brought together a diverse group of people with knowledge and experience of the CPS system to review its current state and make recommendations for reform. This group identified five common problems: (1) Overinclusion—some families who were in the system should not be. Inappropriately included lower-risk families received an unnecessarily adversarial response from the child welfare system. (2) Underinclusion—at the same time some families who should receive child protective services did not. These include some families who voluntarily contact CPS to ask for help (or would accept help on a voluntary basis) but do not receive help because their problems had not yet become serious enough. (3) System's capacity—the number of families involved with CPS far exceeded the capacity of the system to serve them. Not only were the numbers increasing, the problems they presented were becoming much more complex. (4) Service delivery—services were fragmented and culturally insensitive. (5) Service orientation: CPS's one-size-fits-all approach did not serve families well (Waldfogel, 2000).

To address these problems so that CPS better serves children and families, this group recommended a new "differential response" paradigm for CPS. This paradigm had three essential elements: (1) The provision of customized response to families—CPS tailoring its approach to families based on their particular needs and circumstances at the time; (2) the development of a community-based system of child protection—partnerships with other agencies in the community; and (3) the involvement of informal and natural helpers—members of the community or families themselves. In this group's vision, CPS, instead of acting alone to address the problems of child protection, would develop partnerships with a broad range of community agencies such as police, schools, public and private agencies, and informal sources of help such as neighborhood associations, congregations, and families themselves. For the higher-risk cases, CPS would assume primary responsibility but would work in partnership with other community providers as appropriate. In lower-risk cases, if parents were willing to participate in services on a voluntary basis, a non-CPS provider from a public or private agency would take the lead role, again drawing on other community partners, both formal and informal, on a case-by-case basis. Case assignments would be reviewed constantly by CPS and the community partners to make sure that they remained appropriate as family needs and circumstances changed.

The key issue in such a system was the ability to sort out cases by level of risk. This proposal led to the evolution of numerous risk-assessment tools in many states and counties in the mid-1990s (American Humane Association, 1998).

English et al. (2000) describe a Community-Based Alternative Response System (CBARS) in one state. In examining the characteristics and outcomes of 1,263 families referred to this program between 1992 and 1995, they found that even in this sample some families were referred to CBARS who shouldn't have been, while some families were referred to CPS that didn't need to be referred there. This indicates that the level of risk cannot always be assessed accurately or predicted (despite carefully devised risk-assessment instruments), that errors exist. They note that it is possible that if referrals to CPS continue to exceed capacity, there would be a tendency to make more referrals to community-based programs, which could put some children at serious risk. They also point out that the assumption that families will seek or accept help voluntarily is an un-tested assumption—it is not necessarily true in all cases. For successful engagement and intervention, staff of both CPS and the alternative program have to be skilled in assessing parents' willingness and motivation to change.

Participatory Management

The problems of bureaucracy in business and industry became strikingly apparent during the economic recession of the 1980s when the rigidity and centralized decision-making process of the hierarchical organizational structure did not permit industries to adapt quickly to changing economic conditions. Industry leaders came to realize that they needed to be more flexible, and for increased flexibility, thinking and acting could not be compartmentalized to the top and the bottom. It had to occur at all levels. They also came to realize that individual workers were not just cogs in a machine but thinking, feeling, creative human beings who can make decisions on the job and about the job; that often employees who do the job have better ideas on how that job can be done more efficiently than management that is far removed. Since then, progressive businesses have been moving toward new management approaches such as participatory management. Human service organizations have embraced the notion; its implementation, however, is slow.

Participatory management means involving workers in organizational decisions. Workers have a role in making decisions about organizational mission, goals, policies, and procedures, in problem-solving, and in evaluating the organization. It involves a wide range of activities such as strategic planning, total quality improvement, conflict management, team building, etc. It implies a sharing of power and decision-making, a reframing of the relationship between management and labor from an adversarial relationship to one that is more collaborative.

Participatory management approach is especially salient to the field of child welfare where the work is complex and unpredictable and societal problems affecting the entry of children into the system change rapidly so that the system's response requires constant planning and program development. As became evident in the 1980s, when the system faced the challenges of poverty and homelessness, parental substance abuse and addicted babies, family violence, the AIDS epidemic in quick succession, it did not have the flexibility to change rapidly to meet its challenge. In child welfare, service outcomes rely primarily on the quality of interactions between clients and the workers who provide direct services to the clients. To improve service outcomes, it would only make sense to involve workers in a planned process of analysis and improvement of the quality of their work and their workplace environment.

Participatory management has other benefits as well. Participatory groups enable knowledgeable people to get involved, bringing more ideas to the table and increasing the likelihood of greater innovation, as well as creating a synergistic effect of collaboration and thus multiplying each person's individual effort. Staff members develop new skills, knowledge, and new contacts through their participation in work groups, task forces, or teams. Involvement in identifying needed changes helps staff understand why they are needed, be more willing to try new approaches, and be more committed to proposals that are chosen. Other related benefits include increased staff satisfaction, low burnout, increased performance, humanization of the workplace, and empowerment of the workers. As workers feel empowered and valued, they can better empower their clients. In order for the concept to work, however, participatory management requires leadership that is strongly committed to its philosophy and has the interpersonal skills to facilitate group process.

Pine et al. (1998) describe a participatory management project in one state's public child welfare agency whose purpose was to improve the agency's family reunification services. A multilevel task force of volunteers representing the full range of people involved with reunification—administrators, supervisors, line staff, trainers, attorneys, staff members with financial responsibilities, foster parents, collateral providers, and birth-parents—undertook a careful self-study process and intensive examination of the agency's family reunification service delivery system and developed an extensive set of recommendations for strengthening their family reunification policies, programs, and practice. Cohen (1999) describes another project in another state's public child welfare agency. Part of the larger Quality of Work Life Project whose purpose was to transform the large centralized bureaucracy into a more flexible and adaptive organization, this project established a mini-grant program to encourage the developing and testing of innovative ideas generated by child welfare workers.

Interagency Collaboration and Systems of Care

The notion of case coordination and service integration (to reduce service fragmentation and costs) has existed since the beginning of professional social work in the early years of the 20th century. Over and over again different approaches have been developed, tried, and discarded. The most recent thrust in this direction came from the field of child mental health. In 1969 the Joint Commission on Mental Health had drawn attention to the fact that emotionally disturbed children and their families were underserved or served inappropriately in very restrictive environments. In 1977, President Carter established the President's Commission on Mental Health, which issued a similar report. In 1982, the Children's Defense Fund published a seminal study, *Unclaimed Children* (Knitzer, 1982). This study documented that of the three million children with serious emotional disturbances in this country, two thirds were not receiving needed services. Many were not receiving any services at all; those who did received mostly in-patient care that was both costly and restrictive. States did not follow children through the mental health system. Although it was evident that troubled children had multiple needs and were served by education, child welfare, juvenile justice, health, mental health, substance abuse, mental retardation, and other agencies, there was almost no attempt to get the range of child-serving agencies to work together at either the state or the local level. Knitzer contended that these children were "unclaimed"—abandoned by the public agencies that were responsible for helping them. And she referred to the federal role as "unfulfilled promise" (Stroul, 1996).

Knitzer's report and the ones before concurred that a coordinated system of care providing a range of services was required in order to serve these children and their families effectively. Advocates now called for a concerted action to develop systems of care nationwide.

As a result of much advocacy, Congress appropriated funds for a national initiative in the area of child mental health and launched the Child and Adolescent Service System Program (CASSP) under the National Institute of Mental Health in 1984. The goal of CASSP was to assist states and communities to develop systems of care for children and youth with serious emotional disturbances.

CASSP required an interagency approach to system improvement. Soon thereafter Ohio's Governor Celeste issued an executive order that required all the state agencies to form an Interagency Cluster for children. The cluster was to meet regularly to coordinate services across systems and also to review difficult cases that could not be resolved locally. Each county was also to form a local cluster for system planning and coordination and for reviewing difficult cases. This order became state legislation in 1987. Now, several other states have similar legislations; initiatives and demonstration projects have also been undertaken with grants from private foundations. States and communities have created interagency entities for system-level coordination; many communities have also created interagency teams specific to each child.

> A system of care is defined as a comprehensive spectrum of mental health and other necessary services that are organized into a coordinated network to meet the multiple needs of children and adolescents with serious emotional disturbances and their families. (Stroul, 1996, p. 16)

> A primary objectives of these systems is to develop a comprehensive array of community-based services within a collaborative infrastructure for planning, funding, developing, and delivering services. They are intended to benefit children and families by closing gaps in the existing service delivery system, facilitating access to needed treatment and services, providing continuity of care, and increasing the likelihood of positive child and family outcomes. (Rivard et al., 1999, p. 62)

The concept of a system of care represents more than a network of individual service components; it represents a philosophy about the way in which services should be delivered to children and their families. The actual components and organizational configuration of the system of care may differ from state to state and from community to community, but they are all guided by the following common set of basic values and principles: (1) The system of care should be child-centered and family-focused, community-based, and culturally competent. (2) Children with emotional disturbances should have access to a comprehensive array of services that address their physical, emotional, social, and educational needs. (3) Children should receive individualized services, in the least restrictive, most normative environment that is clinically appropriate. (4) Families should be full participants in all aspects of planning and delivery of services. (5) Services should be integrated, with linkages between child-servicing agencies and programs and mechanisms for planning, developing, and coordinating services. (6) Services should include early identification, prevention, and case management.

Stroul (1996) reports the results of a descriptive study of 20 local systems of care initiated in 1990. The development of each community system followed its own unique evolutionary path, but in each of these projects, she notes, three types of critical events were instrumental in moving the process forward. The first was the creation of an interagency entity for cross-system planning and collaboration. Second was the receipt of some type of funding that enabled the development of new services in the system of care. And third, somewhat less tangible, was that at some point in the developmental process leaders made the decision to move beyond traditional approaches and to invest in an array of community-based services. These decisions were significant in that they set the precedent for continued system development as opportunities and funding became available. In all of the communities, the state also influenced the system development process in a variety of ways, including emphasizing and requiring interagency collaboration in service delivery, passing legislation related to system of care development, providing funding, and providing technical assistance to communities.

Mulroy (1997) reports findings from an organizational analysis of Dorchester CARES, one of the nine projects funded by the National Center on Child Abuse and Neglect (NCCAN). In this project, executive directors and frontline practitioners from seven agencies worked for five years to create, implement, and institutionalize a community-based service network of formal and informal family support programs to help prevent child abuse and neglect.

Both Stroul's and Mulroy's studies indicate certain commonalities that contributed to their success. The most outstanding were strong and committed leadership, be it one person or a core group; a shared vision of community-based system of care and a clear acceptance of mutual responsibility; meaningful interagency structures and processes that produce tangible results, not merely have proforma interagency groups; a proactive attitude; and a cooperative approach to problem-solving. Mulroy points out that mutual trust was imperative to generating cooperative behavior. Mutual trust must exist among administrative decision-makers and also among frontline workers. In a neighborhood network it must also exist with residents.

Nugent and Gleason (1999), on the other hand, show a different outcome in one state. Earlier research in this state had suggested that service sectors in this state's children service system competed with one another to *avoid* providing services to the most problematic children. Children with more severe mental health problems were found to experience numerous residential placements and placement ejections, so service providers would not accept the more problematic children. Case managers' requests for services were being refused more and more frequently, so they had to send these children farther and farther away from their home communities.

Noting that children entering state custody are especially at risk of chronic, long-term mental health problems that can follow them into adulthood, Nugent and Gleason (1999) undertook another study to examine whether children's mental health service needs enter either the judicial or service decisions as the children come into state custody, and whether the state's children's services system was responsive or reactive to the mental health problems of the children entering state custody. They define a responsive system as one in which services are provided to meet each child's unique mental health needs, and a reactive system as one in which service providers take actions to avoid providing needed mental health services.

Their findings confirmed the findings of previous research that children's mental health problems and services needs did not play a direct role in the children's receipt of services from public children's service systems. The system was reactive rather than responsive; service providers in the children's service system avoided providing services to children with mental health problems. The reason was unclear. These researchers speculated that it might be because such a child poses problems for the child welfare system; or it might be because service workers, residential placement staff, and foster parents misunderstand children's mental health needs.

The system of care approach rests on the need to build a collaborative infrastructure. Rivard et al. (1999), researching the question of how services become integrated and how barriers posed by fragmented organization of service delivery systems are overcome, describe how interagency linkages involving child welfare and juvenile justice organizations developed within a system of care demonstration project in some counties in North Carolina. The Children's Initiative—one of eight demonstration projects funded by the Robert Wood Johnson Foundation—specifically targeted, among others, children with serious emotional disturbances dually served by mental health and child welfare or juvenile justice systems. In this project, in the 12-month period before the implementation, a multi-level interagency governance structure was established at state, regional, and county levels. Representatives (administrator and case managers) of child welfare and juvenile justice organizations were team members at each level. This multi-level interagency governance structure provided opportunities for collaboration at administrator and direct service levels. As a result, they found, there was evidence of incremental growth in partnerships that supports the system of care model.

Policymakers have identified networks as the most promising model for integrating services and strengthening poor communities. Organizational theorists claim that networks are the most complex forms of interorganizational collaboration (Mulroy, 1997). Practice experience in the last few years seems to support the view of the theorists.

Neighborhood-Based Services

A continuing theme in most of the proposal and recommendations has been that services should be community-based.

The idea of neighborhood-based services is not new. Settlements emerged over a century ago as neighborhood-based services for new immigrants, and they encompassed a wider variety of services including recreation, socialization, acculturation, education, counseling, and advocacy. With the rise of professionalization and bureaucratization of social services in the 1940s and 1950s, neighborhood-based services were pushed into the background, but they never disappeared completely. Many poor neighborhoods sustained a diverse set of recreational and cultural programs for children and youth, health outreach programs, programs to reach out to vulnerable children and families, and street-corner programs to reach out to youth gangs. The 1960s saw the rise of neighborhood-based services; however, the forces shaping neighborhood-based services at this time included the Civil Rights movement, grassroots protest groups that focused on issues ranging from welfare rights to community control of local schools, the federal government's War on Poverty, and the Community Mental Health Services movement. Numerous programs, funded by government or private funds, sprang up in storefronts, church basements, or anywhere space could be found. While each had a distinct purpose and provided different services, most programs tried to be internally comprehensive by adding other services and helping functions. For example, Headstart was not just a preschool program but also included health screening, meals, and service brokerage for the whole family. Neighborhood health centers not only tried to provide health and mental health services, but also started day-care programs and became involved in advocacy for educational and welfare reform.

One by-product of this movement was an even more complex, fragmented, and incoherent local service system for poor children and families. There were more entry points, service sites, categorical programs, and specialized roles. Different types of programs provided almost identical services. Multiple programs served the same family at cross-purposes, and no one program had over-all responsibility for a particular child and family. When a child or family slipped through the cracks of the system, there were no mechanisms to examine that failure, let alone figure out who might be responsible. Many programs were committed to improving community well-being, but their uncoordinated efforts failed to do so. The Model Cities program was initiated specifically to "knit together" the dozens of categorical programs in inner-city neighborhoods. However, there was no vision of what a more coherent local human service system would look and act like from an individual client's perspective, nor how it might be governed and funded (Adams and Nelson, 1995, p. 35). So, along with the war on poverty, neighborhood-based services faded into the background.

Now the notion of neighborhood-based services is gaining attention again. The intertwined issues of substance abuse, mental health, youth gang violence, substandard housing, poverty, economic disinvestment, infant mortality, and child abuse and neglect call for comprehensive planning. Demographic shifts affecting both staff and clients in social agencies have underscored the need to value diversity and use differences effectively to improve both services and workplace climate. The imperative of providing comprehensive services that would prevent problems and promote child and family well-being as well as provide treatment and rehabilitation and partnerships between different levels of government and private sector is being keenly felt. Many communities are attempting to integrate all these elements in designing a neighborhood-based service delivery system. However, a clear concept, vision, or version of such a system is yet to emerge.

In the interest of moving the process forward, this author proposes the following conceptual model. Originally published in NASW California News (November/December 1992), it is being presented here with minor editorial changes and updates. This model should be taken as a conceptual model only, not a blueprint. Each community can adapt it to its own specific characteristics and needs.

DELIVERING SERVICES TO PREVENT FAMILY PROBLEMS: A NEIGHBORHOOD-BASED MODEL OF PUBLIC–PRIVATE PARTNERSHIP

While there is widespread agreement that we need preventive programs, that programs should be neighborhood-based, and that there should be a public–private partnership, what we don't know is how to go about doing all this. One possible service delivery model is being presented here. This model is based on the following research findings and assumptions:

1. Child abuse/neglect is a complex problem. There is no one cause or one set of causes; it results from multiple causes that operate in various combinations. The basic dimension over which other causes superimpose is the cultural acceptance of the use of physical force in child-rearing as the norm. Other causes can be divided into two general categories, environmental/social factors, and individual, inter- and intrapersonal factors.
    If causes are multiple and interactive, then solutions have to be multiple and interactive too. Single, simple services will obviously be of limited effectiveness in resolving problems that are multiple and complex.
2. Child abuse and neglect are related to truancy, juvenile delinquency and adult criminal behavior such as arson, homicide, suicide, drug-abuse, prostitution, and sexual assault. Therefore, reduction in the incidence of child abuse and neglect should lead to reduction in the incidence of these other related problems.
3. A large proportion of the reports made of child abuse and neglect are false. However, they must be investigated before they can be determined to be false. If the number of false reports can be reduced, then resources spent on investigation of these (false) reports can be redirected toward services for families in which the reports are not false.
4. Evaluation studies of the innovative programs since the 1950s show that with multiproblem families, the factors most significant in prevention, treatment, and rehabilitation were (a) multiple, intensive, comprehensive, flexible, long-term services, (b) trusting relationship with a helping person, and (c) services that are coherent and easy to use (Schorr, 1979; Jones, Magura, and Shyne, 1981; Howing, Wodarski, and Kurtz, 1989).

Model—The Neighborhood Center

The neighborhood center is conceptualized as a "cafeteria"-style service center. A variety of services to provide a continuum of care—from prevention to rehabilitation and after-care—is offered; people can select and choose what they need, want, and can use. People in the neighborhood can drop-in, seek and explore services on their own, be referred by others, or be mandated by court.

Since this is a new idea, it is recommended that it be tested as a pilot project as follows:

1. In each voting district/ward or zip-code area of the city, one neighborhood with a high concentration of children is selected. Having different neighborhoods will provide a basis of comparison in evaluation of the effectiveness of services. Geographic boundaries of the neighborhood are to be drawn so that they provide a basis for a neighborhood identity, and the residents can walk from one end to the other in no more than a half hour. Boundaries of elementary school districts could be useful in defining the boundaries of a neighborhood.

2. Once a neighborhood is defined, a large building, as close as possible to the center of the neighborhood and either a public park or school playground, is selected to house the services. This will facilitate use of existing space for recreational activities if needed, thus saving on the need to develop new facilities. The neighborhood elementary school could serve this function.

Primary/Core Services—Publicly Funded

1. *Assessment, intervention, and case management.* Assessment of individual and family needs—environmental, intra- and interpersonal needs—and the barriers to accepting and using help effectively (external/environmental barriers as well as internal/psychological resistances). Services/intervention are based on this assessment. If needed services are not available on premises, then the client is assisted in getting them elsewhere.

2. *Individual (child, adolescent, adult), couple, and family counseling.* Crisis, short- and long-term, including premarital, marital and divorce counseling, will serve as a mechanism for resolution of family problems that can escalate into serious situations, hasty marriages, separations, divorces, or into violent behavior. It will also provide an avenue for "letting off steam" between irate family members and/or neighbors, who now vent their anger by making reports of child abuse.

3. *Family life education.* Social work theory provides an understanding of the family life cycle, with expected, predictable stress points when a family is particularly vulnerable. Families can be prepared to deal with these expected stress periods without breaking down through education and support. This program can also provide information on child development, so that parents do not have unrealistic expectations of their children and vent their frustrations in violent behavior when these expectations are not met. This would also provide a forum for teaching alternate forms of disciplining children.

4. *Out-patient health clinic,* which can serve as the provider of primary health care. This would be significant in reduction of reports of child abuse, false or real, particularly from hospital emergency rooms, where a report of an injury has to be made to determine whether or not it was accidental.

5. *Socialization and recreation programs.* For children, adults, and families.

ADDITIONAL SERVICES—PRIVATELY FUNDED OR WITH PUBLIC–PRIVATE PARTNERSHIP

Additional services can be tailored to the specific needs of the neighborhood. For example, if the neighborhood has a large number of working parents and the need is for child care—preschool or before and after school—then greater resources can be invested in child-care programs. If the neighborhood has a large number of single parents who may be isolated and alienated, services and programs of recreation and socialization, respite care, etc. can be emphasized. Another neighborhood with a large number of teenagers may need to emphasize programs geared to this age group. And in yet another neighborhood that has a larger senior population, services that also meet the needs of this particular population can be emphasized (for example, intergenerational programs). Similarly, programs and services can be adapted to the race/ethnic/cultural compositions of the people in the neighborhood and their needs. Programs and services can change as the composition of the neighborhood changes, or as the larger social and economic conditions change.

Once a neighborhood is identified, business and industry can be solicited to participate in programs like "adopt-a-neighborhood." Interns from all disciplines can be used under the supervision of trained professionals to provide services that otherwise might not be affordable. Other professionals can be encouraged to volunteer some of their time in providing services in which they specialize, or in doing other things they enjoy but do not have a chance to engage in otherwise. For example, an attorney or engineer who enjoys the arts or carpentry or cooking could either teach a youngster or organize events from time to time. People interested in music or the arts or theater or dance could similarly be involved in one-time or ongoing activities with individuals or small groups in the neighborhood. People of any occupation could participate in Big Brother, Big Sister, or foster grandparent programs. The possibilities are endless.

However, while people and services are obtained from the private sector, responsibility for their recruitment, organization, and coordination remains with the publicly funded staff and management.

Staff and Management

The core staff recommended is a team of MSW social workers. MSW social workers specifically are recommended because they have been found to be the most effective in this kind of work. A study conducted in 1987 by Booz-Allen and Hamilton Inc. (an independent, conservative consulting firm) concluded that ". . . The overall performance of MSWs was significantly higher than non-MSWs . . ." and ". . . Education, specifically holding an MSW appears to be the best predictor of overall performance in social service work. . . ." (p. iii, Executive Summary).

A team approach to management and administration, rather than traditional bureaucratic/hierarchical approach, is recommended because it facilitates greater opportunity for flexibility, innovation, and change in responding to the changing needs of the neighborhood. Some of the most successful private industries use a team approach to management because it produces much more innovation and creativity.

The number of staff on the team will depend on the size of the neighborhood. In addition to management and administration of the center as a team, each member will carry a generalist caseload, being responsible for the well-being of around 10–15 families in the neighborhood. Each member will serve as the one helping individual with which a family can establish a long-term relationship. Each member can also serve as a specialist on the team, according to their particular area of interest; that is, one person especially skilled in marital therapy can be a consultant in this area to others, while another person especially knowledgeable about community resources can provide that particular information to the team members.

Medical staff will be needed to staff the health clinic, and recreational staff will be needed to run the recreation programs. Other staff will depend on the nature of services provided, depending on the particular needs of the neighborhood.

Benefits, Anticipated and Unanticipated

In a large city/metropolitan area, the population is much too diverse, and social conditions change much too rapidly to plan and provide countywide services efficiently and quickly. A neighborhood-based structure is much more responsive to the needs of families, providing more services at lesser cost, thus reducing both the incidence and the severity of incidence of child abuse and neglect, which leads to a reduction in the number of children needing out-of-home placement. Such a structure of services will reduce the number of false reports, thereby freeing resources now used in unnecessary investigation, and make them available for services to those families where the reports are not false. (Besides, unnecessary investigation is a violation of a family's privacy.) On the other hand, such an approach may identify families at risk who otherwise might not have been reported, so that the actual number of reports may or may not decrease. What is expected, and can be measured, are the decrease in number of false reports and the decrease in severity of abuse/neglect, leading to a decrease in the number of children needing out-of-home placement.

Other tangible and intangible benefits could also result from such a program. For instance:

1. Availability of a neighborhood health clinic will reduce the number of visits to large hospital emergency rooms. Emergency-room care is much more expensive.
2. Other public and private social services in the neighborhood can be coordinated for greater efficiency, thus avoiding duplication of programs, and developing programs for unmet needs.
3. Because child abuse/neglect is related to status offenses and crimes committed by juveniles and adults, such as crimes involving illegal substances,

property, homicide, suicide, rape, and prostitution, neighborhood-based services are also likely to reduce the incidence of these other social problems. Benefit is not only immediate and confined to the neighborhood, but also long-term and of national consequence in terms of spillover benefits of increased productivity of the people and prevention of loss of revenues necessary for dealing with these social problems.

4. Such a center is more likely to be much more culturally-sensitive and responsive to diverse ethnic and cultural groups.

Evaluation and Measurement of Effectiveness

The value and effectiveness of this plan can be evaluated through pre–post studies (taking measurements before, after, and periodically during the period of the pilot project in each neighborhood) of social indicators such as:

1. The number of reports of child abuse neglect received from that neighborhood, substantiated and false, and the trend and rate of increase in the previous three years.
2. The number of children from that neighborhood placed in out-of-home care and the duration of this out-of-home placement; trend in the previous three years.
3. The number of visits of children to hospitals (emergency room and inpatient care); trend in the previous three years.
4. The number of times police are called to the neighborhood; trend in the previous three years.

These measurements taken before the beginning of the pilot will also serve as indicators of needs. Periodic measurements during the pilot will serve as a feedback mechanism for assessment of programs and need for modification or change.

However, since this is not a controlled laboratory experiment, factors such as changes in the population of the neighborhood, other local/state/federal policies affecting the general population, the economy, and normal developmental changes in individuals and families will also influence the incidence of child abuse/neglect in the neighborhood. The measurements described above are thus to be interpreted in general terms only, as indicators of trends, rather than as absolute evaluative measures of the program.

Possible Objections to This Idea

1. This plan of neighborhood-based human services is a major shift from the established pattern of categorical, centralized, bureaucratic delivery systems and, as such, it represents a shift in the power structure of the current system. The first objection, therefore, is to be anticipated from those who are likely to lose power, and possibly their positions, in this change. Their concern over their loss is understandable; negotiations will need to be con-

(A Public-Private partnership)

1. Identify a geographical area that can provide an identity to a neighborhood.
2. Select a large building, close to a park or school playground, easily accessible to all residents of the neighborhood, to serve as the focus of services.
3. Core services government funded:
   a) Complete assessment of family needs for healthy functioning.
   b) Case management.
   c) Primary health care.
   d) Counseling ranging from prevention to rehabilitation.
   e) Basic social services.
   f) Recreation—all ages.
   g) Advocacy.
4. Additional services geared toward specific needs of the neighborhood—developed with private, indigenous community resources. (e.g., volunteers, industry and businesses "adopt a neighborhood," etc.)

Staff: Professionals assisted by interns, paraprofessionals, and volunteers.

Management: Team approach rather than bureaucratic hierarchy. Is more flexible and quicker to respond to changes in the needs of the neighborhood.

Anticipated Benefits:
1. Cost efficiency.
2. Reduced incidence of abuse/neglect, crime, substance abuse. . .
3. Reduced demand for more expensive health and mental health care.

Effectiveness can be evaluated through pre–post studies of criteria relevant to the neighborhood. Periodic studies can be used as feedback mechanism to make changes if necessary.

Possible Objections:
1. Problems of collaboration between traditionally categorical agencies.
2. Fear of political empowerment of the neighborhoods, as in the 1960s.

Other Civic Organizations

Intergenerational Programs

Big Brother Big Sisters

Formal & Informal Leaders

Recreation and Socialization

Primary Health Care

Adult Education Programs

Church

Foster Parents, Grandparents

Assessment, Referral, and Acvocacy

Core Services (Gov't Funded)

Counseling, Preventive Treatment & After Care Family Life Education

Social Services

Additional Services (Privately Funded)

Elementary School

Arts Music Theater

Child Care

Library

FIGURE 1

Delivering services to prevent family problems (a public–private partnership).

ducted with them so that they can be reassigned to new roles. For this reason also a pilot program would be more acceptable, since that would mean
a slow change to which people can accommodate gradually.

2. The success of the program depends, to a great extent, on the ability of the
    core staff to work together as a team. This will necessitate a careful selec-
    tion of the staff, which can be a basis of argument against the program.
    Measures to overcome such opposition, such as allowing people to rotate
    in or out of teams as needed, gradually expanding into other neighbor-
    hoods, etc., will need to be considered.

3. The fact that there are no absolute measures of success can also be a basis
    of opposition. This fact will have to be accepted, because human services
    can indeed not be evaluated in terms of measurable quantities only. Success
    will also need to be measured in terms of participants' opinions on com-
    parison with the present system.

4. Provision of comprehensive services will necessitate collaboration and co-
    operation between various departments of the government, and other pri-
    vate agencies that now provide categorical services. This coordination/
    collaboration can pose tremendous problems of independent agencies
    working together, which will have to be resolved through perseverance and
    emphasis on cooperation, rather than competition, in service provision.

Figure 1 depicts the various components of such a public–private
partnership.

The success of any idea depends on its implementation. Therefore, it is recommended that the first 12 to 18 months of the project be devoted fully to developing support for the project, within the selected neighborhoods as well as
with public and private organizations currently responsible for the services that
will be most affected by the change. As has been demonstrated in successful
new programs in the past decade, the critical element will be strong, dedicated,
and skillful leadership by one or more people.

AFTERWORD

The field of child welfare is enormously complex. Professional practice in this field requires, in the person of the practitioner, the synergy of basic *values* and *skills* of professional social work combined with and informed by a vast body of *knowledge* on numerous theories and subject areas that help understand the intricately interrelated and interwoven factors that contribute to child maltreatment, and help design interventions to prevent its occurrence, reduce its severity, and alleviate its adverse effects in diverse children and families. Each of these bodies of knowledge is a vast subject of study and research in itself; each of them usually addresses one, or perhaps some, of the innumerable interwoven factors related to child maltreatment in any one family. The challenge of professional practice is to *integrate* this vast and diverse body of knowledge into some sort of a coherent, manageable whole that can be used to guide practice with each individual client differentially, to be relevant to each client's situation.

This is the challenge this book has undertaken in offering a model of practice suitable to the field of child welfare, and in offering conceptual frameworks for assessment and case planning at different points in the child welfare system that could guide workers' decision-making at those points. The intent is to offer conceptual tools that could help workers adapt their practice methods and approaches to the children and families they work with and provide to each client culturally relevant and respectful professional help that preserves the safety of the child, the dignity of the parents, and the integrity of the family.

The emphasis in this book is on *integration*. The conceptual frameworks offered here permit the integration of relevant knowledge of numerous different theories and subject areas in social work practice skills. This focus on integration precludes the treatment of any one subject at length or in-depth. Should a reader wish further study in any subject area or theory, references are cited in this book; they are available in most libraries. Basic social work values and practice skills are addressed by this author in an earlier book (see Samantrai, 1996, 1999).

In the field of child welfare, neither practice nor the teaching of practice can be formulaic. This book can serve as an organizing framework for one or more courses of any length and depth depending on the needs of the specific student group. Teachers can teach the subject matter in any order they wish and choose any supplemental educational materials they wish. This book is not prescriptive; indeed it is intended to stimulate the reader's own thinking and creativity. Readers are encouraged to use it in any way that suits them most.

BIBLIOGRAPHY

Adams, P. & Nelson, K. (Eds.) (1995). *Reinventing Human Services: Community- and Family-Centered Practice.* New York: Aldyne De Gruyter.

Aguilera, D. C. (1998). *Crisis Intervention: Theory and Methodology.* 8th Edition. St. Louis, MO: Moseby.

Ainsworth, M. D., Blehar, M. C., Waters, E. & Wall, S. (1978). *Patterns of Attachment.* Hillsdale, NJ: Lawrence Erlbaum Associates, Publishers.

American Humane Association. (1998). *Twelfth National Roundtable on Child Protective Services Risk Assessment: Summary of Proceedings.* Children's Division, Englewood, CO.

Anderson, G. R., Ryan, A. S. & Leashore, B. R. (Eds.) (1997). *The Challenge of Permanency Planning in a Multicultural Society.* New York: The Haworth Press.

Arches, J. (1991). Social structure, burnout, and job satisfaction. *Social Work.* Vol. 36, No. 3. May. pp. 202–206.

Augustino, M. (1987). Developmental effects of child abuse: Recent findings. *Child Abuse and Neglect.* Vol. 11. pp. 15–27.

Ballew, J. R. & Mink, G. (1986). *Case Management in the Human Services.* Springfield, IL: Charles C. Thomas.

Barth, R. P., Courtney, M., Berrick, J. D. & Albert, V. (1994). *From Child Abuse to Permanency Planning.* New York: Aldyne De Gruyter.

Barth, R. P. & Price, A. (1999). Shared family care: Providing services to parents and children placed together in out-of-home care. *Child Welfare.* Vol. LXXVIII, No. 1. Jan./Feb. pp. 88–107.

Beck, D. F. (1987). Counselor burnout in family service agencies. *Social Casework: The Journal of Contemporary Social Work.* Vol. 68, No. 1. pp. 3–15.

Booz-Allen and Hamilton, Inc. (1987). *The Maryland Social Work Services Job Analysis and Personnel Qualifications Study.* Prepared for the Department of Human Resources, State of Maryland.

Bowlby, J. (1973). *Attachment and Loss*. New York: Basic Books, Inc. Publishers.
———. (1988). *A Secure Base*. New York: Basic Books, Inc. Publishers.
Brager, G. & Holloway, S. (1977). A process model of changing organizations from within. *Administration in Social Work*. Vol. 1, No. 4. Winter. pp. 349–358.
Bremner, R. H. (Ed.) (1972). *Children and Youth in America: A Documentary History*. Cambridge, MA: Harvard University Press.
Bretherton, I. & Waters, E. (Eds.) (1985). *Growing Points of Attachment Theory and Research*. Monographs of the Society for Research in Child Development. Serial no. 209. Vol. 50, Nos. 1–2.
Brooks, D., Barth, R. P., Bussiere, A. & Patterson, G. (1999). Adoption and race: Implementing the Multiethnic Placement Act and the Interethnic Adoption Provisions. *Social Work*. Vol. 44, No. 2. March. pp. 167–178.
Brun, C. & Rapp, R. C. (2001). Strengths-based case management: Individuals' perspectives on strengths and the case-management relationship. *Social Work*. Vol. 46, No. 3. July. pp. 278–288.
Brunk, M., Henggeler, S. W. & Whelan, J. P. (1987). Comparison of multisystemic therapy and parent training in the brief treatment of child abuse and neglect. *Journal of Consulting and Clinical Psychology*. Vol. 35, No. 2. pp. 171–178.
Callard, E. D. & Morrin, P. E. (1979). *Parents and Children Together. An Alternative to Foster Care*. Detroit: Department of Family and Consumer Resources, Wayne State University.
Canino, I. A. & Spurlock, J. (1994). *Culturally Diverse Children and Adolescents*. New York: The Guildford Press.
Child Welfare. March/April 1996.
Child Welfare League of America. (1994). *Kinship Care: A Natural Bridge*. Washington, DC: Author.
Cicchetti, D. & Carlson, V. (1989). *Child Maltreatment: Theory and Research on the Causes and Consequences of Child Abuse and Neglect*. Cambridge: Cambridge University Press.
Cimmarusti, R. A. (1992). Family preservation practice based upon a multisystems approach. *Child Welfare*. Vol. LXXI, No. 3. May/June. pp. 241–256.
Cogan, N. H. (1970). Juvenile law, before and after the entrance of parens patriae. *South Carolina Law Review*. Vol. 22. pp. 147–181.
Cohen, B. J. & Austin, M. J. (1994). Organizational learning and change in a public child welfare agency. *Administration in Social Work*. Vol. 18, No. 1. pp. 1–19.
Cohen, B. J. (1999). Fostering innovation in a large human service bureaucracy. *Administration in Social Work*. Vol. 23, No. 2. pp. 47–59.
Cole, E. & Duva, J. (1990). *Family Preservation: An Orientation for Administrators and Practitioners*. Washington, DC: Child Welfare League of America.
Costin, L. B., Bell, C. J. & Downs, S. W. (1991). *Child Welfare; Policies and Practices*. Fourth Edition. New York: Longman Publishing Group.
Dane, B. (2000). Child welfare workers: An innovative approach for interacting with secondary trauma. *Journal of Social Work Education*. Vol. 36, No. 1. Winter. pp. 27–38.
Davies, D. (1999). *Child Development: A Practitioner's Guide*. New York: The Guilford Press.
De Jong, P. & Miller, S. D. (1995). How to interview for client strengths. *Social Work*. Vol. 40, No. 6. November. pp. 729–736.
Dixon, S. L. (1979). *Working with People in Crisis*. St. Louis, MO: The C. V. Moseby Co.

Dubowitz, H. & DePanfillis, D. (Eds.) (2000). *Handbook for Child Protection Practice.* Thousand Oaks, CA: Sage Publications, Inc.

Dunst, C. J., Trivette, C. M. & Deal, A. G. (1988). *Enabling and Empowering Families.* Cambridge, MA: Brookline Books, Inc.

Eagle, R. (1994). The separation experience of children in long-term care: Theory, research, and implications for practice. *American Journal of Orthopsychiatry.* Vol. 64, No. 3. pp. 421–434.

Emlen, A. (1976). *Barriers to Planning for Children in Foster Care.* Portland, OR: Regional Research Institute for Human Services, Portland State University School of Social Work.

Emlen, A., Lahti, J., Downs, G., McKay, A. & Downs, S. (1978). *Overcoming Barriers to Planning for Children in Foster Care.* Portland, OR: Regional Research Institute for Human Services, Portland State University.

Emlen, A. C. (1981). Development of the permanency planning concept. In S. W. Downs, L. Bayless, L. Dreyer, A. C. Emlen, M. Hardin, L. Heim, J. Lahti, K. Liedke, K. Schimke & M. Troychak. *Foster Care Reform in the '70s—Final Report of the Permanency Planning Dissemination Project.* Portland, OR: Regional Research Institute for Human Services, Portland State University, pp. 1.1–1.15.

English, D. J. (1998). The extent and consequences of child maltreatment. *The Future of Children.* Vol. 8, No. 1. Spring. pp. 39–53.

———. (1995). Cultural issues related to the assessment of child abuse and neglect. *Contemporary Group Care Practice, Research, and Evaluation.* Vol. 5, No. 1. Spring. pp. 31–35.

English, D. J., Wingard, T., Marshall, D., Orme, M. & Orme, A. (2000). Alternative responses to child protective services: Emerging issues and concerns. *Child Abuse and Neglect.* Vol. 24, No. 3. pp. 375–388.

Epstein, N. B., Bishop, D., Ryan, C., Miller, I. & Keitner, G. (1993). The McMaster model view of healthy family functioning. In F. Walsh (Ed.). *Normal Family Processes* (pp. 138–160). New York: The Guilford Press.

Erikson, E. H. (1980). *Identity and the Life Cycle.* New York: W. W. Norton & Co.

———. (1982, 1997). *The Life Cycle Completed.* New York: W. W. Norton & Co.

Ernst, J. S. (1999). Whanau knows best. Kinship care in New Zealand. In R. L. Hegar and M. Scannapieco (Eds.) *Kinship Foster Care.* New York: Oxford University Press. pp. 112–138.

Everett, J. E. (1995). Relative foster care: An emerging trend in foster care placement policy and practice. *Smith College Studies in Social Work.* Vol. 65, No. 3. June. pp. 239–254.

Fanshel, D. & Shinn, E. B. (1978). *Children in Foster Care: A Longitudinal Study.* New York: Columbia University.

Flavell, J. H. (1963). *The Developmental Psychology of Jean Piaget.* New York: D. Van Nostrand Company, Inc.

Fraiberg, S. (1959). *The Magic Years.* New York: Scribner.

Freud, A. (1936). *The Ego and the Mechanisms of Defense.* New York: International University Press.

———. (1963). Regression as a principle in mental development. *Bulletin of the Menninger Clinic.* Vol. 27, No. 2. March. pp. 126–139.

Freud, A. & Burlinghame, D. T. (1943). *War and Children.* New York: Medical War Books.

Freud, S. (1905). Three essays in sexuality. *Standard Edition.* 7: pp. 135–243.

Fox, R., & Carey, L. A. (1999). Therapists' collusion with the resistance of rape survivors. *Clinical Social Work Journal*. Vol. 27, No 2. pp. 185–201.

Gibson, D. & Noble, D. N. (1991). Creative permanency planning: Residential services for families. *Child Welfare*. Vol. LXX, No. 3, May/June. pp. 371–382.

Gitterman, A. & Miller, I. (1989). The influence of the organization on clinical practice. *Clinical Social Work Journal*. Vol. 17, No. 2. Summer. pp. 151–164.

Gleeson, J. P. (1996). Kinship care as a child welfare service: The policy debate in an era of welfare reform. *Child Welfare*. Vol. LXXV, No. 5. Sept.–Oct. pp. 419–449.

GAO/HEHS-98-204. (1998). *Foster Care: Implementation of the Multiethnic Placement Act Poses Difficult Challenges*. Report to the Chairman, Subcommittee on Human Resources, Committee on Ways and Means, House of Representatives. United States General Accounting Office.

Greenberg, M. T., Cicchetti, D. & Cummings, E. M. (Eds.) (1990). *Attachment in the Preschool Years*. Chicago: The University of Chicago Press.

Geddes, J. B. (1977). The rights of children in world perspective. In Gross, B. & Gross, R. (Eds.). *The Children's Rights Movement*. Garden City, NY: Anchor Press/Doubleday. pp. 214–216.

Goldberg, S., Muir, R. & Kerr, J. (Eds.) (1995). *Attachment Theory: Social, Developmental, and Clinical Perspectives*. Hillsdale, NJ: The Atlantic Press.

Goldstein, J., Freud, A. & Solnit, A. (1973). *Beyond the Best Interest of the Child*. New York: The Free Press.

Gross, B. & Gross, R. (Eds.) (1977). *The Children's Rights Movement*. Garden City, NY: Anchor Press/Doubleday.

Harvard Educational Review, Reprint Series No. 9. (1974). *The Rights of Children*. Cambridge, MA.

Harvey, S. & Raider, M. (1984). Administrator burnout. *Administration in Social Work*. Vol. 8, No. 2. pp. 81–89.

Hasenfeld, Y. & Saari, R. (Eds.) (1978). *The Management of Human Services*. New York: Columbia University Press.

Hearings Before the Subcommittee on Children and Youth of the Senate Committee on Labor and Public Welfare. *Adoption and Foster Care*, 1975. 94th Congress, 1st Session, 1975.

Hearing Before the Subcommittee on Select Education of the House Committee on Education and Labor. *Foster Care: Problems and Issues*, Part 2, 94th Congress, 2nd Session, 1976.

Heger, R. & Scannapieco, M. (1995). From family duty to family policy: The evolution of kinshipcare. *Child Welfare*. Vol. LXXIV, No. 1. Jan.–Feb. pp. 200–216.

———. (Eds.) (1999). *Kinship Foster Care*. New York: Oxford University Press.

Henggeler, S. W., Melton, G. B., Smith, L. A., Schoenwald, S. K. & Hanley, J. H. (1993). Family preservation using multisystemic treatment: Long-term follow-up to a clinical trial with serious juvenile offenders. *Journal of Child and Family Studies*. Vol. 2, No. 4. pp. 283–293.

Hess, P. M., McGowan, B. G. & Botsko, M. (2000). A preventive service program model for preserving and supporting families over time. *Child Welfare*. Vol. LXXIX, No. 3. May/June. pp. 227–265.

Howe, D. (Ed.) (1996). *Attachment and Loss in Family and Child Work*. Brookfield: Avebury/Ashgate Publishing Co.

Howing, P. T., Wodarski, J. S., Gaudin, J. S. Jr. & Kurtz, D. P. (1989). Effective interventions to ameliorate the incidence of child maltreatment: The empirical base. *Social Work*. Vol. 34, No. 4. July. pp. 330–338.

Jeter, H. R. (1961). *Children Problem and Services in Child Welfare Programs*. Washington, DC: Child Welfare League of America.

Joint Hearing Before the Subcommittee on Children and Youth of the Senate Committee on Labor and Public Welfare and the Subcommittee on Select Education of the House Committee on Education and Labor, *Foster Care: Problems and Issues*, Part 1. 94th Congress, 1st Session, 1975.

Jones, M. A., Neuman, R. & Shyne, A. W. (1976). *A Second Chance for Families*. New York: Regional Center, Child Welfare League of America.

Jones, M. A., Magura, S. & Shyne, A. W. (1981). Effective practice with families in protective and preventive services: What works? *Child Welfare*. Vol. LX, No. 2. Feb.

Kamerman, S. B. & Kahn, A. J. (1993). If CPS is driving child welfare—Where do we go from here? *Public Welfare*. Winter. pp. 41–43, 46.

Kanter, J. (2000). Beyond psychotherapy: Therapeutic relationships in community care. *Smith College Studies in Social Work*. Vol. 70, No. 3. June. pp. 397–426.

Karen, R. (1990). Becoming attached. *The Atlantic Monthly*. February. pp. 35–70.

———. (1998). *Becoming Attached*. New York: Oxford University Press.

Katz, E. & Dane, B. (1973). *Bureaucracy and the Public*. New York: Basic Books.

Kelly, S. & Blythe, B. J. (2000). Family preservation: A potential not yet realized. *Child Welfare*. Vol. LXXIX, No. 1. Jan./Feb. pp. 29–42.

Kempe, C. H., Silverman, F. N., Steele, B. F., Drougmueller, W. & Silver, H. K. (1962). The battered child syndrome. *Journal of the American Medical Association*. Vol. 181. pp. 17–24.

Kilgore, L. C. (1988). Effects of early childhood sexual abuse on self and ego develpment. *Social Casework*. Vol. 69, No. 4. April. pp. 224–230.

Knitzer, J. (1982). *Unclaimed Children: The Failure of Public Responsibility to Children and Adolescents in Need of Mental Health Services*. Washington, DC: Children's Defense Fund.

Koverola, C. & Pound, J. (1993). Relationship of child sexual abuse to depression. *Child Abuse and Neglect*. Vol. 17, No. 3. May/June. pp. 393–400.

Kurtz, P. D., Gaudin, J. M., Howling, P. T. & Wodarski, J. S. (1993). The consequences of physical abuse and neglect on school-age child: Mediating factors. *Child and Youth Services Review*. Vol. 15. pp. 85–104.

Laird, J. & Hartman, A. (Eds.) (1985). *A Handbook of Child Welfare: Context, Knowledge, and Practice*. New York: The Free Press.

Lamb, H. R. (1980). Therapist-case managers: More than brokers of services. *Hospital and Community Psychiatry*. Vol. 31. November. pp. 762–764.

Littlejohn-Blake, S. M. & Darling, C. A. (1993). Understanding the strengths of African-American families. *Journal of Black Studies*. Vol. 23. No. 4. June. pp. 460–471.

Littner, N. (1972). *Some Traumatic Effects of Separation and Placement*. New York: Child Welfare League of America.

Lum, D. (1999). *Culturally Competent Practice: A Framework for Growth and Action*. Pacific Grove, CA: Brooks/Cole Publishing Co.

Lynch, E. W. & Hanson, M. J. (Eds.) (1992). *Developing Cross-Cultural Competence: A Guide for Working with Young Children and Their Families*. Baltimore, MD: Paul H. Brooks Publishing Co.

Maas, H. S. & Engler, R. E. (1959). *Children in Need of Parents*. New York: Columbia University Press.

Maier, H. W. (1978). *Three Theories of Child Development*. Third Edition. New York: Harper & Row Publishers.

Main, M. & Solomon, J. (1990). Procedures for identifying infants as disorganized/disoriented during Ainsworth Strange Situation. In Greenberg, M. T., Cicchetti, D. & Cummings, E. M. (Eds.) (1990). *Attachment in the Preschool Years.* Chicago: The University of Chicago Press. pp. 121–182.

Manoleas, P. (1994). An outcome approach to assessing the cultural competence of MSW students. *Journal of Multicultural Social Work.* Vol. 3. pp. 43–57.

Maslach, C. (1982a). *Burnout: The Cost of Caring.* Englewood Cliffs, NJ: Prentice-Hall, Inc.

———. (1982b). Understanding burnout: Definitional issues in analyzing a complex phenomenon. In Whiton Stewart Paine. (Ed.) *Job Stress and Burnout: Research, Theory and Intervention Perspectives.* Beverly Hills, CA: Sage Publications.

Maslach, C. & Jackson, S. (1986). *Maslach Burnout Inventory Manual.* Second edition. Palo Alto, CA: Consulting Psychological Press.

McCann, L. & Pearlman, L. A. (1990). Vicarious traumatization: A framework for understanding the psychological effects of working with victims. *Journal of Traumatic Stress.* Vol. 3, No. 1. January. pp. 131–149.

McPhatter, A. R. (1997). Cultural competence in child welfare: What is it? How do we achieve it? What happens without it? *Child Welfare.* Vol. LXXVI, No 1. Jan.–Feb. pp. 255–278.

Miley, K. K., O'Melia, M. & DuBois, B. I. (1998). *Generalist Social Work Practice: An Empowering Approach.* Boston: Allyn & Bacon.

Moe, B. (1998). *Adoption: A Reference Handbook.* Santa Barbara, CA: ABC-CLIO Inc.

Moore, S. (1992). Case management and the integration of services: How service delivery systems shape case management. *Social Work.* Vol. 37, No. 5. pp. 418–423.

Mott, P. E. (1975). *Foster Care and Adoptions: Some Key Policy Issues.* Washington, DC: U. S. Government Printing Office.

Moxley, D. P. (1989). *The Practice of Case Management.* Newbury Park, CA: Sage Publications.

Mulroy, E. A. (1997). Building a neighborhood network: Interorganization collaboration to prevent child abuse and neglect. *Social Work.* Vol. 42, No. 30. May. pp. 255–264.

Nagera, H. (1964). On arrest in development, fixation, and regression. *Psychoanalytic Study of the Child.* Vol. XIX. New York: International University Press. pp. 222–239.

National Association of Social Workers. (1989). *NASW Standards for the Practice of Clinical Social Work.* Washington, DC: Author.

NASW. (1997). *Government Relations Update. Adoption and Safe Families Act of 1997 (H. R.867) Public Law 105-89.* Washington, DC: December.

Nelson, B. J. (1984). *Making an Issue of Child Abuse: Political Agenda Setting for Social Problems.* Chicago: Chicago University Press.

Nelson, K. E. (1997). Family preservation—What is it? *Children and Youth Services Review.* Vol. 19, Nos. 1/2. pp. 101–118.

Nelson, K. M. (1992). Fostering homeless children and their families too: The emergence of whole-family foster care. *Child Welfare.* Vol. LXXI, No. 6. Nov.–Dec. pp. 575–584.

Noshpitz, J. D. & King, R. A. (1991). *Pathways of Growth: Essentials of Child Psychiatry. Vol. 1, Normal Development.* New York: John Wiley & Sons.

Nugent, W. R. & Gleason, C. (1999). Reactivity and responsiveness in children's service systems. *Journal of Social Service Research.* Vol. 25, No. 3. pp. 41–60.

Orrantia, R. (1991). *The Indian Child Welfare Act: A Handbook*. 617 Ingleside Place, Escondido, CA. 92026.

Parad, H. J. (Ed.) (1965). *Crisis Intervention: Selected Readings*. New York: Family Service Association of America.

Parad, H. J. & Parad, L. G. (1990). *Crisis Intervention Book 2: The Practitioner's Sourcebook for Brief Therapy*. Milwaukee, WI: Family Service America.

Pelton, L. H. (1991). Beyond permanency planning: Restructuring the child welfare system. *Social Work*. Vol. 36, No. 4. pp. 337–343.

Pennell, J. & Burford, G. (2000). Family group decision making: Protecting children and women. *Child Welfare*. Vol. LXXIX, No. 2. March/April. pp. 131–158.

Piaget, J. (1977). *The Essential Piaget*. New York: Basic Books.

Piaget, J. & Inhelder, B. (1969). *The Psychology of the Child*. New York: Basic Books.

Pike, V. (1976). Permanent planning for foster children: The Oregon Project. *Children Today*. Vol. 5, No. 6. pp. 22–25.

————. (1977). *Permanent Planning for Children in Foster Care*. Washington, DC: U. S. Department of Health, Education, and Welfare.

Pine, B. A., Warsh, R. & Maluccio, A. N. (1998). Participatory management in a public child welfare agency: A key to effective change. *Administration in Social Work*. Vol. 22, No. 1. pp. 19–31.

Ponteretto, J. G., Casas, M. J., Suzuki, L. A. & Alexander, C. M. (Eds.) (1995). *Handbook of Multicultural Counseling*. Thousand Oaks, CA: Sage Publications.

————. (2001) *Handbook of Multicultural Counseling*. 3rd Edition. Thousand Oaks, CA: Sage Publications.

Powell, G. J. (Ed.) (1983). *The Psychosocial Development of Minority Group Children*. New York: Brunner/Mazel Publishers.

Public Law 93-247: Child Abuse Prevention and Treatment Act. 88 STAT. 4; Date: 1/31/74.

Public Law 95-608: The Indian Child Welfare Act of 1978. 92 Stat. 3069. 25. U. S.C. 1978.

Public Law 96-272: Adoption Assistance and Child Welfare Act of 1980. 94 Stat. 500.

Public Law 104-193: Personal Resopnsibility and Work Opportunity Act of 1996. 110 Stat. 2105.

Public Law 104-235: *Child Abuse Prevention and Treatment Amendments of 1996*. 110 Stat. 3063; Date: 10/3/96.

Puryear, D. A. (1979). *Helping People in Crisis*. San Francisco: Jossey-Bass Publishers.

Rapoport, L. (1965). The state of crisis: Some theoretical considerations. In *Crisis Intervention: Selected Readings*. H. Parad (Ed.). New York: Family Service Association of America.

Rapp, C. A. (1998). *The Strengths Model: Case Management with People Suffering from Severe and Persistent Mental Illness*. New York: Oxford University Press.

Rendleman, D. R. (1971). Parens Patriae: From Chancery to the Juvenile Court. *South Carolina Law Review*. Vol. 23, No. 1. pp. 205–259.

Rivard, J. C., Johnsen, M. C., Morrissey, J. P. & Starrett, B. E. (1999).The dynamics of interagency collaboration: How linkages develop for child welfare and juvenile justice sectors in a system of care demonstration. *Journal of Social Service Research*. Vol. 25, No. 3. pp. 61–82.

Roberts-DeGennaro, M. (1987). Developing case management as a practice model. *Social Casework*. Vol. 68, No. 8. October. pp. 466–470.

Rosenthal, K. (1988). The inanimate self in adult victims of child abuse and neglect. *Social Casework*. Vol. 69, No. 8. October. pp. 505–510.

Saleebey, D. (Ed.) (1992). *The Strengths Perspective in Social Work Practice*. New York: Longman.

Sallee, A. L. & Lloyd, J. C. (Eds.) (1990). *Family Preservation: Papers from the Institute for Social Work Educators*. Riverdale, IL: National Association of Family-Based Services.

Samantrai, K. (1990). MSWs in public child welfare: Why do they stay, and why do they leave? *NASW California News*. Sacramento; CA. Sept.–Dec.

———. (1991). Clinical social work in public child welfare practice. *Social Work*. Vol. 36, No. 4. July. pp. 359–361.

———. (1992). To prevent unnecessary separation of children and families: Public Law 96-272—Policy and practice. *Social Work*. Vol. 37, No. 4. July. pp. 295–302.

———. (1992a). Factors in the decision to leave: Retaining social workers with MSWs in public child welfare. *Social Work*. Vol. 37, No. 5. September. pp. 454–458.

———. (1993). *Prevention in Child Welfare: States' Response to Federal Mandate*. New York: Garland Publishing, Inc.

———. (1996, 1999). *Interviewing in Health and Human Services*. Chicago, IL. Nelson-Hall Publishers.

Samantrai, K. & Lum, D. (1995). *Ethnic Sensitive Child Welfare Practice: Three Videos.*
1. *Background to Ethnic Sensitive Social Work Practice* (30 minutes).
2. *Legal, Psychological, and Social Issues Facing New Immigrants* (83 minutes).
3. *Assessment and Intervention Issues with Minority Families* (84 minutes).
Available at the California Social Work Education Center (CalSWEC) Resource Library, California State University, Long Beach.

Schorr, L. B. (1979). *Within Our Reach: Breaking the Cycle of Disadvantage*. New York: Anchor Books, Doubleday.

Seagle, W. (1937). Family law. In *Encyclopedia of the Social Sciences*. New York: Macmillan and Company. pp. 81–84.

Seita, J. R. (2000). In our best interest: Three necessary shifts for child welfare workers and children. *Child Welfare*. Vol. LXXIX, No. 1. Jan./Feb. pp. 77–92.

Silverman, A. B., Reinherz, H. Z. & Giaconia, R. M. (1996). The long term sequelae of child and adolescent abuse: A longitudinal community study. *Child Abuse and Neglect*. Vol. 20, No. 8. August. pp. 709–723.

Singer, D. G. & Revenson, T. A. (1978). *A Piaget Primer: How a Child Thinks*. New York: New American Library.

Siu, S. & Hogan, P. T. (1989). Common clinical themes in child welfare. *Social Work*. Vol. 34, No. 4. July. pp. 339–345.

Stein, T. J. & Gambrill, E. D. (1977). Facilitating decision making in foster care: The Alameda project. *Social Service Review*. Vol. 51, No. 3. September. pp. 503–513.

Stein, T. J., Gambrill, E. D. & Wiltse, K. T. (1977). Dividing case management in foster family cases. *Child Welfare,* Vol. LVI, No. 5. May. pp. 321–331.

Stroul, B. A. (Ed.) (1996). *Children's Mental Health: Creating Systems of Care in a Changing Society*. Baltimore, MD: Paul H. Brookes Publishing Co.

Sullivan, M., Spasser, M. & Penner, G. L. (1977). *Bowen Center Project for Abused and Neglected Children: Report of a Demonstration in Protective Services*. Washington, DC: U.S. Department of Health, Education, and Welfare, Public Service Administration, Office of Human Development.

Taylor, S. H. & Roberts, R. W. (Eds.) (1985). *Theory and Practice of Community Social Work.* New York: Columbia University Press.

Thomas, M. P. Jr. (1972). Child abuse and neglect. Part I: Historical overview, legal matrix, and social perspectives. *North Carolina Law Review.* Vol. 50. pp. 293–349.

Tracy, E. (1995). Family preservation and home-based services. In R. E. Edwards (Ed). *Encyclopedia of Social* Work, 19th Edition. Washington, DC: National Association of Social Workers. pp. 973–983.

U. S. GAO. (1995). *Child Welfare: Opportunities to Further Enhance Family Preservation and Support Activities.* Washington, DC: USDOC GA 1.13, HEHS 95-112.

———. (1999) *Foster Care: Kinship Care Quality and Permanency Issues.* Washington, DC: USDOC GA 1.13 HEHS 99-32.

U. S. Department of Health and Human Services, Administration for Children and Families, Childrens' Bureau. (2000). *Rethinking Child Welfare Under the Adoption and Safe Families Act of 1997: A Resource Guide.* Washington, DC.

Wagner, R., van Reyk, P. & Spence, N. (2001). Improving the working environment for workers in children's welfare agencies. *Child and Family Social Work.* Vol. 6. pp. 161–178.

Waldfogel, J. (2000). Reforming child protective services. *Child Welfare.* Vol. LXXIX, No. 1. Jan./Feb. pp. 43–57.

Walsh, J. A. (1987). Burnout and values in the social service profession. *Social Casework: The Journal of Contemporary Human Services.* Vol. 68, No. 5. May. pp. 279–283.

Webb, N. B. (2001). *Culturally Diverse Parent-Child and Family Relationships.* New York: Columbia University Press.

Weber, M. (1958). Bureaucracy. In Girth, H. H. & Mills, C. Wright (Eds.) *Essays in Sociology.* New York: Oxford University Press.

Weil, M., Karls, J. L. & Associates. (1985). *Case Management in Human Service Practice.* San Francisco: Jossey-Bass Publishers.

Wells, K. & Biegel, D. E. (Eds.) (1991). *Family Preservation Services: Research and Evaluation.* Newbury Park, CA: Sage Publishers.

Werner, E. E. (1979). *Cross-Cultural Child Development.* Monterey, CA.: Brooks/Cole Publishing Co.

Zunz, S. J. (1998). Resiliency and burnout: Protective factors for human service managers. *Administration in Social Work.* Vol. 22, No. 3. pp. 39–54.

INDEX